Amish
Literacy

Amish Literacy

What and How
It Means

Andrea Fishman

With a Foreword by Glenda L. Bissex

Heinemann
Portsmouth, New Hampshire

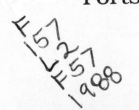

HEINEMANN EDUCATIONAL BOOKS, INC.
70 Court Street   Portsmouth, NH 03801
Offices and agents throughout the world

The following has generously given permission to use material in this book:
From "Toward an Ethnohistory of Writing in American Education" by Shirley
Heath in Marcia Farr Whiteman (ed.) *Variation in Writing: Functional and
Linguistic Cultural Differences*, 27-29. Copyright © 1981 by Lawrence Erlbaum
Associates, Inc. Reprinted by permission.

Library of Congress Cataloging-in-Publication Data

Fishman, Andrea.
    Amish literacy : what and how it means / Andrea Fishman.

        p.   cm.
    Bibliography: p.
    ISBN 0-435-08455-0
    1. Lancaster (Pa.)—Social life and customs.   2. Amish—Education-
-Pennsylvania—Lancaster.   3. Amish—Pennsylvania—Lancaster-
-Intellectual life.   I. Title.
F157.L2F57 1988
306'.09748'15—dc19

                                            87-34487
                                            CIP

Designed by Maria Szmauz, Szmauz Design.

Printed in the United States of America.

10   9   8   7   6   5   4   3   2   1

To the Fisher family, without whom this book never would have been written; and especially to Anna Fisher, who taught me that through love and faith not just books but all things are possible.

CONTENTS

FOREWORD

What have educators and researchers to learn from this study of an odd and tiny culture, whose attitudes about literacy and education we may find not particularly admirable or congenial? Why should those of us concerned with public education read a book about literacy learning among people who have made every effort to separate themselves from mainstream, modern society? Perhaps for the same reason that its author, an English teacher from a mainstream high school, became so engrossed in this research. Her book is not just a study of the Amish; it is a book about how learning to see through the eyes of another culture helps us to see ourselves and to liberate our thinking.

When Andrea Fishman returned to her classroom after her close observations of school and family life in an Amish community, she was not the same teacher as before. The fact that she returned to her classroom after doing doctoral research is in itself remarkable, but more remarkable is her detailed account of how her research experience changed her way of teaching and her vision as an educator. I don't know of anywhere else that this story has been told. I say "story" because Fishman is a natural storyteller, and her book is a rich intertwining of several stories: the story of the lives of Anna Fisher and her Amish family; of Verna, the teacher at Meadow Brook School; and of the author's journey as a researcher as well as a teacher. Because she re-creates these stories in such live detail, because this is a book of scenes rather than of abstractions, readers share much more than her "research findings"; we experience these stories for ourselves, expanding our own lives and thinking, perhaps becoming more conscious of our own perspective and examining it as we would otherwise not have been called upon to do by the usual contexts of our lives and work.

I emerged from reading this book more aware that mainstream

education, like Amish education, exists in a cultural context; that literacy exists in more forms than schools recognize; and that the cultural contexts of educational institutions both limit and shape the ways in which change can occur within them. I recalled some of the students I've taught who struggled with school, and I wondered what more I might have learned about *their* literacies and whether these might have appeared as resources for learning rather than as obstacles to instruction. I saw the kids for whom my discussion questions were meaningless, kids who just wanted to answer factual questions and pass through school into a life that made more sense. I saw my English-teacher self, convinced of the singular rightness of my view of reading, writing, and meaning making. There was one literacy—that being, of course, the form I knew with the particular values I attached to it. If, as Fishman demonstrates, there are other literacies, how do these affect a teacher's role as transmitter of a single literacy in a multicultural society? If I shift my focus away from weeding out the deviant forms, can I then, within a school setting, learn to broaden and extend all my students' notions of literacy?

As a researcher, I reflected on how quantitative methodologies distance us from literacy as a lived experience. Ethnographic observation, description and analysis, as used by Andrea Fishman, yield a study of literacy as lived in the home of one family and in the classrooms of two teachers, Verna and Fishman herself, not a study presented in terms of abstractions and numbers. It is a study not of *the* Amish, but of individuals who are part of one Amish community and culture. The humanness of people whose lives and beliefs differ from my own confronted me as a human being—an awareness probably more crucial for our ultimate survival in this world than possession of literacy skills.

Amish Literacy has a great deal to say to teachers and educational researchers that is of urgent importance if our schools are to be revitalized and educational research do more than justify mainstream academic values. The book may be seen as one vision joining others in a current paradigm shift: a questioning of traditional assumptions about the nature of knowledge and the structure of authority in educational institutions, a revision of our notions of how we know, of what we know, and of who can know. The increased acceptance of ethnographic and case-study methodologies in educational research has extended our ways of knowing and enabled questions to be asked that are outside the scope of traditional hypothesis-testing. The appropriateness of these methods for inquiry in classroom settings has enabled teachers to become researchers as well. Teachers empowered by their own inquiries are no longer merely receivers of university-generated research. And students in classrooms with a more reader-oriented approach to literature and a more student-centered approach to writing are no longer mere receivers of knowledge from teachers. Because this shift has originated largely at the university level, one of the unique contributions of Fishman's book is that it speaks not only *to* but *from* schools.

Why has this piece of research had such a dramatic effect upon

Fishman's thinking and teaching, while educational research is commonly regarded by teachers as irrelevant? First of all, of course, because the same person did the research and the teaching. The research became part of Fishman's understanding of education, schooling, learning, teaching, literacy, and meaning making—part of her way of seeing as an educator. No cumbersome and delaying translation of "theory" into "practice" was required.

Furthermore, this research was undertaken not to justify particular educational practices or theories but to extend a teacher's understanding of literacy by exploring it in a different cultural context and by trying to see it through the eyes of people within that context. Thus the nature and purpose of her inquiry led Fishman to new awareness and questionings. As she reflects on where meaning is found or how it is made, she remarks that she "never knew those were things to wonder about." Such wonderings can change our view of the world and shake our certainties as teachers. Once we see differently, we act differently.

The research approach Fishman took—the careful observation of individuals in their cultural contexts rather than the gathering of discrete bits of data to test a hypothesis—assured that this study would be more than an intellectual exercise. As a researcher and as a teacher, she was engaged with whole persons in natural settings; she did not make them into detached objects, though of course she was able to pull back and reflect on what she had observed—to make meaning. One of the strengths of her research is in the very connectedness she appreciates as existing between these people (her "subjects") and herself, their school and hers. It is from these connections that she makes her meanings.

But neither her position as researcher and teacher combined nor the nature of her inquiry would necessarily produce research with such a powerful effect. The final and crucial reasons for the power of her research, on her and on her readers, lie in Fishman's openness to people and to their differences—whether these persons are Amish folk or students in her classroom. She is able to see their differences from her, as a person and a teacher, as a challenge to her understanding rather than as a threat to her authority. Above all, she is open to reexamining her own beliefs and actions, and she possesses the courage to act on her new understandings and questionings. Lacking such courage to act, people hesitate to reach out in their thinking, sensing that they may not be able to move where it points. Andrea Fishman's openness to looking and wondering—her courage to see and then to act upon what she sees— are qualities her book lets us experience and grow from.

Amish Literacy: What and How It Means will help us think about literacy learning by broadening what we know and challenging what we think we know.

Glenda L. Bissex

NOTE TO THE READER

The names of all individuals have been changed to protect their privacy. The names used in this study were chosen from a list entitled "Amish names: Number and frequency in the three largest Old Order settlements," in Hostetler 1980, 242. Most other names come from the same source.

The name of the family's school was chosen from the "Pennsylvania Amish School Directory" published in the Blackboard Bulletin *(November 1981).*

O N E

The Beginnings

"We 've been invited to the Fishers next Saturday," my husband told me one evening. "All three of us. For the day."

"What Fishers?" I asked absentmindedly, attending more to my two-year-old's dinner-table needs than my husband's dinner-table news.

"You know . . . the Amish couple I told you about. That's how they want to thank me."

That's how it all began for me, as unobtrusively as that. It had been months since my husband first told me about the Fishers, about how a local real-estate agent had sent them to him as a "nice young lawyer in town," one just establishing his practice, who would be willing to do the extra work required by inaccessible out-of-town clients buying a local farm. At the time, I had thought how interesting it would be for Steve to actually meet and deal with an Amish family. When he had gone to their rural Lancaster County home to solve sale-related problems, I had been vaguely jealous of the opportunity, but I never expected to have such a chance myself.

Then the Fishers' invitation came, followed by the appointed snowy February Saturday. I dressed cautiously that morning, in a skirt—not slacks—despite the weather, careful to wear no bright colors and no noticeable jewelry. After a hurried breakfast (hurried because I had changed clothes several times), we bundled ourselves and our son into the car and set off. Having been there before, my husband drove nonchalantly from the heavily traveled highways lined with tourist attractions to the two-lane, unlined rural roads winding through snow-silent farmland. He remained calm, but the closer we got, the more curious, excited, and nervous I became.

As we drove up the Fishers' lane and I caught my first glimpse of the windmill, the plain white clapboard house, and the woman in her dark blue dress, black apron, white covering, black stockings, and black shoes hurrying out to greet us, all I could think about was whether my calf-length blue corduroy skirt was too short, my flat-heeled but knee-high leather boots too fashionable, and the small gold studs in my pierced ears too pagan. In that instant, too, I wondered what I would say to Anna Fisher and how she would reply. I wondered whether I would make some terrible social gaffe and what her husband would be like. I wondered whether their children were friendly and whether my son would cry. I wondered what seemed like a hundred things in those first moments of meeting, but I never once wondered whether the people I was about to meet were literate.

Then, as that first visit passed in a blur of warmth and welcome, full of good food, fascinating conversation, and much laughter, I must have assumed the Fishers were literate for I never consciously considered the alternative. I noticed a Bible and several other black, leather-bound, apparently religious books on one table in the living room; I noticed a stack of newspapers near the couch; and when the four Fisher children took my son to their playroom, I noticed that he was comfortably surrounded by books, paper, crayons, and pencils as well as toys. So the Fisher home seemed not too unlike my own in terms of being a so-called literate environment, and my family was very comfortable there. Besides, Anna and Eli were so easy to talk to and we enjoyed each other's company so much—how could they not be literate?

The next day as I sat at my desk happily recalling the details of our visit, I started to write a thank-you note to Anna, but what I intended as a "note" grew into a multipage letter full of feelings, impressions, reactions, and what I thought were rhetorical questions. Several days later, however, Anna's thank-you for my thank-you arrived in a letter even longer than mine had been, full of her feelings, impressions, and responses to my questions. Though slightly disconcerted by the lined tablet paper Anna used as stationery, I was instantly enthralled by her articulate written voice, which strongly and clearly evoked her spoken one, and I could hear her talking to me as I read the letter repeatedly, mentally accumulating the stuff of my response. Her spelling and punctuation were so good that only an English teacher would see errors; instead, I noticed how much more legible her handwriting was than my own. At that time, I did not know Anna had only an eighth-grade education, nor could I have guessed that from her letters. To me, Anna was unquestionably literate, her literacy consistently confirmed by our correspondence over the next several years.

Ironically, perhaps, as I got to know Anna better, I realized we did not share the same levels or kinds of literacy, and I was often the less literate one. Anna knew the Bible much better than I, and she spoke and read Dutch and German in addition to English while I spoke and read neither. I had read few of the books she had; I subscribed to none of the same periodicals; and while we read cookbooks with equal facility,

Anna could make sense of quilting, sewing, and farming texts that were virtually inaccessible to me.

When I began to see my own illiteracy this way, I began, for the first time, to truly understand researchers who claim that while "literacy invariably involves people interacting with the written word, there is more than one kind of literacy and more than one way to be literate" (Anderson and Teale 1981, 4). Until I began moving in Old Order society, I knew that, like avocational literacies, various occupational literacies existed, and I knew I was illiterate when confronted by computer, engineering, or medical texts, but those seemed tangential to the one central literacy, the kind I believed I possessed. After all, the world in which I lived suggested I was truly literate: I could extract the "real" meaning from "real" literature, both British and American; I knew the philosophical differences between the *Washington Post* and the *New York Daily News*, the *New Republic* and the *National Review*; I understood the humor of Mark Russell and Lily Tomlin, the political religions of Ronald Reagan and Ted Kennedy, and the religious politics of Pat Robertson and Jesse Jackson. I could write anything from a letter to my immigrant grandfather to a doctoral dissertation, and I frequently did the *New York Times* Sunday crossword puzzle (though, admittedly, I rarely finished it). Surely, I was authentically literate.

As I got to know the Fishers, however, I learned there are different core literacies as well as different occupational ones and that my urban, white, Jewish, college-educated, middle-class variety is only one kind. The people who had taught me, both explicitly and implicitly, that the literacy of academe prepared me for all the most valid, valuable occupations and situations had been wrong. It took Anna Fisher to teach me that literacy truly is a cultural practice, not a decontextualized, universal set of skills and abilities automatically transferable across contexts. It is not the technology or isolated skills of reading and writing that count, but the understanding and application of those technologies and skills within particular cultural frameworks that truly matter.

I explicitly realized few of these things during the first eight years I knew the Fishers, however. During that time, I rarely thought about Anna's or Amish literacy, per se, nor did I realize that literacy—Anna's, mine, or anyone else's—was something to study concertedly. That realization came quite apart from my relationship with the Fishers when I decided to return to graduate school as a doctoral student in the Writing Program at the University of Pennsylvania. While Anna, Eli, and their children could not begin to understand why a thirty-five-year-old woman, who was a wife, mother, and English teacher would want to go back to school, they wished me well and only hoped my new occupation would not keep me any busier and keep us apart more often than my old one had. None of us ever imagined that my reincarnation as a student would involve them almost as much as it did me and bring us even closer.

It was in my first fall semester at Penn that literacy presented itself as an issue I had to consider. As a student in a course entitled "Literacy: Social and Historical Perspectives," I had to do a small-scale literacy study to meet course requirements. While I sat and listened to the professor describe the nature of the assignment, visions of the Fishers appeared before me. What an interesting paper they'd make, I thought, and I wondered if my professor would approve it. He said we would need his approval before starting, so after class I told him my idea, and he enthusiastically agreed. But his enthusiasm did not stop there. In the weeks that followed, he began systematically and relentlessly encouraging me to write my dissertation on Amish literacy, too. And not only did he encourage me, but he enlisted other professors and the dean of the graduate school in his cause as well. My concerns, fears, and objections were no match for their concerted efforts, so that semester I became an ethnographer among the Amish.

The idea of becoming an ethnographer was more than slightly daunting even with all that professional encouragement and support behind me. I knew ethnography was the anthropologists' method of choice, and I knew that in some senses my work among the Amish would be at least quasi-anthropological, but I feared that ethnography was as foreign and esoteric as the cultures to which it is most often applied. What I did not realize then was that I had been an ethnographer with the Fishers from day one of our relationship and that ethnography was both the most natural and most appropriate method for the formal study I was about to undertake. In fact, what ethnography is and how it works may be best illustrated by an event that occurred during the second year of the Fisher-Fishman alliance, long before I had ever heard the word.

That particular winter had been notably hard, paralyzing central Pennsylvania with its snow and icy cold. Anna Fisher and I had written increasingly long letters for months, sharing news of children's colds, husbands' crankiness, and our own longings for spring and each other's company. Though we had known each other for only a year before the season's siege began, that year had been filled not only with letters but with monthly visits during which weekends of making hay, canning produce, and washing endless dishes had combined with family outings, backyard baseball games, and endless conversation, all of which promoted an unusual but wonderful relationship. So when spring finally arrived and my family embarked for Lancaster once more, I could hardly wait to see Anna again.

As we drove up the winter-rutted lane, I could see Anna's husband, Eli, standing in the muddy yard talking to several other Amish men. Heedless of the mud or the other men, I responded to Eli's smile of welcome by bounding from the car to throw my arms around him in a hug and kiss of long-awaited greeting. In the midst of my excitement, however, I caught an unexpected glimpse of the three other men over Eli's shoulder; their faces were passive, but their eyes revealed both shock and amusement as this "English" woman in blue jeans and sneakers embraced their married friend. In that same moment, I realized Eli's face and body had stiffened—his arms and shoulders drawn in, his lips pressed tightly together, his eyes staring straight ahead. He was struck dumb, but I was mortified and he knew it. Though I quickly released my hold and Eli quickly took my hand in the traditional Amish handshake of greeting, I had to get away. Overwhelmed by confusion and embarrassment, I fled toward the protection of the house ostensibly to find Anna, who had witnessed the entire scene from a kitchen window.

That was in 1975. I remember it vividly—as does Anna—because it became a significant incident in our developing relationship and remains one we still laugh about when recalling our shared history. Yet the "hugging incident," as we now call it, was not a significant moment in my formal ethnographic research into Amish literacy because I was not a self-conscious ethnographer when it happened. In 1975, I was a temporarily retired high school English teacher turned full-time wife and mother, and one fortunate enough to have made Amish friends quite by chance. Therefore, when I realized what I had done and how Eli felt by putting myself in his position, I was not an ethnographer analyzing her data but a person trying to make sense of her experience. According to the faces and body language of Eli and his friends, I had made a terrible social move, and I needed to understand what I'd done wrong so I could both apologize and keep from making the same mistake again. In order to understand, however, I had to see Eli not just as a friend I had missed for months but as an Amishman surrounded by his Amish friends in their rural Lancaster County context where behavior appropriate to my upbringing did not work at all. In other words, I had to see the world and myself as others did at that moment, not as my usual unexamined ethnocentric perspective would have it.

Though I quickly figured out that the hugging, kissing, and verbal exuberance I expected at reunions both shocked and embarrassed men unaccustomed to such displays, I never suspected Anna's well-concealed reaction until she, months later, told me how she felt. Because I live in a world where married and unmarried women sometimes kiss other women's husbands and where it takes more than a cheek-directed kiss of greeting to provoke jealousy or possessiveness, I never perceived my actions as a personal threat to Anna. So while I understood the men's reaction to my blatant performance—and I could imagine Anna being similarly shocked—I would never have inferred her deep discomfort and uneasiness without her help. Yet Anna could not share those feelings with me immediately for two reasons—first, because she felt a conflict between her understanding of me and her culturally instinctive response to my behavior, which kept her from acting on either, and second, because though we were fast becoming close friends, we were not yet close enough for her to risk disclosing such personally powerful, important feelings. Not until we had shared nearly another year's experiences and confidences was there enough mutual trust for Anna to reveal how she had felt that day.

In short, the hugging incident involved several important human propensities and abilities that characterize ethnographic research: 1) participating actively in another culture; 2) seeing the world through other people's eyes; 3) understanding the concepts, practices, and beliefs that shape others' perceptions; and 4) developing personal relationships that facilitate both access and understanding. What I did in this instance people do all the time, on both large- and small-scale, short- and long-term bases. Getting to know an Asian merchant, an Indian student, or a Latin American colleague involves these skills and perspectives even if only briefly or occasionally. Moving to another region or neighborhood, starting a new job, or having a child immerses people in new cultures more completely and for a longer time. If we try to make sense of the world as we experience it in these daily ways—instead of condemning, dismissing, or simply muddling through—we are functioning as ethnographers. We just don't realize that on a day-to-day basis any more than I did the day I first hugged Eli Fisher.

In addition to being an unconsciously conducted human practice, however, ethnography is also a self-conscious research method, and as such is most often defined not in terms of what it is but rather in terms of what it's not. (See Magoon 1977; Mischler 1979; Emig 1981; Hymes 1982; Heath 1983; Harste, Woodward, and Burke 1984; and Calkins 1985 for helpful versions of such definitions.) As the hugging incident suggests, ethnography is not traditional experimental, positivistic research. It does not deal in researcher-created procedures conducted in researcher-created settings, and it does not aim for generalizable, context-free laws. Ethnography does not view subjects as objects; it does not think in terms of input, output, correlations, variables, or controlling hypotheses; and it does not rely on statistical models or computer programs for its data analysis. Briefly, that is what ethnography is not.

Briefly or otherwise, it is difficult to define ethnography in terms of what it is for several reasons. First, because it originated in anthropology, ethnography was designed to serve anthropological purposes that are only partially shared by researchers in other disciplines who have adopted the approach. This makes the usual definitions cast in anthropological terms seem only obliquely relevant to other fields, including education. Second, because ethnography is a fairly recent approach to fields like education, these new ethnographers are still discovering and trying to articulate what the method does or might mean to them. (See Gilmore and Glatthorn 1982 for a series of important articles on this topic.) And third, because different educational researchers doing different kinds of research claim ethnography as their method, ethnographic practices and studies seem conflicting, if not contradictory, even among self-identified practitioners.

So rather than attempt to define ethnography in some decontextualized, generalizable, supposedly objective way (which, in itself, would be antiethnographic and which, I suspect, would be of little interest to anyone but students of ethnography), I want to explain how ethnography facilitated this study and why it became my method of choice. Readers will then know how this study was conducted, understand its conception and perspective, and be better able to place it on the continuum of educational research as they have experienced that field.

First of all, after reading most of the extant literature about the Amish, I saw ethnography as the only method that would enable me to avoid what I came to think of as the "museum approach" many researchers take toward these people. Using traditional survey or other descriptive methods, they make what I consider an important inaccurate assumption: they seem to assume that all Amish—men and women, children and adults, Pennsylvanian and Iowan, eighteenth- and twentieth-century—can be displayed in the same case, as though a chronologically ordered stack of data and artifacts can be cross-cut along social, religious, or customary lines, revealing a representative tableau for visitors to view. While Amish quilts and clothes can be hung this way and Amish history factually laid out, somewhere in all of these patterns, somewhere creating all of these artifacts, there are people— not just A People, but individuals. Despite their apparent homogeneity, the Amish are distinct individuals who intentionally choose to maintain their shared appearance. Some previous research has helped make the strands of the Amish cultural web visible (Geertz 1973); I wanted to acknowledge a few of these individuals and discover their reasons for continuing to weave as they do.

Second, I realized that only through participant observation and subsequent "thick description" of these people in the context of their culture (Geertz 1973, 14) could I begin to discover and disclose both the basic humanity and cultural complexity central to understanding Amish society. Unlike research that focuses on what makes people different, reinforcing an us-them dichotomy, ethnography enables empathy without overlooking distinctiveness. It allows the researcher to be both insider and outsider—sometimes simultaneously, sometimes contrapuntally—and thereby allows her to discover what makes people ordinary as well as what makes them extraordinary. Such a sense of normalcy is not usually granted a "peculiar people," making ethnography particularly appropriate for learning about the Amish.

More particular complex concerns influenced my methodology choice, too. Confronted by at least three arenas for consideration—inside the home, outside the home, and inside the school—I needed an approach that would permit these separate foci but not require their total separation, a method that would enable me to consider each arena separately but would not let me forget their fundamental connections. In addition, confronted by a culture about which I knew little (and about which little is written) and by a community about which I knew little more (and about which nothing is written), I needed a method that did not require a pretense of knowing much. I needed a method that allowed relatively unencumbered inquiry, attributing no particular world view to the Amish nor encouraging premature closure through an early hypothesis on my part. Finally, confronted by the prospect of research into the lives of people I had known for years and who meant a great deal to me personally, I needed a method that would not reduce them to subjects or in any way manipulate them, a method that would respect their feelings, their complexity, and their integrity. Ethnography turned out to be that method.

Perhaps the simplest reason for choosing ethnography, however, was that it attempts to answer the two questions foremost in my mind at the outset of this study as they were when the Fishers and I first met: What is going on here? (Heath 1982; Smith 1983) and "What the devil [do] they think they're up to?" (Geertz 1976, 224).

While my choice of ethnography may seem self-evident for quasi-anthropological consideration of an Amish home and community, ethnography in the school may need further justification. Even before I realized how much my study would have to consider home and community, when I saw myself only as a teacher investigating teaching and learning, I realized the usual educational research methods would be inappropriate, for they seemed to miss the point in an Amish context. Pre- and post-testing, handing out surveys, counting student and teacher behaviors, assessing personality and leadership types, or evaluating adequacy of physical plant and extracurricular activities seemed somehow insufficient or irrelevant at Meadow Brook, the Old Order school the Fisher children attended. Yet none of the traditional school research I read seemed willing to more than tangentially admit that any school was other than generic, any students other than typical, any teacher not just "the teacher." Most research on schools and education seemed to assume

> that schools are primarily and exclusively agencies of formal education (rather than being social institutions); that pupils are isolated individuals (rather than social beings who participate in the life of peer societies, ethnic groups, and the like); that formal education is synonymous with education; and that the principal task of the teacher is to educate. (Wax and Wax 1971, 3)

None of which seemed to be the Old Order case. And since most traditional education research rests on such assumptions about what education is for, I had to find a method with assumptions that would not preclude all but its own intentions.

Finally, I realized that any method other than ethnography would severely limit the scope of my research, producing not just an incomplete study but a misrepresentative, misleading one. Meadow Brook, like all other schools, is created and influenced by its social and cultural situations. Without a method aware of and able to accommodate these outside influences on the children and on the school itself, my study would be of limited value as it ignored or precluded patterns existing and created across contexts.

For all these reasons then, I realized that if I wanted to study Amish literacy seriously, I had to become a serious, more self-conscious ethnographer than I had been the day I hugged Eli. But as I self-consciously began my fieldwork, I experienced many of the problems common in ethnographic pursuits—problems in establishing a participant's role in the community, problems in establishing and maintaining relationships with community members, and problems in collecting data. The one area in which I had no problem, however, was finding an inside informant (or informants) willing and able to assist in data analysis.

Because of my long-standing relationship with the Fishers, my access to the field was automatic and my role was that of friend; yet this pre-existing entrée carried it's own potential problem—the possible damage a change in my status from friend to researcher friend might create. Several times during the first months of my formal data-collection period, Anna commented, more often seriously than not, that she feared my research would interfere with our relationship. Most damaging, she thought, might be a change in her children's perception of me, perhaps leading to their alienation. "I don't want your book coming between us," she emphatically warned.

Nor did I want my professional interests to eclipse my personal ones. There were times, particularly during the writing of the study, that I confronted information ethnographically significant but humanly damaging, when an incident or comment revealed more about an individual's perspective than that individual wanted known. Although such unanticipated, unpredictable reactions from informants often gave me the insights that make ethnography so valuable, I had to distinguish carefully between what would help me and what would hurt them. As an ethnographer I was my own research instrument, and, through much fine tuning, I learned to make the distinctions I thought necessary to separate exploration from exploitation.

To the nuclear Fisher family, then, I was a trusted friend with outside interests rather than a friendly, interested outsider, and I became that to their extended family and close friends as well. We had shared many meals, swapped many stories, and experienced each other's families and feelings for many years before my fieldwork formally began. We had a history of mutually explorative discussions; their questions about Judaism, higher education, learning to drive, gender and religious discrimination were as numerous and as freely asked as mine about Amish religion and custom, parochial schools, birthing cows, and being a tourist attraction in your own hometown. When my yellow legal pad became omnipresent, it was accepted, too, as just a manifestation of my work, which they recognized as part of me in the same way their work is part of them.

To Verna Burkholder, the Meadow Brook teacher whom I met through the Fishers, my role was that of fellow teacher with an outsider's perspective, not just an outside teacher. I came asking for her help to increase my knowledge of teaching, a desire with which she easily empathized. In some of our earliest conversations, Verna learned that, like her, I had confronted unhappy parents and insensitive school boards, that I sometimes felt isolated in my classroom and frustrated by "unreachable" students, and that I still believe teaching to be one of the most difficult but most rewarding professions there is. Verna knew without my suggesting it that she might learn something from my study, and she enjoyed the idea of collaborating on such a mutually beneficial project. As my research continued and we ate lunch, took walks, washed blackboards, and spent long after-school hours together, more personal matters arose; Verna felt free enough to ask me questions similar to those I asked her, and we both felt relaxed enough to move from the professional to a more personal level.

It was with some surprise, therefore, that I received the news of my school banishment from Anna alone (see chapter 3 for that story), with the addendum that Verna had concurred with the parents' decision and had declared the final spring picnic for families and "scholars" only, successfully precluding me. Several weeks after school ended, however, I received a letter from Verna, apologizing for what had happened. She hoped my project was not ruined, and she offered to meet me at the school for any further discussion I might want, suggesting that "if [I] didn't have enough to write about before, [I] certainly did now." In the last analysis, I was still a colleague but still an outsider, too.

To the Meadow Brook parents I never became more than an insider's outside friend, instead becoming less. They never saw any benefit for themselves in my work or in my presence, showing little interest in my intentions even at our initial interview when my explanation of the proposed project (including assurance of anonymity) was met with averted eyes, and my offer to let them read the manuscript, with shrugged shoulders. Only my connection to the Fishers seemed to matter ("When Verna mentioned that you were a friend of Eli and Anna, we decided it was okay," the school treasurer told me), along with some vague apprehension about outsiders who want to come in ("We know we can't shut the door to people from outside if we want to keep our schools").

My de facto alignment with the outside finally overrode my relationship with the Fishers, however, when after five months a group of school parents decided that "too much [was] getting out" and I should not return. Although at first I was both frustrated and angry about not being told of their discomfort sooner and not being given the opportunity to further explain or clarify my intentions, with hindsight I see that my relationship to the school community developed neither as slowly nor as personally as did my relationships elsewhere. Despite my presence at meetings, my enjoyment of programs, and my participation in projects, I interacted with a group, not with individuals, and because this group constantly guards itself against people like me, my sudden, seemingly impersonal approach had done nothing to mitigate their fears.

Perhaps if I had gone more slowly, perhaps if I had gotten to know individual families separately and shared more meals and more stories with the other women, my outsider's status would have become background to more acceptable, personal qualities. Then again, perhaps not.

The majority of my data collection occurred through participant observation in these three roles as family friend, teaching colleague, and community participant/visitor, and much of the data consisted of verbal interactions, including interviews. While ethnographic procedure may include both formal and informal questioning, the latter often occurring spontaneously, the former seemed inappropriate in an Amish context. Within what superficially appear to be rigid formal patterns, the Old Order Amish and the Old Order Mennonites tend to be somewhat informal by outside standards. People work side by side across situations, without distinction between host and guest, family member and friend, and with everyone on first name bases, without distinctions of age, sex, or status. That meant that at times, though I had a "formal" set of questions to ask, I could elicit better answers while doing dishes, washing the blackboard, or driving the car than by sitting still attending to pencil and paper.

The need to collect such conversational data raised a methodological dilemma inherent in my particular research situation (and one I suspect may affect many ethnographers, regardless of circumstance). Though field notes are the traditional ethnographic currency, audio- and video-tapes are often recommended as the most comprehensive, accurate, reproducible methods of data collection, especially in classrooms (Spradley and McCurdy 1972; Spradley 1980; Shultz 1983). Yet recording equipment is less than common in most contexts, creating a particularly notable intrusion in mine.

Standards of the Old Order Amish and Older Order Mennonite Parochial and Vocational Schools of Penna., the governing document of Old Order schools, says "No radios or tape recorders allowed" (p. 28). This rule comes under the heading "Rules for Children," but it is listed between "No photographing in school building or on school grounds" and "Library books shall be such as is conducive to building christian character." From this I inferred that the presence of recording equipment would not be welcome, regardless of who brought it, so I never considered recording other than by hand at Meadow Brook School. I happily discovered, however, that the ability to record verbatim can be learned, and though my handwriting suffered and my abbreviations evolved slowly, I became increasingly able to record classroom talk. (Occasional bits of discourse were lost to my notes, as some examples in chapter 5 reveal.)

Recording at home and in the community was a slightly different, though related, problem. One day I brought my battery-operated tape recorder to the farm and let the children play with it, recording and listening to their own voices. Eli and Anna were curious too, at first, then amused, then annoyed. They enjoyed it when the five children decided to sing hymns, but they did not enjoy having their own conversations "interrupted" by the presence of the machine, which is no larger than a small transistor radio. I thought that in time everyone would forget about the recorder and life would go on around it, but I was wrong. Perhaps because of the novelty or perhaps because of something less benign, neither parents nor children were able to forget that "it" was there, not even when it was under a sofa cushion. Anna asked that I not bring it back.

I never even attempted to use the tape recorder at community functions. Just as the family was unable to ignore it, I sensed that other families and individuals would react similarly. My presence among these people was intrusion enough; in most cases, they accepted me more completely than I dared anticipate. I believe, however, that their willingness to tolerate my inappropriate clothes and strange manner would not have extended to my modern contrivance.

So for me, data collection meant field notes written unobtrusively in the field and/or rewritten voluminously as soon after as possible. But it also meant lists of questions taken to Anna and hours of focused discussion in her kitchen or on her porch swing, sometimes involving Eli or the children, but most often just the two of us. Anna's role in this research cannot be overestimated, for she was not only the primary informant but became a collaborator in the best ethnographic tradition. Though at first we both assumed the research task was mine, soon Anna began articulating questions of her own and discovering meaning she never realized before my research made her "think about things." At first, the notion that an ethnographic study can be useful to those studied (Spradley 1980, 20–21) seemed ludicrous in this context, but as the research evolved, both Anna, as informant, and I, as investigator, gained clarity that reshaped both our individual thinking and what became, in some respects, our mutual research.

What follows here, then, is a topic-oriented ethnography, the product of years of participant observation, ethnographic interviews, artifact collection, and close researcher-informant relationships. It is at once the study of a culture and of literacy, the story of two families' and two women's relationships, and the product of one writer's significantly raised consciousness. Both Anna and I welcome you to our world, to enjoy and perhaps to learn from it as we have.

T W O

The Family at Home

• *The Context* •

On a November Thursday in 1966, twenty-one-year-old Eli Fisher married nineteen-year-old Anna Stoltzfus in a traditional Old Order ceremony. Their first home was a small, rented house in rural Lancaster County where they would live until they could afford to buy or rent land and begin the farming life they both desired. Until then, Eli would work in a trailer factory while Anna kept house and "went to market" (sold produce) for a neighbor. One year after their marriage, their first child—a daughter named Sarah—was born. Two years later, they were able to rent a seventy-six-acre farm and start their own dairy operation, albeit on someone else's land.

For eleven years Eli and Anna rented that farm, postponing the dream of buying their own, because they realized the rented one had certain advantages: It was within a barefoot walk of Anna's parents', sister's, and brothers' homes and within a buggy ride of Eli's; it kept them near their friends and other relatives; and it was affordable.

Yet renting had significant disadvantages, besides the feeling of impermanence. Their non-Amish landlord expected his tenants to make any repairs, no matter how large, and the house needed a new roof. The barn needed work, too, and the lane was pitted and rocky, both problems for a farmer with dairy cows to house and frequent milk-truck pickups to accommodate. More complicated, perhaps, were problems presented by what the farm did offer—electricity and a telephone, neither of which the Fishers wanted but neither of which could be removed since future tenants might want them.

Because farming was their chosen life-style and Lancaster County was their home, Eli and Anna patched the roof, repaired the barn, and fixed the lane repeatedly, never wanting to make long-term investments but unable to ignore immediate needs. They used the existing electric lights after dark because the lanterns they would have preferred were prohibited by their landlord's insurance policy, and they used the telephone on the kitchen wall when calling someone seemed necessary. Four of the five Fisher children arrived while they lived on that farm; three were actually born in that house. The three oldest children attended the one-room school down the road, and all the Fishers called Lancaster home.

Finally, however, the frustrations of renting grew intolerable. The family needed a place of their own as much as they wanted one, so the search for their own farm began. Though they wanted to stay in Lancaster County, farmland there sold for between $8,000 and $10,000 an acre that year, an economic reality that forced Eli and Anna to look westward as had many other Amish they knew. They looked in areas several hours away from Lancaster—but always within established Amish church districts—until they found what they wanted and could afford: 120 acres of good land with a useless barn and a barely inhabitable house. The owner wanted to sell; his current tenant could not afford to buy but wanted to stay, so Eli and Anna offered money to the owner and time to the tenant. They would buy the farm but remain in Lancaster until their children were older and could help manage the larger operation. Then they would build a new barn, rebuild the house, and the tenant would have to leave.

Three years later the building began. Vanloads of Amish men traveled with their hired drivers from Lancaster every day to build the barn and the house and returned to Lancaster every night, a round trip of more than four hours. They built the barn first, according to Eli's specifications for the herd he hoped to develop. They started the house only after the barn was finished, demolishing most of the old shell to construct a new kitchen, new summer kitchen, new bathrooms, new living rooms, and new bedrooms for the family, saving the habitable older portion primarily for guests and storage. They removed all electric wiring and telephone lines from the property. This would be Eli and Anna's home.

Eli and his brothers, uncles, and cousins worked through the winter, each day building a fire in what had been the kitchen of the old house to create one warm space in which to eat lunch and thaw out. (That portion of the ramshackle structure remained until the very end of the building process, when with great pleasure the men reduced it to a pile of rubble behind the new house. The heap of bricks, mortar, and boards stayed alongside Anna's garden for months until she convinced Eli to remove it and with it, the last physical reminder of how far they had come.) The traveling crew built the house almost entirely themselves, contributing their individual blueprint drawing and carpentry skills, and calling no professionals until plumbing problems arose. Finally, on a gray, snow-dotted March day, months after the process began, the family, with their cows, horses, mules, and machines, tearfully left Lancaster for the diaspora, joining other Amish exiles leaving present homes for future survival.

• *The House* •

Though an Amish farm in conception and construction, little marks the Fisher home visibly as such. The white aluminum siding and pale brick exterior of the two-story house, the well-kept lawn with flowered borders, the white barn, maroon carriage shed, maroon-and-white horse barn and storage buildings are not particularly "Amish." Only the windmill and its metal tank in the yard permanently suggest anything unusual. In fact, what is absent marks the farm more than what is present. When all is quiet, the scene is unusually pristine for the 1980s: no modern farm equipment, no trucks or cars, and no power lines are in evidence.

When all is not quiet, however, the farm becomes a vibrant anachronism, with the family buggy or pony cart unhitched in the front yard, identical black trousers and pastel shirts in graduated sizes swinging from the clothesline, men in straw hats and women in long dresses, many with bare feet, busily moving between house and barn, calling to each other in Dutch. Because none of this can be seen from the road—the lane too long and the trees too plentiful—once there, the farm seems like a bubble in time.

Inside, the house itself is no more evidently Amish than outside. Its main living space, a kitchen–dining–living-room combination, contains a modern, white, two-door, gas-powered refrigerator (bright with children's artwork), a four-burner gas stove, a double-bowl stainless-steel sink, modern wood cabinets, and pale green formica counters. The central wooden table is large and highly polished, comfortably seating twelve on surrounding wooden benches and chairs. A wood stove shares one corner with a wooden-cabineted sewing machine. Upholstered furniture, including a brown vinyl recliner and a large green-tufted rocker, sit along the opposite wall. Heavy green sun-blocking window shades hang from the four large windows, protecting the living area from afternoon glare. Pale green-and-white pebble-textured vinyl covers the floor; the walls are paneled in wood to chair-rail height, vinyl papered pale green above.

The bathroom is equally modern and efficient. A long cabinetlike vanity with a white-and-gold flecked formica top and white fiberglass sink faces a white fiberglass bathtub and shower combination and a modern toilet. Two large built-in wooden closets hold linens and toiletries, while a large, sliding-door closet holds hanging clothes. Beneath the single window covered with its white lace curtain sits a traditional silver-painted radiator.

Like the outside of the house, the kitchen and bathroom are notable for what is not there as much as for what is. Both seem to have inordinately long expanses of counter space, but the dimensions are not unusual; the absence of toaster, blender, electric can opener, and coffee maker in the kitchen and of cosmetics, curling iron, hair dryer, and razors in the bathroom leaves considerable uncluttered space. Also "missing" from an otherwise modern house are the dishwasher, clothes dryer, vacuum cleaner, and other small electric appliances. A wringer washing machine sits in the corner of the summer kitchen and must be connected to the sink and the floor drain for use.

The house does have a few features that mark it as unusual, however. A gas lantern hangs from a green-and-white metal shade over the kitchen table and a tank-based gas floor lamp sits between the couch and the rocking chair. An oil-burning hurricane lamp sits on the bathroom vanity, an ashtray for used matches beside it. The summer kitchen, across the hall from the regular kitchen, is outfitted with an old four-burner gas stove, a gas-powered refrigerator, a sink, a large brick canning oven, and the "bucket-a-day" coal stove that heats the bathroom and one bedroom. Serving as a mudroom all year, a place to wash before completing the trip from barn to house, it is busiest in summer when Anna and the girls can their garden produce (jars of which line the walls of the cavelike cellar).

In addition, the house has a formal living room, notable for its size and appearance. Reached through a door in the sitting area, the living room is empty but for the many wooden chairs and one small couch lining its four walls. This may be the most definitively "Amish" part of the house, for this room was built specifically to accommodate church services, quiltings, and other large community and family gatherings. It remains empty and unused except at such special times.

Though not as cluttered as non-Amish houses may be with devices and decorations, the Fisher house is neither bare nor stark. In addition to the plants hanging in macramé holders near most windows and the quilted pillows and crocheted afghans in the sitting area, pictures and signs appear everywhere. Immediately inside the front door, opposite a desk holding the family business and personal papers, hangs a large cross-stitch sampler—"Friendship is a rainbow between two people"— on which the word *rainbow* dominates, embroidered in appropriate bright colors. Facing the door is a poster picturing wheat stalks bending in summer sunshine, with the motto "The test of our love to God is the love we have for one another." Another embroidered piece hangs further down the hallway (a picture of Jesus Christ and the words "Peace I leave with you, my peace I give unto you. . . . Let not your heart be troubled, neither let it be afraid"), and another poster hangs in the bathroom (a picture of a mountain waterfall with the words "God is my rainbow in the storms of life").

The living area, too, displays such decorations. An armetale bread tray with the motto "Give us this day our daily bread" and an engraving of two men harvesting wheat leans against the backsplash near the sink. Directly behind the table hangs a bulletin board covered with newspaper clippings, greeting cards, public-sale handbills, and slogans, the latter handwritten by Anna on white paper trimmed with pinking shears and culled from various sources. Though these change periodically, some of the longest-lasting ones include:

When you study the scriptures "hit or miss," you are likely to miss more than you hit.

We must adjust ourselves to the Bible—never the Bible to ourselves.

Never sacrifice the spiritual condition of your children for the physical condition of your house.

How confusing when someone gives good advice but sets a bad example.

If you give what you do not need, it isn't giving.

The formal living room, too, has its wall hangings. Made by Anna's mother as gifts for the family, "Family Records" are displayed there. Hand-painted in black on white glass trimmed with pink roses are the birthdays and anniversaries of two generations.

Yet another room, the glass-enclosed porch-playroom is decorated by its contents stored primarily on open-shelf bookcases of varying heights. Toys insufficiently contained by wooden toy chests abound—Fisher-Price, Playskool, Matchbox, Lego, and other major manufacturers are evident. Crayons and colored pencils, lined and unlined paper, pencils and pens are kept here, as is the family library. Amish religious books sit between bookends atop the highest bookcase, accessible only to the tallest people. Fiction and nonfiction, paperbacks and hardbacks, reference and recreational reading fill the shelves below and spill into the living area itself, often stacked on convenient tables.

• *The Individuals* •

Who are the seven people living in this house? Eli Fisher, two years older than his wife, shares essentially the same background, though he was one of eleven children in a Lancaster County Amish farm family and she, one of four. Neither tall nor fat, Eli has the presence of a very large man. A black beard and heavy black eyebrows cloud his face, making even passive expressions seem ominous. When he frowns in displeasure or confusion, darkness looms. When he frowns to cajole or tease, however, light shines from his dark eyes, removing any threat. His voice is deep and somewhat harsh, his smile broad and heartening.

Eli's hands may be his most revealing feature. Thick, heavily calloused, and permanently lined with grime, they attest to work done with few labor-saving devices. Horses and mules pull his buggy and plow. A diesel engine cools his milk tank and powers his semiautomatic milkers. Otherwise, Eli plants and harvests tobacco, corn, and hay, tends and milks his cows and heifers, uses and maintains his equipment, feeds and houses his animals and family with his own hands and the daily help of only his wife and children. Eli's hand controls most others it takes in the characteristic Amish single, downward handshake of greeting, and it does other things with equal firmness and equal pleasure, including swing a baseball bat, use a fishing rod, and hold a child.

Anna Fisher is a thirty-six-year-old mother of five, married to a dairy farmer, living on their own farm and helping to make it home. Born and raised in Lancaster County, Pennsylvania, she attended a one-room public school through the eighth grade, as did her sister, two brothers, and both parents. Anna cleans, cooks, bakes, sews, quilts, gardens, milks cows, bales hay, plants tobacco, and cares for her family, among other tasks. Yet no list of relevant facts, no matter how extensive, could reveal the joy she experiences watching her children hunt for Easter eggs, the pleasure she finds in a moment of seated silence, the exuberance she brings to games of Score Four and shuffleboard (or her glee when she beats her husband), the concern she feels for a sick friend or an ailing marriage, or the faith that dominates and undergirds her daily life.

The duality of Anna Fisher becomes most apparent when she dresses to "go out." One evening when I arrived early for our planned trip to market, I stood in the kitchen, looking down the hall, so she and I could talk while she got ready. Padding from bedroom to bathroom and back again, Anna's stockinged feet made wispy sounds against the vinyl flooring as her concerted steps vibrated through the floorboards. I watched the transformation as unencumbered Anna, youthful in her loose-fitting forest-green dress and black stockings with her waist-length hair falling freely, became an Amish Woman, black apron tied tightly above her waist, white net prayer covering fixed firmly on her center-parted, tightly knotted hair, and heavy black oxfords guarding her feet, removing all softness from her step. The smile of pleasure on her smooth unlined round face told me it was Anna coming down the hall, but she looked, for all the world, like a no-nonsense, commonsense woman in plain clothes, an exemplary Amish woman.

Sarah, the eldest Fisher child, is sixteen and has started "running with the young folks," as the Amish call the social activities of their unmarried children between the ages of sixteen and their early twenties. While still in school Sarah considered becoming a teacher because school and books were her greatest pleasures. During her "three-hour" year (between completion of eighth grade and her fifteenth birthday when she went to school three hours each week), she sometimes substituted for her former teacher and sometimes worked as her unpaid assistant. Also during that year, however, Sarah began working three days a week for Lapp's Meat and Cheese, selling at a local farmers' market, and her pleasures began to change. Teaching school looked increasingly restrictive, with too many regimented hours and too many take-home activities. It lacked the excitement of market, of people and freedom and spontaneity. Her life began to revolve around market on Thursdays, Fridays, and Saturday mornings, and the young folks on Saturday evenings and Sundays.

But Sarah was missed at home. Her father missed her company and assistance in the barn, her mother in the house. As the fun of market became commonplace, Sarah missed them too. So now Sarah works at home during the week and looks forward to weekends of gabbing, game playing, and singing with her friends. She made the crucial decision to "join church" at sixteen, but that does not keep her from wishing there were more than one Saturday in the week.

Daniel is fifteen and just out of school. For the first time no "hired boy" lives with his family during the week, because Daniel now has the time and ability to work alongside his father in the barn and in the field from early morning until late at night. When Eli comes in for supper, caked with dirt and more exhausted than hungry, Daniel is not waiting in the house with the children but comes in right behind his father, looking and feeling the same way. And when Eli returns to the barn at 9:00 P.M. to repair equipment or complete unfinished business, Daniel goes too. Anna keeps adjusting the sleeves in Daniel's shirts to accommodate his increasingly well-muscled arms, and though Eli can still wrestle Daniel to a fall—a fact Eli reluctantly demonstrates when necessary—the match grows progressively more even.

Though he has assumed his place at home, Daniel is still too young to run with the young folks and watches Sarah, impatiently awaiting his sixteenth birthday. Occasionally her friends invite him to play baseball, and Daniel makes his sister smile at the astonishing strength and grace he brings to his favorite game. Caught temporarily between childhood and adolescence, Daniel combines the unfettered joy of playing ball with new-found concern about the obstinate curl in his hair on humid days. Sarah can provoke unexpected fury by commenting on how his "ears were lowered" after a haircut, but Anna still receives boundless filial appreciation for putting a new band in his mandatory hat.

Katie was always the family tomboy. Preferring fieldwork to housework, the barn to the kitchen, Katie's mule-driving voice at age seven had the same tenor and confidence at the reins as her father's. Her smudged face, unruly hair, scabbed knees, and constant motion contrasted markedly with Sarah, who was sewing, cooking, and reading at the age that her sister was still running with their brothers, wrestling with their pet dogs and cats, and singing while she worked.

Now twelve, Katie still sings and still runs, but she has slowed down enough to learn fundamental embroidery and sewing and to start cooking and baking; she has even started reading more. She watches Sarah blush when her boyfriend's name is mentioned, both teasing and wondering about what happens when the young folks gather. As the oldest

Fisher child still in school and the only girl at home to help her mother on weekends, Katie seems to both recognize and welcome her new female responsibilities. But she still looks forward to the arrival of the family's two Fresh Air Fund children each summer, especially Aleesha's, a girl her age with whom she plays tag, jumps rope, and rides the pony.

Small, slim, and dark, Amos could get lost among his more assertive siblings. Spending most of his time alone or with Eli, Jr., Amos once favored Matchbox cars and trucks over people and conversation. Even at school he found himself alone in his grade, with no one to recite or commiserate with. Amos did his schoolwork and chores, obeyed his teacher and parents, and stayed in the background, speaking more Dutch than English, until recently.

In fourth grade, the year he turned eleven, Amos discovered his true love: reading. He had always liked books, reading whatever he found at home, but he began to pursue them actively. When not working, Amos was reading. After chores, before and after meals, in the buggy on the way to church, Amos read, by flashlight if necessary. He even started taking a book to the barn, concealing it inside the front of his pants. When Eli discovered this cause of poorly or incompletely done chores, however, Amos's barn reading stopped. Little House books and Walt Disney books, *Young Pilot* and *Ranger Rick*, things already in and coming to the house were not enough. Subscriptions to *ZooBooks* and *Cards of Knowledge* soon started in his name, and he reads each one over and over again. He has read all of Daniel's Hardy Boys books and borrows others from friends, sometimes finishing a book in only a day or two (a feat that particularly amazes Katie). Amos will play baseball, smashball, or other games with the family, but his eyes shine most brightly when he can share a book with someone else.

Eli, Jr., is the only Fisher child who does not remember life in Lancaster. Though born there, he moved with the family before he was two and has grown up into the life of a boy on his family's farm, without the daily presence of aunts, uncles, cousins, and grandparents. Whether that will make a difference cannot be foreseen, but Eli has taken his place in the nuclear family rapidly and with remarkable commitment.

At six, Eli, Jr., is independently driving the mules and doing chores his father sometimes hesitates to assign his youngest child. Despite the pudgy cheeks and big, dark eyes reminiscent of his baby days, Eli's willingness and determination to please his parents and prove himself mark the set of his mouth and the intent innocence with which he meets others' gazes.

Eli started school with the same attitude he has at home. Determined to succeed as a "scholar," he became a model first grader, bringing home excellent papers and getting superior report cards. Aligning himself with the only brother still in school and the one with whom he used to play most often, Eli follows Amos, reading almost as much and requesting his own magazine subscriptions. Looking to Daniel for batting instruction and Sarah for more personal help, Eli knows he is the baby of the family, but he is not a baby anymore.

• *Reading at Home* •

At home, at the center of the Fishers' lives, reading fills almost as many hours as conversation does. Reading entertains and edifies; it exercises and strengthens faith; and it maintains links with family and friends. In the few minutes preceding a meal, after supper, at the end of a day, or at any time on Sunday, one, a few, or all seven family members may be reading in the living area. And not infrequently, when everyone else is working, a younger boy will return to the house and his reading, only to be summoned back outside by Eli's command. Individuals may be engrossed in their own texts; two children, snugly seated in one large chair, may share a book, newspaper, or magazine on their common lap; or a parent and children may share—Eli, Jr., for example, encircled by his father's newspaper-holding arms, reading inside pages, while Amos, seated beside his brother, reads the outside ones.

On a cold January Sunday night four adults and four children were playing separate games of Dutch Blitz (a card game resembling double solitaire played with a special deck), other children were building with Dominoes, and both Elis were reading, the little one with a book on the couch, the big one a newspaper in the recliner alongside.

"Where are your new books?" father asked son, referring to a set of Walt Disney books my son had outgrown and given to Eli and Amos.

Eli, Jr., pointed to a stack on the floor from which his father chose *Lambert, the Sheepish Lion*. As Eli, Sr., began reading aloud, Eli, Jr., climbed onto the arm of the recliner and snuggled against his father. Eli's reading was so dramatic, however, particularly in the dialogue between Lambert and his lioness mother, soon everyone was listening to the story instead of playing their separate games. Laughing out loud at the antics of the cub who preferred cavorting with the sheep to stalking with the lions, Eli held his enlarged audience through the rest of the story.

As most of us returned to our games when he finished the book, Eli asked, "Where's the *Dairy*?"

Daniel left his game and walked toward the couch. "It's in here," he said, rummaging through the newspapers and magazines stacked in the magazine rack beside the couch until he found a thick newsletter called *Dairy World*, published by IBA, the Independent Buyer's Association to which Eli belongs.

Eli leafed through the publication, standing and walking over to the wood stove as he did. Leaning against the stove, he began reading aloud without preface. All conversation stopped as everyone again attended to Eli's loudly expressive reading voice:

A farmer was driving his wagon down the road. On the back was a sign which read, "Experimental Vehicle. Runs on oats and hay. Do not step in exhaust."

Everyone laughed, including Eli, who then read the remaining jokes on the humor page. All our games forgotten, we shared remembered riddles and jokes until it was time for bed.

While reading aloud happens frequently among the Fishers—parents or older children reading to younger ones, or an individual sharing with the group—worth noting is the current absence of a bedtime oral reading ritual. While prebed reading is common, it occurs downstairs or upstairs, as often silently as orally, as often individually as not. Anna recalls reading to Sarah and Daniel when they were small enough to be tucked in, but now singing accompanies any tucking in of the younger children who, in most instances, have read for themselves earlier in the evening.

One variety of oral reading does remain regular and ritualistic, however, occurring on nonchurch Sunday mornings when everyone gathers for family devotions. Then all the Fishers take turns reading Bible verses aloud, on holidays reading the appropriate Scripture, at other times reading individual selections. Before Eli, Jr., could read, someone would read a verse slowly, pausing every few words so he could repeat what was said. Eli and Anna insist the children read aloud for two reasons: "so we can hear what they're saying" and because "they keep it a lot better than if we read it."

(The Fishers use the King James Version of the Bible, Anna citing Revelations' command not to change the words of the Scripture as the reason. "Revelations says not to change words because changing words would change meanings, but some feel changing words brings out meanings," she explained, so "some [Amish] use The Living Bible, instead." The Fishers also read a German edition of the Bible and "take the two together" for their understanding.)

A second kind of family devotional oral reading comes from *Martyrs Mirror*, a large, heavy tome full of graphic descriptions and woodcut illustrations of the tortured deaths of early Anabaptists. I had assumed that only Eli and Anna read this book, even then reading "not too much at one time [because] it makes [Anna] feel sick to think what those people suffered for their faith," but everyone listens as Eli reads on Sunday. "We think it's important that they know their own history," Anna explained.

Also during Sunday devotions, the children recite verses their parents assigned for memorization earlier that morning. Sarah, Daniel, and Katie receive the same assignment; Amos and Eli, Jr., get an easier one. Memorization selections may come from the Bible or from Amish hymns, verses "that have the most meaning . . . that you build on [i.e., use in many contexts and as the tune basis for further learning]." In both cases,

Eli and Anna choose portions their parents once cited as important. "What we learned at home is what we teach ours," Anna said.

Text-based hymn singing, too, is part of Sunday ritual. The Fishers take turns choosing and leading songs, using *Kinder-Lieder* (Children's Songs)—a book Anna and Eli used when they attended Saturday "German school" to supplement their public school education—and *Dos Neue Kinder-Lieder*, which combines *Kinder-Lieder* content with *Gesang-Buch* (Song-Book) content (songs sung at nonchurch "singings" which generally have faster tunes and some English equivalents).

None of these is the hymnal used in church services, however. That book, the *Ausbund* (Selection), is a collection of hymns written by imprisoned sixteenth-century Anabaptists about their experiences and their faith, making the song texts similar to that of *Martyrs Mirror*. The Fishers have several copies of the *Ausbund*, Eli using one in which he has made tune notations when he attends "practice singings" with other male church members. No one takes a copy to church because the congregation owns a set of books that moves with the benches from each church location to the next.[1]

Eli and Anna carefully attempt to control all reading material that enters their home. Some books are standard Amish volumes, including the Bible, the song books, *Martyrs Mirror*, and what they call "the Directory."[2] Others are standard reference volumes—e.g., German and English dictionaries, bird and animal identification books. There are Bible-story collections, children's classics, such as *Black Beauty* and *Heidi*, and inspirational fiction and nonfiction—*Dorie, the Girl Nobody Loved* by Erwin Lutzer and Doris Van Stone, *Tortured for Christ* by Richard Wurmbrand, *Faith Despite the KGB* by Hermann Hartfield, and *In My Father's House* by Corrie Ten Boom, to name only a few.

Anna buys their books primarily from a local Christian bookstore and from an Amish-operated dry-goods store, both of which she trusts not to stock objectionable material. When she sees interesting books in other places—in the drugstore, the book-and-card shop, or at a yard sale—she uses the publisher's name as a guide to acceptable content. Though she once frequented the local public library with the children, its out-of-the-way location and due-date constraints make it an inconvenient source. During the school year, however, the school library and other children supply acceptable books for the Fishers that are more easily obtained and returned.

Gift-giving occasions also bring books for the children, people who know them selecting individual- and family-appropriate titles. One year at Christmas, for example, Amos received *Stories of the Patriarchs* from his grandfather and Daniel got *The Shattered Helmet* (A Hardy Boys adventure) from a cousin. Each child has received a songbook from their maternal grandparents as a birthday gift at one time or another. My family, too, often gives gifts of books, Hardy Boys for Daniel, Little House books for Sarah and Katie, Disney and other children's books for Amos and Eli, Jr. (When my son's elementary school was discarding outdated texts and workbooks, we offered those to the Fishers. They accepted several cartons of books, keeping single copies at home "for playing school" while giving the rest to their actual school for supplementary use.)

In addition to trusting stores, publishers, and individuals for known categorical guidance, Eli and Anna trust them for specific recommendations as well. Anna often borrows or buys books suggested by her mother and sisters. As our relationship developed, she came to trust my judgment as I learned to exercise it in her behalf. Early in our relationship, for example, I brought Anna some summer fruit recipes clipped from a national women's magazine. Anna's enthusiastic response prompted me to offer the magazines, uncut, as I finished with them, at which her smile immediately faded.

"No, no thank you," she replied, shaking her head for emphasis.

"Why not?" I wondered.

"I trust you," she replied. "Just bring me what you think I'd be interested in. I don't want the rest of the magazine. That doesn't interest me."

Since then I have given Anna various recipes, articles, and newspaper clippings I thought she would find interesting (the most recent a discussion of magic drugs and miracle-cure quackery that appeared in the Sunday newspaper *Parade Magazine*), all of which have been well received.

Some texts enter the Fisher home not by choice but by necessity. As a farmer, Eli finds certain reading mandatory. Feed and equipment salesmen offer written information touting and explaining their products, which Eli must read, first to select among them and then to use the chosen items properly. (A recently purchased fertilizer spreader came with only metric directions, however. Eli had no book with conversion information and had to ask a friend to "translate" for him.) A contract binds him to his milk cooperative, and a receipt accompanies every milk check, both contract and checks required reading, too.

Other institutions demand reading, as well. The Production Credit and Federal Land Bank loans that financed the Fishers' major equipment purchases came with contracts. The Internal Revenue Service sends annual forms and last year sent a letter announcing an audit, which meant rereading a year's financial records. The complexity of such texts and their attendant rituals, however, years ago led the Fishers to hire an attorney and a certified public accountant, as many Amish do.

As a farm wife and mother, Anna's required reading exceeds Eli's. Cooking, sewing, cleaning, gardening, and shopping all have attendant texts in labels, tags, instructions, catalogs, and advertisements. Anna's recipes, for example, come from three major sources: *The White Horse Fire Company Cookbook* (which Eli once took to the barn for its measurement chart and never returned); *The HomeStyle Cookbook*, "compiled by the patrons and friends of the Linville Hill Mennonite School" (which Anna's cousin gave her to replace the White Horse book); and a set of handwritten index cards recording favorites learned from her mother, grandmother, and others. Though much of Anna's daily cooking, like much of her regular sewing, is done from remembered instead of read text, special baked goods or desire for a change sends her to these sources. When Sarah became a serious cook, she, too, started compiling favorite recipes, copying them into a notebook specifically reserved for that purpose.

Anna also manages the family checkbook, making deposits and withdrawals and paying bills. Though she is unsure why Eli has little interest in this task, she describes the checkbook as "the least of his worries." Recently, sixteen-year-old Sarah became interested in family "bookwork," and now she relieves her mother of most such reading and writing.

Another source of unsolicited reading is the mail. The Fishers receive offers of magazines, records, tapes, Pocono vacations, and Florida condominiums, most of which go directly into the trash. However, one such offer, "Cards of Knowledge" from the Magrace Corporation, included several sample cards with laminated pictures and accompanying paragraphs about events and individuals in American history and culture. Eleven-year-old Amos kept the cards while the offering letter went into the garbage. Several months later, another set of cards arrived, again unsolicited. Again, Anna gave the cards to Amos and again she discarded the rest. This time, though, Amos rescued the membership application from the trash and convinced his parents to let him join. Amos now receives three cards every two months in categories including Entertainment, Wars Abroad, The Black Man, Westward Expansion, Government, Thought and Culture, and Daily Life, and he files them in a sectioned, blue plastic case that accompanied his first regular shipment.

Books and magazines I bring to the farm for my own purposes—to read or study while everyone else is in the barn doing the milking—generally attract little attention. *Adventures in British Literature*, *Lord of the Flies*, and *What Is The Short Story?* (all texts from which I teach) usually go unnoticed, except the first time I brought the former. A new, large textbook, its shiny, full-color cover picturing a traditionally outfitted huntsman leaping a hurdle on his horse, attracted one of the children who picked it up and began leafing through the pages. This activity attracted Eli, who sat beside his son to peruse the text.

"What kind of book is this?" Eli asked.

I explained that it is a collection of poems, essays, plays, and stories written in England that I use in school.

Eli shook his head. "Your students read this?" he asked.

I nodded, and he continued flipping pages and shaking his head until he reached the end and set the book aside.

Another book I brought, however, attracted considerably more attention. The cover of John A. Hostetler's *Amish Society*, a trade paperback, shows an Amish mother and daughter in traditional dress looking at each other (instead of the camera) on the cover. Anna noticed the book on her kitchen counter and said, without other preface, "She's not Pennsylvania."

Hearing her mother's comment, Sarah came over, looked at the picture, and asked, "Why do they do that?" referring to the clothing style differences that had prompted Anna's statement.

"That's the way they have it," Anna matter-of-factly replied, as she took the book and sat down in her chair.

Leafing through the pages with Sarah at her shoulder, Anna recognized many of the pictures as having appeared in issues of the Lancaster daily newspaper. She laughed at how frequently some have been reprinted—particularly a barn raising, a group of children sledding outside a schoolhouse, and a clothesline hung with identical trousers in increasing size order. "That's where I went to school! I remember that pump," she exclaimed at one point. And she recognized several houses and farms pictured, pointing out one as "where Eli's brother lives."

When Anna left the room, the book remained on her chair. As the children filtered in from the barn, they noticed it, and three of them squeezed into one large chair to peruse it together. I could not hear their whispered comments, but they spent at least fifteen minutes reading. After supper Katie picked up the book again, then left it on the table where her father noticed it. Eli, too, took time to look at the pictures, but he never commented.

One thing I bring specifically for Eli always prompts comments, however. As a Philadelphia Phillies' fan without access to radio or television, Eli follows the team through the Lancaster newspaper, keeping track of individual and team performance. Forbidden to attend sporting events, he has never been to a game, so when my family goes, we buy programs for Eli and once each season a team yearbook as well. He begins reading these by looking at the players' pictures (particularly interested in those players shown with their families), then reads the individual descriptions, individual and team statistics, moving on to all the other facts, anecdotes, charts, and souvenirs displayed. Daniel shows almost as much interest as his father, reading with and after Eli, but interest is not solely male. Anna and the girls also enjoy the individual player information, often standing or sitting around Eli as he reads silently or out loud.

As prominent as books in the Fisher household are subscription-ordered periodicals. Two general-interest newspapers (*The Lancaster Intelligencer* and the local daily), one Amish-specific newspaper (the weekly *"Die Botschaft"*), one farmer-directed newspaper (the weekly *Lancaster Farming*), one farm-interest magazine (the monthly *Farm Journal*), and five child-oriented publications (*Young Pilot, Ranger Rick, Country Kids, ZooBooks,* and *Cards of Knowledge*) arrive regularly. In the course of this study other subscriptions came and went. *Hoard's Dairyman*, a farmers' bimonthly was allowed to lapse because of perceived duplication with others received. *Jack and Jill*, for the children, was discontinued for lack of interest.

While local news is important as a matter of personal interest and perceived economic need (for example, Anna reading advertisements and sale announcements and teaching her daughters to be wise shoppers), the Lancaster newspaper, which arrives by mail one day late, is read more thoroughly and with greater enthusiasm than the local one. Not only does Eli follow the Phillies through the *"Intell,"* as they call it, accent on the first syllable, but he follows businesses, fire companies, and individuals who still live "at home." Anna, too, reads the *Intell* for personally important information, and both read its general-interest news reports. In fact, all the Fishers read the Lancaster paper for one reason or another; "everyone goes right for the comics," Anna smiled.

For several months one winter, the family went without the Lancaster paper, however. Frustrated by the actual distance between their farm and Lancaster and fed up with headlines proclaiming urban crime and mayhem, Anna did not renew their subscription when it expired. "We get enough other papers," she decided, and she added a new one, *Grit*, which features good news instead of bad and which does not include columns like "Dear Abby," to which Anna particularly objects.

"I don't suppose you think about it much," Anna said, referring to my son's exposure to such material, "but can you imagine the questions my children have reading some of those ["Dear Abby"] letters? I don't see any reason for them to have to worry about such things or even know they exist."

Not all the children had been reading the column. Daniel displayed no interest in it, and though Katie read it, "she forgot about it as soon as she finished." Sarah had been reading, questioning, and "worrying about" what she read in "Dear Abby," however, each day's column staying with her for several days. I wondered if Anna attributed that to her age or to the fact that she's a girl.

"It's just the way Sarah is," she told me. "She worries about everything she notices, and she notices everything." (For *worries*, read *wonders* or *thinks*.) "I just won't have that newspaper in my house anymore," Anna concluded.

For months, she did not. When baseball's spring training began, I brought the sports sections from the closest big-city newspaper to Eli each week. When the season began, I continued bringing the sports, but as much as Eli appreciated that, he missed the personally important news he could get only from the *Intell*. By summer, Anna relented and resubscribed, without telling Eli. "If you had said to me when I first stopped the paper that I would do this, I would've had to admit that you were probably right," she acknowledged, shaking her head over the inevitability of it all.

Getting equal time and attention from the family is *"Die Botschaft,"* "A Weekly Newspaper Serving Old Order Amish Communities Everywhere," published in Lancaster. (See chapter 3 for detailed discussion of this newspaper.) Written by its readers with a minimum of editorial interference, it is available only by subscription, and the Fishers look forward to its weekly arrival. The whole family reads *"Die Botschaft"* though no one reads all of it. Most important to everyone are the letters written by family and friends. Anna is the scribe for her district, her father the scribe for his, and their letters receive immediate attention. Other scribes are cousins and friends, and all but the youngest boys read those, at least.

One week, when I had been unable to find Anna's letter in my copy, I asked why she had not written. She had written, she told me, but she had been unable to find her letter, too, until Katie discovered it.

"They forgot to put [the name of their town] at the top," Katie explained. "But I found the letter when I saw mom and dad's names [at the end]."

The children's response to what Anna writes is not always positive, however. The week that Anna "introduced" her children to her readers, she described Katie as eleven. "How could you do that?" cried Katie, who was an angry twelve.

In addition to the letters, "Ivverich und Ender . . . A Column for the Housefrau" interests the older Fishers. Anna particularly enjoys the household and health hints sent in by readers, though she has never considered sending any herself. The poetry pages and other features take more time than Anna—or Eli—willingly spends at one sitting, so those may be scanned over the weeks that each issue remains in the living-room magazine rack.

While I was learning to read *"Die Botschaft,"* Anna and I would pore over clippings at her kitchen table as she translated occasional Dutch and German phrases, explaining the rituals and history many of the words represented, but we were rarely alone. One or more children almost always stood near us or knelt on the bench opposite, eager to both listen and help teach. One day Amos stayed at the table for nearly a half hour, reading my clippings upside down and occasionally commenting on what we said. At one point, I misplaced a clipping with a particular word.

"Ordnix, ordnix, ordnix," I muttered, sifting through papers.

"Here it is!" Amos pointed.

"When did you start reading so well upside down?" I teased, getting a blush and a smile in return.

While *"Die Botschaft,"* other newspapers, and farm-related publications arrive addressed to Eli, the children's subscriptions name individual children. For many years, only Daniel received such mail, *Ranger Rick* and *Young Pilot* addressed to him though read by his brothers and sisters, too. Recently, however, Amos began receiving *ZooBooks*, a monthly series produced by Wildlife Education, Ltd., each issue about a different animal or animal group, including Endangered Animals, Birds of Prey, The Apes, Wild Horses, Bears, Big Cats. Again, though everyone (including Eli and Anna) reads these colorful, beautifully photographed volumes, they "belong" to Amos.

Several months after *ZooBooks* began arriving, Eli, Jr., asked why he was the only one without a personal subscription. Anna promised the next subscription would be his and soon heard about *Country Kids*, a bimonthly magazine "featuring the children of America's farmers and ranchers." Published by Reiman Publications of Milwaukee, Wisconsin, *Country Kids* includes articles, stories, riddles, artwork, and recipes submitted by its readers, ranging from preschool to junior high school children. Filled with color photographs of both the writers and subjects of its text, the magazine appeals not only to Eli, Jr., but to his brothers and sisters—and parents—too. In fact, Katie recently submitted a riddle which, if published, will win her a "Country Kid" tee shirt. ("When will you wear it?" I asked her, knowing the strictly observed traditional limits on her attire. "I don't know," she grinned. "Maybe over my bathing suit.") Eli, Jr., enjoys sharing his magazine and hopes to see Katie's riddle in it; he also enjoys the subscription label addressed to "Eli Fisher, Jr."

While Eli, Jr., felt he was "the only one" without a personal subscription, in truth, he was the only boy without one; neither of the girls receives a magazine in her name. Sarah, who has always been the most serious reader among the children, reads all the family periodicals, *Farm Journal* and *Lancaster Farming* excepted. In the past few months, however, following her entrance into the "young folks," she has started reading *True Story* and *True Confessions*, two magazines she buys at the local drugstore. Full of stories about unrequited love and troubled relationships, with sad endings and sadder-but-wiser heroines, they fascinate Sarah who reads and discusses those of greatest interest with her mother.

I was amazed that Anna allowed Sarah to read such things. "She likes reading about other girls' experiences," Anna explained to me. "Sometimes she can't believe that people could treat each other the way they do in some of those stories. . . . I told her 'there are some things in there we don't believe,' and she said 'I know that!' "

"She's feeling her way . . . seeing what it's like," Anna continued in a later conversation. "I know there are things in there she doesn't understand, in the stories and in the advertisements. When she wants to know, she'll ask me and I'll tell her. She's not seriously involved in these magazines, though. She doesn't want to subscribe. The other day she thought about buying some when we were shopping but bought a book instead. . . . She does keep them put away, though, so the other children won't see them."

Like Sarah, Katie receives no magazines personally either, but her interest in reading is a most recent development. Though she had read several of the Little House books, Katie's preference used to extend to any "books with big print because [she] can read them easier," she told me. ("Because you can read them faster," Anna amended, making Katie smile.) Interested in some *"Die Botschaft"* content, Katie limited her reading to letters of personally known scribes, particularly her mother's, and relied on family conversation to supply the rest. "Katie sings instead of reading," Anna once said, "and instead of thinking." (Anna sees reading as requiring concentrated thought, singing as requiring little. Katie has always been "[her] singer.") This year, however, Katie has started reading more. She likes *Country Kids* and *ZooBooks* and "true stories about real people." In fact, Katie brought a book to our first picnic of the summer, in case she got bored—an act so significant that Anna made sure I knew.

The book Katie brought that day exemplifies an interesting phenomenon among the Fishers, one noted several times before. While each child and adult has his or her own particular interests and particular reading preferences, "everyone reads everything." Though Anna's statement oversimplifies, it contains a considerable degree of truth. *The Emancipation of Robert Sadler*, the book Katie brought, was the one Sarah had purchased instead of magazines, and it attracted almost everyone's attention. During the week Sarah brought it home, both she and Katie started reading it, Katie telling Anna, "You're gonna like this book. You're not gonna get too far until you have tears." Anna and Daniel decided they would read it when the girls finished, and even Eli picked it up, read the covers and the first few pages, prompting Daniel to ask whether his father, too, wanted time with the same book. Only Amos and Eli, Jr., expressed no interest in reading the book, though Amos had heard others discuss it and seemed interested in hearing details of the story. In truth, almost everyone reads almost everything; and everyone reads something regularly with pleasure.

• *Writing at Home* •

Like reading, writing serves multiple purposes for the Fishers, helping them communicate, conduct business, express and identify themselves, and enjoy leisure. Although all family members write and all find some satisfaction in doing so, writing is pursued less eagerly than reading by most.

What seems to be the primary purpose of writing—communicating with others—is perceived as work by some, as fun by others, but as necessary by everyone. All the Fishers write letters with more or less regularity. Anna tries to write weekly for *"Die Botschaft,"* monthly in two "circle letters," and as often as she can to individual friends and relatives. (She and I corresponded monthly for five years while the family lived in Lancaster.) Eli writes in one circle letter when Anna presses him to do so. Sarah writes in a circle letter with Lancaster friends and individually to Lancaster cousins, sharing her circle letter with Katie, who does not have one of her own.

These circle letters involving the three oldest Fishers are a common phenomenon among the Amish but one I had never heard of before I got to know the family. Circle letters are written by self-selected groups of friends, relatives, former schoolmates, members of the same occupation, or any other shared interest or background group. When a circle letter arrives, a participant adds his or her new pages and removes the pages he or she wrote for the previous circuit before mailing it to the next person.

Sarah's circle of eleven same-age girls began three years ago. When her circle letter arrives, after reading it herself, she shares it with Katie, who is equally anxious for news about the older girls in Lancaster. Last year Sarah's circle was broken twice by someone not doing her part. When Sarah asked her mother what the girls should do, Anna said they must figure out who keeps breaking the circle and ask her to drop out. She should not be allowed to ruin it for the others, Anna concluded.

Anna herself is part of two different circles. One is a group of women—some relatives, some friends, all approximately the same age. The other she shares with Eli; it is a family circle with his eleven brothers and sisters. Each couple in that group writes one page—husband on one side of the paper, wife on the other. "It takes Eli a half hour to write one side of a piece of tablet paper," Anna teased. "And he needs stationery with lines."

When asked what would happen to one of her circles if she did not take her turn or decided to drop out, Anna hesitated. "Why would anyone not write?" she asked. "That's how we keep in touch. You'd never hear the news if you dropped out!" In fact, to keep the circle and the news moving, anyone who keeps the letter for more than three days is expected to enclose a stamp for the next person's use as his penalty.

The other four Fisher children don't participate in circles letters, but they do write to friends and relatives on their own. Daniel, though old enough to write more, writes only to his favorite cousin, Samuel, "maybe twice a year." Katie writes to same-age cousins and to Aleesha, one of the two Fresh Air Fund children who spent the past two summers on the farm. Amos, too, writes to his cousins, as does Eli, Jr., who used to dictate his messages to Sarah and sometimes copied her writing, always enclosing his own signed drawings.

At the beginning of my research, I tried to make use of the family propensity for writing and brought three notebooks to the farm so Sarah, Daniel, and Katie could keep journals for me. The children were not home, but Anna smiled wryly. "You're optimistic," she said and asked what I expected them to write.

"They could write about anything," I replied. "Anything they do . . . anything that happens. . . . If Daniel and Sarah had a fight, they could write about it. . . ."

"They'd never do that," Anna interrupted sharply, then paused to change her tone. "They'll have more time now, but I don't know about this summer," she continued, wondering how long I wanted them to keep writing.

As it turned out, Anna gave them the notebooks, but none of the children wrote more than a single page.

One evening when Sarah, Katie, and I were preparing supper while the others were in the barn, the girls explained the notable writing-related differences between Fisher males and females, the conversation started by Sarah who noted that Daniel had begun keeping his journal for me but that she doubted he would do it well or for long.

"Boys don't care for writing as much as girls do," she explained. "They're more interested in sports. Amish girls aren't as interested in sports as your girls are. I hardly ever think about it anymore [since she finished school]. . . . Some boys take interest in writing just like a girl," she continued, "but mostly it's a regular thing—boys hate to write."

"Boys quick go over their lessons so they can read," Katie added.

"Boys hate school more than girls," Sarah concluded. "They want to be outside. Girls like book work and housework."

Without my having to make the connection, Katie added a postscript about her father. "Dad hates it [writing]. He won't write circle letter. You really have to get him to," she said, corroborating what Anna had told me, that Eli hates writing, requiring lined paper and a half hour to write one page.

A variation on letter writing constitutes part of the family's non-church Sunday routine. After family devotions, the children combine art and writing to create cards for special occasions or "spiritual art pieces" to decorate the refrigerator or bulletin board. When their grandmother was ill, for example, all five children used construction paper, tablet paper, crayons, pens, glue, and a box of received greeting cards Anna had saved to create get-well cards for Grandmother. Some cut out pictures from the cards; some cut out or copied verses; and some used the professional cards as inspiration for pictures and verses of their own.

In fact, the Fishers mark most birthdays, anniversaries, and other occasions with greeting cards, and cards they receive from others are displayed on the bulletin board or tucked under wooden molding on the kitchen wall to create a decorative border. Though the children usually create their own for parents and close relatives, Anna keeps a general-audience supply in her desk for last-minute mailing. Sometimes she buys special ones, however, as she did the week I took my comprehensive doctoral exams. I received a card that read, "To wish you good luck, I went out to get you a rabbit's foot! And do you know what I found out?" Inside, "Rabbits fight back! Anyway, Good Luck." The card was signed, "Guess who is thinking of you! Love ya! Only me." But even printing could not disguise Anna's hand.

Writing to conduct business, the Fishers' second overt purpose, rarely exceeds filling the blanks of a subscription renewal form or those of a fabric order blank. Anna cannot recall ever writing a letter of inquiry or complaint or any kind of at-length business communication. Complex, official business correspondence, the kind required by the Internal Revenue Service, for example, is left to the family lawyer and accountant.

While only some family members actively enjoy writing letters and none enjoy business correspondence, all enjoy playing games requiring writing, particularly Scrabble (using tiles) and Boggle (using pencil and paper). I once arrived at the farm to find Sarah, Daniel, and Amos involved in a three-hour Scrabble contest while waiting for the others to return from a visit. On another occasion I found Sarah and Katie playing Boggle at the kitchen table, and Anna, Amos, and Eli, Jr., playing Scrabble on a folding table in the same room, while Eli and Daniel were in the barn.

My husband, son, and I have all participated in Boggle and Scrabble games with various combinations of Fishers, and we have adjusted to their variation of the rules. In any game, the oldest person or people playing may assist the younger ones. No question of fairness arises unless only some players go unaided. The older players may also receive help from someone else playing or someone else in the room. Score is always kept, and while some moves are ruled illegal (nonexistent, misspelled, or German words, for example), age or aid received neither bars nor assures a winner.

Another writing-involved game, one played exclusively by the children, is School. While I cannot describe the game at length because the children always move to their separate "schoolroom" on the porch, I have seen the "schoolroom" set up, have heard Anna ask Katie to bring back the Bible she "used to play school," and have overheard Katie "teaching." From these fragments and from Anna's accounts, the game, though imaginary and without box-lid instructions, consistently follows its real-life model, with "pupils" using actual textbooks and workbooks and doing what could be actual lessons. This game has a long family history; in 1975, Sarah was the teacher, and Katie and Daniel were the pupils. Now Katie teaches Amos and Eli, Jr.

While family involvement in writing is intellectual, social, and sentimental, and is shared to some extent by everyone, Anna and Sarah are the most personally interested. When Anna learned that the Meadow Brook children wrote compositions for me, she asked to see them. The day I brought the papers, both Anna and Sarah sat reading them on the couch, immediately engrossed.

"Daniel's drawing style is sure catching on," Anna remarked when she saw Richard's signature framed with colorful zigzag lines like Daniel's pictures.

"His handwriting is, too," Sarah added. "Doesn't this look like Daniel's?" she asked, pointing out Davie's similar capital *D*'s.

"They seem to be used to misspellings," Anna groused. "There are so many of them, but no one seems to notice."

Though her first appraisal of the compositions focused on their appearance and form, later that evening, while we were washing dishes, Anna returned to what she had read in the student papers, this time considering content, instead. She noted the number of students who wrote about Verna, their teacher, and described her negatively—as big or heavy—or revealed negative feelings toward her. "I knew they didn't like her very much, but I'm surprised they wrote it down and told you," she remarked.

Anna also reads her children's regularly assigned compositions and clearly recalls some from one year to the next. When I was writing about Daniel and Katie's farm-sale papers (discussed in chapter 4), I mentioned them to her and she remembered a surprising number of details though she had not seen the papers for over a year, and what she remembered was content, particularly the length and details of Katie's. Aware of the characteristic styles her children were developing, Anna noted that when she and Eli are away in the evening, the children leave notes telling what they did and saying good night. Daniel's notes are typically brief and direct, she told me, but Katie's are long, narrative, and clearly hers. "I really enjoy those," Anna smiled.

While both parents review most papers brought home from school, some receive special attention. When Eli, Jr., returned from "preschool day" at Meadow Brook (described in chapter 4), Anna saved the sheaf of papers he handed her, bringing them out to show me the following week. By mistake, I picked up those papers along with my own when I left for home. The next day, when I went to market with Anna, she asked if I had taken Eli's papers. "I wouldn't care if they were any other papers," she apologized, "but I always feel something special for the first school papers, and I like to save them."

• *Meaning at Home* •

The way the Fishers deal with text seems to reveal their assumptions about where meaning is found and how it is made, yet family experiences sometimes contradict these assumptions, teaching interesting lessons to those involved. Perhaps partially because of her extensive involvement with both reading and writing and partially because she is who she is, Anna seems most aware of how complex meaning can be, and each such experience only heightens her sensitivity.

Looking first at the Fishers' reading, text appears to represent an authoritative voice requiring attention and acceptance. Texts contain truth, and readers must decode, recall, and apply that truth, whether by extracting and using the relevant information or lesson (from a recipe, set of instructions, or story) or by memorizing and reciting it (from the Bible or hymnal). Newspapers and magazines differ in form and content from books, but their reader demands are the same: accept and recall.

While granting books authoritative status, Anna does not necessarily read them from cover to cover, giving equal attention to everything printed. Returning her copy of *Martyrs Mirror*, I commented on something in the introduction. When Anna did not recognize my reference, I asked with surprise if she had read that section. "No," she replied, looking equally surprised. "Isn't that how you read any book? You go to the part you want?" she responded, subtly pointing out that the purpose and meaning I find in reading the *Mirror* differ considerably from its purpose and meaning for her.

The family's preference for "true stories" is particularly interesting in this regard. Of all the regularly read material, only Daniel's Hardy Boys books are consciously acknowledged as fiction. The Little House books and the Jeanette Oke pioneer heroine series are read as though rooted in fact, as are *The Emancipation of Robert Sadler, Faith Despite the KGB, True Story, True Confessions*, "Jesus to the Iron Curtain" (a "newsletter"), and all other such texts. Each involves people, not *characters*—a term I never heard used by anyone at home, in the community, or at school; each represents "somebody sharing"; and each, according to Anna, has "more meaning because it's an experience of somebody else" from which everyone can learn something personally applicable.

In fact, Fisher use of the word "story" to refer to anything "told" by or about someone took some time for me to comprehend. The night many years ago that I first broached the idea for my dissertation, which ultimately led to this book, we discussed what I called my "study" and my "paper" for a while but moved to other subjects and activities for the remainder of the evening. As I was leaving, Anna asked when my "story" had to be finished. I had no idea what she meant until she elaborated: "What you want to write about us."

Lessons learned from stories, then, become matters of subjective personal identification with those involved rather than matters of supposedly objective intellectual assessment of the people, their actions, or their circumstances. In the tradition of the *Ausbund* and the *Martyrs Mirror*, appropriate reader response to any story combines sympathy and empathy, readers vicariously experiencing, internalizing, and responding to others' feelings. Just as the pain and suffering of early Anabaptists require no explicit interpretation or analysis by the family, they perceive no need to interpret the trials of pioneering, slavery, political oppression, growing up, or remaining faithful in a faithless world. For them, text demands response, not reification.

This reader-text relationship contrasts interestingly with Anna's awareness of meaning as interpretive. Anna knows that different people can find different meanings in the same print text or even in the same picture. One day Amos brought home a penmanship paper with the word *dolphin* on it. Anna asked if he knew what that meant, and Amos said he did because he had seen dolphins when we all went to Dutch Wonderland (a Lancaster amusement park) several summers earlier. Finding the pictures we took of that dolphin show, the children agreed that Eli, Jr., now looks "exactly" like Amos did then, and they showed Anna the pictures for her concurrence. Anna disagreed, not seeing the resemblance. "You see?" she asked me. "We all looked at the same pictures but saw different things, got different meanings."

Anna also knows that despite the legitimacy of individual interpretations, sometimes shared meaning is more desirable, so she discusses books and newspaper articles she's read with others who have read them to confirm what they mean to her. Yet while their mother knows to confirm meaning by consulting the reading community, her younger children, like most, do not always know or want to know that their individual interpretations may be wrong according to some external standard. When differences involve children, understanding that multiple meanings exist and accepting someone else's may require social development not yet accomplished, a point illustrated by both Anna's youngest son and older daughter.

In the case of Eli, Jr., conflict arose over interpretation of a preschool-day paper that required writing capital and lowercase A's in three lined columns, copying the teacher-written model in the top left-hand corner. While Eli had copied the letters precisely, writing A a in the first column, he wrote A/a in the second and third, prompting his teacher to circle each dividing slash in red ink, indicating that he had not done as he was told and that those lines should not appear. Unfortunately, Eli read her circles differently. He had recently participated in a home Bible-study program for children, conducted by an Evangelical group, for which he completed worksheets that were marked and returned. On those papers, capital C's meant "correct"; on his Meadow Brook worksheet many of the red circles were incomplete or misconnected, resembling C's. Despite Anna's explanations, Eli insisted that his teacher's marks meant that he did well, not that he made mistakes.

A variation on this same meaning theme occurred when Sarah, in Lancaster with her mother, wanted to buy a souvenir for a girl friend who had been unable to make the trip. She picked out an oversized pencil decorated with hearts, flowers, two kissing Dutch children, and the slogan "From Intercourse to Paradise" then showed it to Anna. Assuming that her daughter understood only the words' geographical meaning (Intercourse and Paradise are Lancaster County towns), Anna explained the other possible interpretation. Sarah, disgusted, chose to buy another souvenir.

This awareness of interpretive differences among readers affects Anna as a writer. She believes that "the writer is more responsible for [making] meaning than the reader, and [she] should provide whatever the reader needs." Many *"Die Botschaft"* writers, she senses, "don't think about who's reading. . . . [these writers] are not self-conscious enough," not asking themselves, "Will others understand as I do?" When scribes use a lot of German words, for example, Anna wonders whether readers "will get out what the writer intended," so she avoids German, sometimes seeking Eli's help to translate particular, usually church-related, vocabulary.

"I'm never sure what mistakes I make," Anna said about her spelling and grammar, but despite their importance, she worries primarily about content. "I worry that readers won't get my meaning," but will take other, possibly negative or contradictory messages from her letters. "I never know what readers will make of what I write," she sighed. When her letters first appeared in print, it felt "strange . . . exciting. But you get used to it. Now I just worry about what others will make of it."

Our relationship has affected Anna's *"Die Botschaft"* writing recently. When she writes her weekly piece, she now wonders, "Will Andy understand this?", and she tries to state things so I will. She also thinks of me when she reads the paper, wondering whether I choose to read the same letters she does, whether I understand all of what is written, and what I "make of some of the things people say," always aware that my meaning and hers may differ.

Collaborating on my research has heightened Anna's awareness of meaning in general, my search for understanding and meaning affecting hers. One day when I asked a question she had never considered, Anna said, "I can't believe how much I am getting from your writing this. It gives me so much to think about. I never realized how precious so many of the things we have are. We always just do them; we don't think about them. But your talking about them and asking questions makes me realize what we have."

It is through Anna, then, that family notions of meaning become explicit. For writing, she posits meaning in the writer and the reader, expecting both to use their larger contexts and their awareness of each other to construct it. For reading, she knows individual meanings may legitimately differ, but she also knows community negotiation or arbitration is sometimes necessary and desirable. While her writer's awareness seems almost always conscious, her reader's knowledge most often seems to operate implicitly, allowing Anna, as a good Amishperson, to posit meaning in the text.

T H R E E

The Family and Their Communities

When I first tried to write about my research experience with the Amish, I did not know where or how to begin. Years of accumulated field notes, artifacts, journal entries, and notes to myself merged before my eyes in a single, fragmented, overlapping, kaleidoscopic image. The Fishers, their relatives, friends, and acquaintances, their church and their school, their work and their play, their travels and their time at home seemed distinct yet inseparable. I could write about particular individuals, incidents, or relationships, but I could make no coherent sense of it all. Every day for weeks I wrote about what I knew, but what I wrote one day seemed to have no meaningful relationship to what I wrote the next.

Then one day, after weeks of struggling, when I fled my desk—again—and went for what I always hoped would be a mind-clearing, sense-making walk, it happened. As the rhythm of my steps began shaking loose my mental blocks, vague categories emerged in my mind. By the time I returned home, I had the categories that would organize and make coherent sense of my data; I had suddenly recognized the four "communities" operating in the Fishers' lives, communities that had always been there but that I had been unable to see.

I record this here not because of what it reveals about how ethnography (and I) work, but because I want readers to understand that the communities identified and discussed in this chapter are not communities the Fishers or other Old Order members necessarily perceive or acknowledge. Rather, they are explanatory communities I devised to make sense of the seemingly ineluctable complexity of my data and the world it represents. These categories are "elegant" in that they account for everything I discovered; they are artificial in that they arose from my view as observer, not my experience as participant.

As I said, it took four communities to make sense of what I found.

The first or *immediate community* as I call it includes the Fishers' relatives and friends, people the family knows personally and interacts with regularly, whether Amish or English (as they call anyone not in an Old Order). These people may live nearby or may live—as many do—in Lancaster. Their immediacy derives not from membership in any group or residence in any place but from their personal connection to the family.

Second is the *larger community*, the one including all Amish everywhere. Because the Fishers' identification with this group is the primary fact of their lives, it matters not that Eli, Anna, and the children do not know most of these people personally. That they, too, are Amish makes them automatically significant and makes theirs a community in which the Fishers live.

The *church community* is the third group, the only one geographically defined. While to Anna's mind "the Church" is synonymous with the larger community, in her daily life, the church community is the East District in which her home is located and its Amish residents with whom she gathers each fortnight for prayer and intermittently for other reasons.

The *school community*, group four, does not include the school's student body but consists of the parents whose children attend Meadow Brook. While also part of the immediate community, these people might not have entered the Fishers' lives were they not school-affiliated. Like the church community, the school community places certain demands and constraints on the Fishers, directly affecting their actions and activities.

Though these four communities overlap—some people members of all four simultaneously—their separate identification makes possible an orderly approach to reading, writing, and meaning. Since each group makes specific demands on the family yet each group's demands are notably similar, their separate investigation helps reveal the internal coherence behind their external complexity.

• *The Immediate Community* •

READING "Everyone I know reads something," Anna once told me, and while I can't claim to have substantiated her assertion, I did find wide reading, wide interest in reading, and nothing to the contrary in her immediate community. Most community members' occupations require some amount of reading, and in their leisure time those people read as well, for books read, books recommended, and books of interest are frequent topics of discussion, as is information gleaned from Amish and English newspapers. Even when publications are not the topic of discussion, Anna's friends and relatives often allude to them as support or justification for their opinions and ideas, such citation requiring no academic precision but sufficing simply as having been read.

Many of the Fishers' friends and relatives also farm, keep house, and sew, and they read the same kinds of task-related texts as those discussed in chapter 2. Some have less traditionally Amish occupations, however, and do other kinds of occupational reading. Anna's brother, Reuben, for example, is a housepainter—complete with panel truck driven by an employee—who must deal with suppliers and discriminate among products often through reading about them. Anna's father, Daniel, a retired farmer, works for a Lancaster business that manages mail-order campaigns for other companies. His job involves receiving orders, with their accompanying coupons, labels, and box tops, and filling them. And Anna's sister-in-law, Mary, operates Mary's Stitchery, doing not only the kind of reading associated with sewing and quilting but the kind necessary for running a retail business as well.

With their immediate community, both at home and away, the Fishers participate in discussions about books read for other than occupational reasons. For example, at supper one evening Eli's brother, Elam, reported on a book he had read about the Volga Germans—"about this thick," he indicated with thumb and forefinger, "maybe 400 pages"—as part of a conversation about our various immigrant backgrounds. Later his wife, Lydie, in discussing their new home, expressed interest in reading *The House of the Seven Gables* because their house fits that description. In another instance, one Sisters' Day at Anna's grandmother's, Anna's Aunt Rebecca held several dozen women spellbound by recounting episodes from "a book by a persecuted Swedish Christian" about people tortured, imprisoned, and killed for their faith. And during a Sunday afternoon visit, Anna's friend, Susie, claimed to enjoy reading "any book by James Michener." These four examples represent not only the variety of reading and reading awareness evident in the community, but they illustrate what these people consider important about books. Titles and authors are haphazardly remembered by most; publishers are, for the most part, insignificant and unnecessary. Content is memorable, however, and is the only thing that consistently matters and is consistently useful.

Of the many book-related conversations I heard or participated in, Susie's reference to Michener was the most intriguing. I wondered both why she initially selected a Michener novel and why she chose to tell me about it as we sat around Anna's kitchen table. I asked the first question of Susie herself, and she explained that she had found "a shelf-ful" of Michener books in a local Christian bookstore (confirming what Anna had once said about the primary source of books among her friends).

Not wanting to make Susie uncomfortable, I waited until she left to ask Anna why she thought Susie chose to tell me about her "find." "She knew you'd be interested," Anna explained. "She wouldn't tell anybody she didn't think would be interested. 'What's it to you?' she'd figure." I wondered aloud whether it would be "safe" for Susie to reveal what seemed a mainstream interest to most other Amish. "You know what kind of things different people are interested in," Anna replied tactfully, choosing interest rather than safety as the operative consideration.

Perhaps more common than book-centered conversation is newspaper-focused talk, involving both English and Amish papers. One Friday evening several married Amish couples sat around a picnic table at the local farmers' market, visiting and reviewing the week.

"Saw your picture in the paper," one man said to Jake.

"Ach, I know," replied Jake, evidently disgusted by the local newspaper story about farmers preparing their fields for spring, illustrated with a photograph of Jake behind his mule-drawn plow.

"Did you know they were taking it?" asked Aaron.

"Yeah, I knew, but I ignored them," Jake replied. "I'm so used to the college kids doing that. They park along the road and take pictures. They don't need to get close; they just aim their cameras . . ."

The conversation soon turned to business and newspaper reports about government surplus food. Could there be as much of a surplus as the local newspaper and the *Lancaster Intelligencer* had reported? "The paper said the government's been supporting us [farmers] for twenty years," Reuben noted, "and we didn't know it until they pulled out."

"Huh!" Jake snorted. "I told my wife the other day we'll be standing in line for that free butter and cheese they write about soon."

English newspapers provide more than business news and personal annoyance, however. Sometimes they report news of more immediate community interest. On Memorial Day weekend in 1983, a group of Amish girls from Lancaster County went to Ocean City, New Jersey, to help open a summer house belonging to a child-welfare agency. While there, the girls went for a walk along the water's edge. One of them got caught in the undertow and, unable to swim, was pulled away from the shore. Several of her friends tried to help, as did two young men who happened to be nearby. The Lancaster newspaper, which Anna showed me the day after the event, reported that the first girl drowned, as did one of her male would-be rescuers.

Two days later Anna and I went to Lancaster for Sisters' Day. We spent some time visiting alone with her mother (Sarah Stoltzfus) and her married sister Fannie, and it was while the four of us sat on the Stoltzfus porch that the "Ocean City story" came up.

"Did you hear about those Amish girls in Ocean City?" Anna asked her sister.

"The one who almost drowned?"

Anna nodded. "Was it Benny King's Mary? I looked it up in the *Directory*, and she was the only one I could find."

"Yes, it was Mary, and Levi Esh's Sarah and John Lapp's Emma," Fannie confirmed.

Neither Anna nor I realized immediately that Fannie had said Mary *almost* drowned. Then Fannie said, "For a while they thought Mary was dead, too."

"You mean she isn't?" Anna asked. "We thought she was."

"I can't believe the paper made that big a mistake, saying she was dead when she wasn't," I commented.

"Well, it was eight hours before they knew the truth here," Fannie said.

Mrs. Stoltzfus then explained that first reports from the New Jersey police said the girl had died and not until late that night did her family learn she was alive and on life-support systems, which was "why the newspaper printed what it did," she concluded.

"Do you know anything else about what happened?" Anna asked, "because the newspaper story didn't make any sense to me."

Fannie recounted the details she had heard, including one about the girls walking in shoulder-deep water.

"Up to their shoulders?" Anna exclaimed. "The newspaper said up to their ankles!"

"I know," Fannie replied calmly, her patience with journalistic misstatement far exceeding my own.

(Interestingly, Anna's father reported the same event in his *"Die Botschaft"* letter that week. For what he wrote, see page 45.)

More common than English-newspaper-prompted discussion, however, is talk based on *"Die Botschaft."* The Fishers, their friends, and their relatives frequently talk about individual scribes' letters and particular reported events, using the paper as a link both to the larger community and to each other. For example, Lydie Fisher, who lives several hours further away from Lancaster than Anna, reads the same scribes Anna does (those they both know from their Lancaster County days) before scanning the rest of the paper, a fact discovered accidentally during a conversation about what they had read the previous week and one that set both women laughing.

When Lydie realized I could follow the conversation because I, too, read *"Die Botschaft,"* she seemed delighted but unsure how I understand what I read because sometimes she does not. "When you see a lot of names in a letter, do you skip over them?" she asked. "I do. It's too confusing when you don't know them," she confided, revealing something about her reading process and her sense of what matters in a text.

Conversations need not revolve around texts that have been read for texts to be mentioned, however. Anna's relatives and friends often allude to what they have read or heard about texts as support for what they are saying. Often such allusions are religious—for example, Anna referring to New Testament doctrine when discussing church voting procedures or mentioning the Articles of Faith when discussing "running with the young folks"; Mrs. Stoltzfus using the New Testament to make a point about marriage; and Jake King using the same text to make a point about women.

Allusions may refer to secular texts as well. "That's what I found in the *Directory*" or "I read it in the *Botschaft*" often establishes validity, as does the less specific "I read it somewhere." Two examples noted earlier, the book about the Volga Germans and the book "by a persecuted Swedish Christian," were mentioned initially to support opinions expressed on issues separate from the books themselves. Even without complete identification, those references to supportive texts lent credence to the arguments of the speakers who made them.

WRITING   Perhaps it may also be said that almost everyone the Fishers know writes something at one time or another. Again, such a claim cannot be fully documented, but again I encountered no one evidently unable to write in at least "functional literacy" terms. Labeling, business communication, personal communication, and publication all occur regularly in the Fishers' immediate community.

A seemingly insignificant form of writing, labeling matters a great deal in this community, necessitated by the size and similarities within and among families, and it appears both within households and at extended gatherings. Amish boys' and men's hats, Amish girls' and women's bonnets look essentially alike. Eli and Daniel, Amos and Eli, Jr., Sarah and Katie are as likely to pick up each other's as their own. At family gatherings or church services when dozens of equally similar hats appear, finding one's own would be nearly impossible without the initials Anna and the other women sew or mark in hatbands and bonnet linings. Similarly, cooking pots, baking pans, and food storage containers look more alike than different, especially in Anna's family where all the women use the same manufacturer's pots and the same brand of plastic containers. On holidays, Sisters' Days, and regular visits, when everyone contributes food prepared at home, finding one's own containers after they all have been emptied and washed would be impossible without the initials laundry-markered on the bottoms. Christmas and Easter require labeling, too, of gifts and baskets, particularly for the Easter hunt when only names distinguish hidden treasures, and the rules require ignoring those found that are marked for someone else.

Businesses require another form of labeling. Many Fisher friends and relatives sell food and crafts to the general public. J and A Meats, operated by Jake and Annie King at a local farmers' market, labels its products by variety and price. Signs also announce sales and services available, including, weekly specials and a call-ahead hoagie take-out service. A week before the annual quilt consignment sale held to benefit the Amish schools, Jake and Annie displayed a state-bird quilt, with embroidered state names, at their market stand and posted a sign announcing the date, location, and time of the sale. (Anna worked for Jake and Annie for six months while their oldest daughter substituted for the teacher in a local school. Curiously, during her tenure, all of J and A's signs were in Anna's handwriting.)

Businesses also require other forms of writing. Mary, who operates Mary's Stitchery mentioned earlier, does considerable shop-related writing. In addition to the written work any small business requires—the receipt writing, record keeping, licensing, and tax filing, for which she retains a CPA—Mary must advertise, particularly because of her rural location. While small signs mark the road to her house, business cards and handbills introduce the Stitchery to customers in other shops where Mary's professionally printed information sits on counters and beside cash registers. For several summers, Mary also purchased space on paper placemats used by local tourist-attracting restaurants, and she supplied the text to be printed there.

As noted in chapter 2, personal communication among Fisher friends and relatives occurs regularly through individual and circle letters. Also noted earlier, Anna's father writes a weekly letter for *"Die Botschaft,"* having become a scribe before his daughter did. Dad's letters follow the newspaper format as hers do; their most distinguishing feature, though, is his signature. Dad always signs himself "D.B. Stoltzfus," an appellation that makes Anna laugh and sometimes teasingly call him "D.B."

The Ocean City story, discussed in terms of reading, fell within D.B.'s purview as scribe from the district in which the girls involved lived. He told the story in his next scribal letter, recounting it in *Botschaft*-appropriate style, after discussing the weather, current farm work, that day's Sisters' Day gathering, Sunday visitors, a Monday funeral, and yesterday's tractor accident. His account, however, gives the facts the English newspaper missed and adds details an Amishman would consider important.

> Last week a group of girls went to Ocean City, NJ to help to prepare a summer home for use by the Christ's Home for Children, located in Paradise. Before returning home Mary King and Emma Lapp, both school teachers of Ronks R.D., were wading in the ocean. A strong undertow pulled Emma in and Mary trying to help her also got pulled in. A 24 year old boy heard them screaming and rushed in and had Emma, but was also pulled in and he drowned. His body was washed up to shore around 3 hours later. Both girls were rescued by a policeman and other passerbys. The policeman and both girls were admitted to the hospital. Mary came home yesterday, but Emma remains in the hospital yet on a life-support system and still unconscious and showing no signs of improvement as of yet. She is a dau. of Mr. and Mrs. John Lapp, Little Beaver Road, Ronks, PA.

MEANING Like the family, the immediate community grants authority to text, sometimes based on faith, as with the Bible; sometimes on familiarity, as with *"Die Botschaft"*; and sometimes seemingly on nothing more than the fact of publication, as with Elam's and Rebecca's books. Their writing, too, reflects a sense of text trustworthiness, writing to establish ownership, to conduct business, and to communicate information and feelings.

Interestingly, this assumed authority is not destroyed by instances of erroneous text. When the Lancaster newspaper mistakenly reported Mary King's death, Mrs. Stoltzfus understood how such an error occurred; she could read the newspaper in light of meaning she acquired in other contexts and brought to her reading. Such exceptions seem only to prove the rule: a writer is responsible for the accuracy of and understanding derived from his text, so writers must and do tell only the truth as they know it. The newspaper reporter was wrong because he could not help but be wrong; had he known the truth, he would have written the truth. Instead, he wrote the only truth he knew.

Awareness of writer responsibility for meaning also arose in a car ride to Mary's with Mary, Anna, and Mrs. Stoltzfus. As we drove past a small wooden arrow reading *QUILTS* and pointing down the road toward the Stitchery, Mrs. Stoltzfus said, "Maybe that sign should be bigger."

"Reuben thinks it should have more on it," Mary replied, referring to her husband. "He thinks it should say how far to the shop from here."

"Maybe you should put one across the road," Anna suggested, as we pulled into Mary's driveway. "Or you could put one further in that direction," she nodded pointedly, "that says 'You missed it' or 'Quilt shop one mile back.' "

So Mary and her family, too, wanted to be sure their readers knew as much as they needed to make sense of what they read.

Though they seem to know that different meanings do exist and can be legitimate, the community still believes that one shared meaning is more desirable than several different ones, and they work toward that goal in what they read as well as in what they write. As Anna once noted and my experience bears out, during a quilting or a Sisters' Day, many topics of conversation arise often involving books or articles the women have read. Sometimes "everyone has a different meaning" for the same book or on the same subject. After discussing their interpretations, however, they "have the same meaning" at the end.

• *The Larger Community* •

While the larger Amish community, consisting of Old Order Amish in settlements around the United States and Canada, is no more monolithic than the Fishers' immediate community, *"Die Botschaft"* may represent the Amish at large. Available by subscription only, this "weekly newspaper serving Old Order Amish communities everywhere" is written by randomly chosen scribes, some self-selected, some district selected, with anywhere from 150 to 170 individuals' letters printed in each issue. These writers are male and female, married and single, young and old. They are farmers, businessmen, self-employed, or employees. They are Old Order Amish and Old Order Mennonite, some more conservative, some more liberal. Their only common characteristic seems to be their commitment to Old Order life and, thereby, to each other.

While *"Die Botschaft"* offers fascinating reading for anyone interested in current Amish culture and society, I found it particularly interesting as an ongoing literacy event. The newspaper not only illustrates what the Amish read and write, but it reveals how they read and write, what they think about reading and writing, and how they define literacy for themselves, both explicitly and implicitly.

Throughout this section readers may be surprised or appalled by the sentence fragments, run-ons, misspellings, and grammar and punctuation errors not only in the scribes' letters but in the professionally written parts of the paper as well. I was both surprised and appalled when I first read *"Die Botschaft,"* for not only did the scribes seem "illiterate" to me then, but I seriously questioned the professional competence of those who edit and publish the newspaper. What I discovered over the years of my subscription, however, was that if I understood what the writers were saying, their mechanics became not only less distracting but disappeared almost completely from my conscious awareness. In other words, when I shifted from my roles as English teacher/mainstream literate into that of Old Order participant, mechanics no longer mattered. Then I read to understand, not to evaluate. From this personal shift, I began to recognize and understand the Amish definition of literacy—of what "counts" as reading and writing—and how a definition so different from the one I was accustomed to could be acceptable to others and to me (a point more fully explained in chapter 6).

As a result, when I shifted back to my role as classroom teacher, I found that I could read my students' writing the same way—looking for meaning instead of mistakes—which made their writing and my response both more positive and more meaningful. Of course, mechanics still counted, but they no longer came first, no longer obscured my view nor obstructed my students.

"Die Botschaft" offers several kinds of reading material to its audience. Scribes' letters comprise the bulk of the newspaper, offering news, narrative, and comment from settlements in fifteen states and Canada. (Settlements represented in *"Die Botschaft"* are in Illinois, Indiana, Kansas, Kentucky, Maryland, Michigan, Minnesota, Missouri, New York, Ohio, Pennsylvania, Tennessee, Texas, Virginia, Wisconsin, and the province of Ontario.)

"Ivverich und Ender . . . A Column for the Hausfrau" contains "odds and ends of information about cooking and household tips," providing a forum for reader requests, responses, and unsolicited contributions on these topics. While this column may occupy from one to three pages in a single issue, poetry does the same, on pages without specific heading usually following "Ivverich und Ender" and offering reader-submitted and sometimes reader-written poems and song lyrics. Descriptive, narrative, persuasive, and argumentative columns also appear throughout the paper, written by named but otherwise unidentified individuals on topics ranging from the religious to the secular (for example, "The Chastening of the Lord" and "History of Tobacco-Man Beheaded"), from the personal to the public (for example, "Old-Fashioned Parents" and "Polio Now More Rampant Than Ever"). "Obituaries," "Births," "Exchange Column," and "Classified Ads" complete the paper, making it both superficially similar to but substantively different from its mainstream counterparts.

READING Through its content variety and Old Order writers, *"Die Botschaft"* serves the same reader purposes as the other texts many Amish read regularly; it entertains, edifies, exercises and strengthens faith, and helps readers stay in touch with each other. In addition, *"Die Botschaft"* provides a forum in which to discuss reading—to evaluate and recommend books, to articulate the often assumed but unspoken reasons to read. And in doing this *"Die Botschaft"* illustrates the power these readers vest in text; writers, like the speakers discussed earlier, cite published sources to support their personal ideas and statements.

In their letters, columns, request responses, and ads, *"Die Botschaft"* reader-writers reveal some of the other reading they do and illustrate their attitude towards reading and books. Occasionally a writer relating a personal narrative mentions a personally important book, as did this individual, telling the story of his open-heart surgery and subsequent low-blood-sugar problems:

> I have a book called Nine-day Inner Cleansing and blood wash for renewed youthfulness and health—printed by Parker Publishing Company, Inc., West Nyack, New York. I was on this diet in Feb. and feel I am completely cured from low blood sugar. I went to a health food store for the fruit and vegetable juices. Good luck. Andy Kurtz, Jr.

Writers also support personal opinions with text citation, both secular and religious.

> I feel there are two books that every Amish and Mennonite who uses horses should read. "Black Beauty" and "Beautiful Jos". I am afraid we have some very poor horsemen among our Plain People who regard their horse as mear article of machinery or tools. Stop to think they are our lively hood and I am sure a symbol that are associated with our Christian Faith, which the outsiders see in another light than we do. These are God's creation and in the Christenplicht one can read. Und lasse uns, deine Creaturen and geschepfe nicht verderhen, sondern das mir zur eigen Seligkeit megen gebracht and erhalten werden.

(*Christenplicht* is the statement of one's Christian duty in which it says, according to Anna, "And let us not your creations and works destroy, so we may have eternal salvation.")

In response to requests for information or advice, writers often suggest books. For information on reflexology, one respondent suggested two:

> one is called Helping Yourself with Foot Reflexology. Another one Helping Yourself with Pointed Pressure Therapy. Price of books, about $5.00 each plus $1.50 postage. Address: Parker Publishing Co., Inc., P.O. Box 472, West Nyack, NY. 10995. We find all 3 books helpful. Wouldn't want to be without. They show how to cure about all sickness. A reader.

Product ads cite books for validation, too. An interesting scribe/advertiser/request respondent, "S. Yoder" operates a health-food store and makes it difficult to distinguish his letters from his responses to others' queries and his ads. In each circumstance he writes about experience with and knowledge of diseases, their treatments, and their cures, and most of the time he emphatically attributes his knowledge to "reputable" sources, from

> Gomez Pamo's 'Tratodo de Materia Farmaceutica Vegetal' which runs more than 1,600 pages is in the colection of the National Library of Medicine in Bethesda, Md. The information on Aveloz (his cure) appears in Vol. 11, pages 745–746.

to "Nutrition News" to "For You, Naturally," without further identifying the latter two.

Like most newspapers, *"Die Botschaft"* occasionally needs brief fillers to complete its pages, and one of these offered a rationale for reading *"Die Botschaft,"* the Bible, *Physicians' Desk Reference,* or *Black Beauty:*

> If you don't read, you don't know. If you don't know, you don't care. If you don't care, you don't give, if you don't give, you don't receive. If you don't receive, you don't succeed, if you don't succeed, you'd better read.

WRITING As *"Die Botschaft"* provides the opportunity for its readers to seek and share information, feelings, and ideas, so it allows its regular writers to do the same. *Botschaft* scribes can also respond more directly to what they have read, communicate more pointedly, and more actively foster further writing and reading.

Scribes' letters run from several paragraphs to several columns in length and follow a predictable format. Most begin with a salutation, from a simple "Greetings" or "Dear Reader" to "Friendly greetings of love," "Greetings of love to all readers and writers," "Greetings to all out there in Botschaft land," or even "Greetings of love to you all I send, in the name of our dear Lord and friend." From there most move to a weather and farming report, including recent temperatures and rainfall (or snowfall) amounts, status of seasonal crops, and current chores underway (whether hay making, tobacco cutting, manure hauling, fruit canning, or quilting). Then, in no particular order, they describe the most recent church service—where it took place, which ministers took which parts, and what out-of-district visitors attended; they list recent births, deaths, and marriages in the district, report who is ill or injured (often with graphic descriptions of their conditions), who is recovering, who visited whom, and any other event that seems notable (which may include runaway horses, school meetings, building of new church benches, or even recent crimes reported in their local newspapers). In addition, scribes frequently call for "showers" and circle letters as well as provoking comment and response. "Sunshine Showers," "Get-Well Showers," and "Birthday Showers" involve sending letters and cards to people who are unhappy, ailing, or celebrating. Scribal letters and "Ivverich und Ender" requests often suggest such showers, explaining their perceived need and supplying the name and address of the proposed recipient.

"Die Botschaft" 's form and format seem to be cooperatively created by its scribe readers and its editor. As a newspaper *"Die Botschaft"* is defined by its format—framed by its titles, column headings, and an identification box on page two.

The title on page one is in Gothic type and quotation marks and, as noted earlier, "A Weekly Newspaper Serving Old Order Amish Communities Everywhere" appears below it. Instead of headlines, geographic locations mark each letter in dark, capitalized type only slightly larger than that of the letters themselves. Articles have titles, but those match their geographic equivalents in just slightly more noticeable form.

Larger divisions of the newspaper have larger identifying headings. "Ivverich und Ender," the largest specialized division, has not only a larger, italicized title, but an accompanying logo depicting an old-fashioned, steaming tureen, bordered by symmetrical carrot and celery scrolls, surmounted by a round fruit or vegetable on each side. Below the illustration, "Ivverich und Ender" reads:

HERE'S A COLUMN FOR THE HAUSFRAU

Odds and ends of information about cooking and household tips. We encourage our readers to send items to be used in this column. Maybe a favorite recipe or a household tip or hint that will be a help in other homes. Send your items today to "Die Botschaft," Box 807, Lancaster, PA 17603.

Each of the other specialized columns begins with a decorative motif, though none as elaborate as "Ivverich und Ender," and provides a similar statement of purpose and constraints. The "Exchange Column" asks:

Do you have something you would like to sell, or maybe exchange or trade. Are you looking for something you would like to buy and can't find it. If you are a "Die Botschaft" Subscriber you can run an AD free in this column. Just send your AD in 20 words or less to "Die Botschaft Exchange Column," Box 807, Lancaster, PA 17603 or phone (717) 392-1321. (*Sorry NO Business Ads Accepted in This Column.*)

"Obituary and In Memoriam," more simply bordered, states:

We will print obituaries at no charge. However, memorial poems and articles to be used after three months will be charged for at the rate of 3 cents per word paid in advance.

And, straightforward in appearance, "Die Botschaft Classified Ads" instructs:

Classified ads will be run at 5 cents a word or a minimum of $1.00 an ad prepaid. Items for the free exchange column will be run at no charge for our subscribers. 6 ads per year.

Do you have something you would like to sell, or maybe exchange or trade.

Are you looking for something you would like to buy and can't find it. If
you are a "Die Botschaft" Subscriber you can run an AD free.

Just send your ad in 20 words or less to "Die Botschaft Exchange Column,"
Box 807, Lancaster, PA 17603 or phone (717) 392-1321. (*Sorry NO Business
Ads Accepted in this column.*)

In other words, the paper explicitly provides guidelines for those
who would be published as other than scribes. The most significant
directions, however, may be the most general and least explicit—the
global constraints implicit in the Dutch titles, their old-fashioned appearance, and the stated intention of "Serving Old Order Amish Communities Everywhere," which clearly contextualize this literacy activity.

There must be an editor behind these explicit and implicit guidelines, yet in the two years of this study only once has this individual
written in his own voice, making a statement necessitated by a breach
of the usually accepted, implicit *Botschaft* appropriateness rules. The
breach was called "The Great Race to Chapter 11," a more-than-three-
column story about the Spendthrift brothers and Cadillac Ed, neigh-
boring farmers who constantly tried to outdo each other in production,
acquisition, and income-tax evasion. While John and Ben Spendthrift
and Cadillac Ed buy tractors and farm machinery not permitted by the
Amish, they still drive carriages instead of cars and carry pocket watches
instead of wearing wristwatches. While they replace their telephone bells
with more functional electric horns, they continue to employ a neighbor
full-time "to take them to every pole in the country and some outside."
One keeps a calculator inside his checkbook to keep track of his crop
sale profits. Another invests in iron and tin—"Omega Software Fetch
Facts Systems," among other producers—"an arena where the limits of
technology could not stymie him as it did with farm equipment." The
story ends with Cadillac declaring a Chapter 11 bankruptcy and, not to
be outdone, the brothers declaring a Chapter 13.

The editorial response to this story constitutes the only extant statement of newspaper policy and philosophy I have seen.

Dear Readers,

We here at Die Botschaft office generally try very hard to see that no
objectionable material gets printed, but once in a while we come up short.
This was the case two weeks ago when an article was printed concerning
a Race to Chapter 11.

Unbeknown to the staff here at the paper, some one was using us as
an opportunity to make trouble and bring disparagement. The writer did
not even have the decency to write his name, but instead used fictitious
initials. [The article was signed 'K.G.B.,' which is an enemy identified and
identifiable in much Evangelical Christian-written and Amish-read literature.]

We wish to apologize to the people who were hurt by this article and
assure you, our readers, that we will endeavor to be more careful in screen-
ing out this type of material.

It is just a very sad commentary on the times that we have people who would stoop so low as to use this method to bring hurt and humiliation to others.

We hope that all our scribes will in the future try to write constructive materials and refrain from including items which are degrading and hurtful to others.

Thank you
The Editor

Who is The Editor? His name appears only once each year in the federally mandated "Statement of Ownership, Management, and Circulation" printed in greatly reduced type, but that does not matter. The editorial role exists independently; it is a function of the activity, not the individual. What constitutes "the staff" does not matter either. The staff is responsible to the editor, who, in turn, is responsible to his readers, his situation, his community, and his context. What is "objectionable"? Making trouble and bringing disparagement. Not claiming one's own writing. Bringing hurt and humiliation to others. Being degrading. *Not* being constructive. But what is it that brings hurt and humiliation to others? What makes trouble or constitutes unacceptable disparagement? How is one to be constructive? For those answers, like the editor and staff, participants must look to the larger context where those answers implicitly reside.[1]

While most *Botschaft* writers generally follow the rules and work within the established format of the newspaper and its individual departments, these boundaries allow considerable freedom. Scribes freely write of events they personally consider interesting and appropriate, sometimes provoking the displeasure of others (as did the male scribe who wrote about a daunting moment in changing his son's diaper and who was chastised by another scribe in the next issue). Non-scribal requests for information and their responses range from how to prevent men's suspenders from scratching chair backs and how to keep jar lids from rusting in a "damp cave" to how to prevent dandruff and pimples. Requests for poems and song lyrics range from "For Those Tears I Died" and "The Golden Rule" to "The Prisoner at the Bar"—an English ballad about "the maiden fair with golden hair" who proved "love always finds a way"—and "Twenty Froggers Went to School," with John Denver, John Russell Lowell, and Henry Wadsworth Longfellow in between. (Some of these poems and lyrics may seem markedly un-Amish to outsiders but are apparently acceptable inside. I would suggest that the way these inquirers read the texts they request may vary considerably from the way outsiders do. Love finding a way, for example, can be seen as an important Christian precept, not just as a romantic dream. See discussions of meaning throughout these chapters and chapter 8 in particular to further contextualize this idea.)

SCRIBES AS WRITERS In their letters, *"Die Botschaft"* scribes demonstrate considerable awareness of their role, their writing, their newspaper, and their readers. As a group they tend to be self-critical, mutually supportive, and consistently concerned about the text they individually and jointly create. Aware of an editor through whom their letters appear, scribes seem to associate editorial presence more with production and typographical matters than philosophical ones, except in nonscribal departments where editorial decisions are questioned when they seem contrary to scribe-shared standards (for instance, when scribes question why some poems appear two or three times in the same issue or why some poems, considered inappropriate, appear at all). Scribal standards are nowhere explicitly stated; operating implicitly, articulation becomes necessary only when standards are breached.

Scribes often consider what it is like to be a writer. A Canadian scribe offered the following anecdote to describe life as a scribe:

> Last Thurs was with a van load to Toronto after different items and material. Bought mostly for others but was an enjoying worthwhile day. On way home others asked if I'll write this in *"Die Botschaft"*. 'Don't write about me,' they all said, except Mrs. Abram Martin of North Woolrich, who said I can write all I want about her. Imagine she was the oldest (and wisest) fellow traveller while I was the youngest.

News gathering and content decisions are not the scribes' only problems, however. One scribe explained her decision to stop writing in more personal terms:

> I noticed some of the scribes were introducing themselves, well there isn't much to say of me that you don't know, and I'm bidding adieu, quite often I realize my natural way of writing is not what it takes to write a news letter, I don't care to make an outline, I prefer personal letters and through writing these weekly letters I'm neglecting to get those written, and it also eats stamps, I will ease myself of this strain of writing the world over, but nothing is lost, you'll just keep on reading the Penn Valley News, wait and see.

Such potential problems make the decision to assume a scribe's role difficult. One tentative writer concluded his or her first letter,

> Since no one seemed interested to write from this area I guess I'll give it a try. The other Curtiss scribe is not of our group. But before I sign my name I want to test it out. See how it goes and listen for remarks, criticism or whatever. Might chicken out!!

The letter is signed only "Best Wishes" with the date.

Not all first-time scribes are so hesitant, however. One explained her initial letter in its opening paragraph:

> Dear Readers, greetings of love to all *Botschaft* readers. After enjoying *"Die Botschaft"* for quite a while I decided to add a few lines along with all the interesting letters.

She then wrote a typical weather-church-visiting-births-deaths-illnesses-events letter, signing her name at the end.

Writing on a regular basis can become difficult, so scribes encourage each other, welcoming newcomers and returnees, teasing or cajoling potential dropouts, including themselves.

> Welcome Barbie (Newburg scribe) to the list of writers. It's getting to be quite interesting to see where the next new scribe hails from.

> Published to be married were sister Ruth to Levi King. A December 13 wedding is planned. The Leola scribe can give others who were published that day. Thought it was nice she started writing again.

> And did the smiling, hustling, corner ball player that lives along the 741 lose his writing credentials. Give him a pencil please.

> Dear *Botschaft* Readers Greetings from Peacedale. Dear me. Finally I seated myself to write to *"Die Botschaft"* once again. I guess you thought I quit writing ha. Something you can easily push off.

As this last example suggests, sometimes it's not the difficulty of writing itself but the difficulty of giving writing priority over more pressing work that interferes. Other obligations are often cited as excuses for ending a letter—or as excuses for not having written—stated bluntly or otherwise.

> So I feel I don't have much time to sit here writing now, as I should be getting some things ready yet [for church the next day].

> Sorry I didn't get this out last week. I was getting ready for church and neglected it.

> Greetings to all. Here I am perched on my rear to see if I can add a few lines here. I haven't written for some time, but I don't think that is a crime. I had things that were more important to do than push a pen. In other words I thought I didn't have time. I know there are the same amount of hours in a day for us all, but people are a little like cars, they don't all get the same miles per gal. I don't get as much accomplished in a day time as some, so I don't get everything done I'd like to.

Sometimes potential excuses are recognized but dismissed.

> Greetings of love to all. Will see if I can get a letter together yet before the mailman goes. Should have done this last night but my head was too tired to think. Also have a head cold, which doesn't make a person feel better, but a cold is a minor ailment.

> Oh, my, shame on me! I feel I'm almost too busy to write. I washed this morn, now I'm making catsup, tomatoes are still so nice since we had rain.

> Greetings of Love to all this snowy winter evening. We didn't get our *Botschaft* yet this week so thought that might be a good excuse not to bother writing. Someone with lots of influence didn't let me get by with that. Hubby thought it was kind of alright we didn't get it yesterday like we usually do as we were very busy cutting hickory logs for Landis Wood Products. We cut around 2100 bd. ft. that day. That should give a lot of ax handles. There

were some long faces when the paper still didn't come today. I like to read it before I write again.

That scribes read their own columns is apparent from the frequent comments they make about their writing, sometimes focused on content and sometimes on mechanics, but usually intended to correct. While some scribes take responsibility for errors (and some errors do originate with the writer), others ascribe mistakes to the editor, and still others correct but do not assess responsibility.

It struck me very funny how my last letter was goofed up by saying that Bro. Ammon is a first grader. I bet he's ready for me! He happens to be a 16 year old, but I do admit it's still easiest for me to imagine him a first grader though.

I want to take this opportunity to correct a mistake in my letter printed in Nov. 23 issue of *"Die Botschaft"* in my brief explanation of Hirschbrungs disease. I have incorrectly stated that it is a "genetic disorder." Actually it is not genetic but it is hereditary. I am not a genetisist nor a geneologist, so I don't know what the difference between genetic and hereditary is, but there is a difference.

Sorry I had the wrong date of the Benefit Auction in my other letter. It was last Sat., Nov. 19, and was a tremendous amount of donated things there to be sold, and an overflowing crowd.

My letter of 2 wks ago had a few misspelled words toward the end of the letter which gave the words kind of a different meaning. So hope you just put 2 and 2 together at your liking or you see it best fit.

I'd better brush up on my writing as I noticed several small mistakes in last weeks letter. One misprinted word can change the meaning considerably.

While some call their own mistakes "misprints," others attribute misprints to the printer or editor.

As for Elmer Keupfer's riddle in his form of "Canadian Amish" German, I can decipher that one all right, as I happened to be familiar with those expressions, as my late mother was a Canadian and used those words. But in the *Botschaft* riddle, some of those words were sadly misspelled but have been due to typographical errors.

We hope it was the editor's mistake to have signed my name wrong last time, as why would one sign entirely another name after using the same for over 25 years? If so, it would surely prove "old age" plus "carelessness" on the writer's side.

When the printer/editor is clearly responsible for errors, scribes note that, too.

I tried to keep my letters as small as possible and the other issue it was printed twice. I thought wasn't really that interesting and nice! A neighbor just asked if they print important people's letters twice. I said I don't know haven't talked with any of them yet! Because I really haven't them met! I guess my is pretty big in size.

I see that there were at least six scribes in this last issue who were important enough to have their letters printed twice! Perhaps that is part of the reason why there was not room for all the obituaries and poetry.

Some scribes choose to correct errors without assessing blame, providing more accurate information and letting readers decide what happened if they care to.

My column had a misprint, which should have read: "how many readers feel that every Sunday morning is too often to sing Das Loblied?" Hope everyone got the idea.
P.S. A correction in my other letter, it should have said David Brubakers from CA. were at Jason Martins, in stead of from PA.

Scribes frequently address writing problems and issues, criticizing and correcting each other's content and form. Sometimes the criticism is specific and is specifically addressed.

To Mary Weaver from Maryland, so you think Mary Byler from Ohio has topped them about all. Well I think it was nice of you to congratulate her, but wasn't that just another way to do a little advertising with new hopes for the future. Nix fur unqute [No offense intended.] Mary. I have heard of such cases before.

Can't help but correct Rachel Fisher. We all know you're a Hertzler and still you claim you don't like to correct. Question mark! If you keep us informed on the Hertzler stunts and Barb Kurtz on the peanut outfit, then Rebecca Stoltzfus can fill in on the rest of the late John B. Ebersole descendants and we'll have a circle letter that comes once a week. But this is getting kind of personal.

Sometimes issues are more universal, scribes attempting to articulate desirable standards of form, style and content.

Lets see the full names signed below each *Botschaft* letter. Not just initials. Is more interesting to see where they come from. Also lets write them all in English so all can read.

Lets write Communion and Council Meetings instead of ordnix and gros gmay, and who had des merry dale [*Des merry dale* refers to the main sermon delivered by the second minister at church, constituting the major part of the service. According to Anna, the word is *merre*, the *y* ending here being someone's error.] I enjoy reading the little paper, and would appreciate proper English.

Please, writers, if you want to write then give the complete name. Not just U. Dave or what ever name it happens to be or mom. Who is mom if the writer is unknown to the reader? Some letters are so confusing with a long letter but has no meaning, no object or point of view. The—I mended or I cleaned—are not interesting to the majority. It also amazes me how some can remember all the names of the guests at a wedding. I could not get half way and what difference does it make unless it is an interesting point to it. Otherwise it is just a list of names.

While some scribes sense a need to standardize and upgrade, trying to promote such improvement themselves, at least two scribes suggested that such guidelines might come from those behind the paper itself.

To Neil Hertzberger, Dover scribe. I also wondered already what the Editor opinion is on initial for signature. A State Board of Health person once told me that initials only, will not go through. But initial for the first name and the full last name is passing. But each organization can have different rules.

Yet scribes seem to ignore grammar and mechanics as aspects of writing that should be improved or standardized. As illustrated by examples throughout this section, spelling errors, run-on sentences and fragments, misplaced and missing commas are common and apparently acceptable. Nothing indicates editorial effort to standardize; letters seem to appear as submitted. While scribes often debate language and content choices, they neither write about nor attend to mainstream "correctness" criteria. What counts as good writing, therefore, seems to be that which conveys the most appropriate meaning most effectively, that which can be most easily understood. While it cannot be said that scribes do not care about grammar and mechanics, those considerations seem to have power only to the extent that they may interfere with communication, and rarely, if ever, do they obscure meaning completely.

Occasionally a specific aspect of publication draws criticism from various scribes. The poetry pages attract considerable comment, one writer addressing the signature issue in rhyme:

There was a poem in here last week
From one who's playing hide and seek.
He says, he likes, to write a rhyme
Whenever he can find the time.
But he would never sign his name!
Because he don't want any fame!
I find the reason very poor!
Most everyone agrees, I'm sure.
If it is fame you're worried about
Why you can quickly throw that out.
What a coward, you must be
Because you don't want folk to see
Of what you write, you're so ashamed
That you would never, sign your name!
Please stand up to the things you do
Then you won't get into a stew.
To me your words don't mean so much
Unless you add the finishtouch
So sign your name, be brave and true
Then folks will think, lots more of you
So please don't write another rhyme

Unless you're brave enough to sign.
Lets never write an unsigned thing
Because it has an empty ring.
Lets all be honest, brave and good,
And sign our name, we really should.
Its just too bad, if you take time
To write your thoughts into a rhyme
But then you hide without a name
Because you don't want any fame!
A poor excuse, we all agree
Its just you don't want folks to see.
Or know the things, you stand up for.
Or unsigned works, lets have no more.
Now I'll be true and not ashamed
To stand up tall, and sign my name.

Naomi Byler

Over the years of this study the poetry page became the poetry pages, sometimes as many as three full ones in a single issue, and duplication in and across issues was common. Scribes discussed this topic in an ongoing "conversation" for three weeks in a row, each writer collaborating with his predecessor. One week appeared:

> Who sends all the poetry to the *Botschaft* office? Surely it wouldn't shouldn't be necessary to print so much and so many of them repeats, sometimes in the same issue. I'm sure it costs to print them, and I wonder who reads them all, I don't.

The next week:

> In full agreement with the Gettysburg, PA scribe concerning the poetry. I also wondered who sends them in, and is there some one who reads or likes them, very likely there are some that might enjoy them. But I don't get them read other than a few. It looks to me as a space waste. Although there are some that are nice and have deep meaning.

And the third week, responding to a comment about inappropriate content:

> A hearty "Amen!" to the comments concerning the questionable poetry and writing in the Ivverrich and Ender pages. We quit the other weekly newsletter publication *The Budget* in hopes of having a "clean" paper coming instead. So we hope the "censors" will be on the job before it gets too far out of hand.

Sometimes scribes are admonished by readers who are not also writers. One wrote a letter printed under the heading "Request":

> Dear Botschaft Scribes: there is something I have noticed already in your writing. And I just could not keep quiet after an issue of a couple weeks ago. If you must write about people with mental problems, then state the facts and let that be it. For most such people it's enough to have their name linked with such an illness Let alone making such a fuss in a public paper.

After noting that too many people treat mental illness as a disgrace, the reader includes herself, saying:

> Please let us be more careful of our actions. How do we know that that person worried too much or didn't look enough on the bright side that he suffered a breakdown. Isn't that kind of judging? Nobody ever was what yourself weren't at one time, could become, or are. So those of us with strong bodies and minds, let us not be quick to judge. But rather help our weaker brothers along. For each of us have weaknesses. Maybe some of us our weakness is to talk too much. Best wishes to you all.
>
> A Reader.

The question of what the *Botschaft* should be is occasionally articulated by scribes without reference to any particular problem:

> Greetings of Christian love to all readers of this dear little paper, with its many encouraging thoughts shared with one another. We hope it may stay clean of envy and strife, as well as "silly talk," for such surely cannot be pleasing to God. And we are remembered only by what we have done, be it good or evil, when we have "gone the way of all flesh."

In sum, scribe awareness of audience, medium, and purpose combines to heighten self-consciousness in both positive and negative ways. The range of scribe feelings about writing for *"Die Botschaft"* is best represented in their own words:

> Greetings once more to all friends who may read. I'm not a good writer, but I'll try to succeed in writing some news that won't bore your mind, but doing so sure isn't easy I find.

> Emma decided to give it up this time, so it is my job to write. In my weakness I will give it a try as I do like to read the *Botschaft* letters.

> Greetings of Christian love to friends far and near. While writing here one's thoughts go mostly to the ones far off, bringing them the news, if there be any. We get so much enjoyment in reading others' letters but cannot believe anyone gets much from my poor remarks. Our talents are not the same and it is good so. God knows we need one another in our everyday life and much more so in the spiritual.

> Swipe a piece of paper, try and find the ink. Sit and chew your pen awhile, scratch your head and think. Try to write a letter fitting to be seen, tis no trifling matter to be writing to *"Die Botschaft."* Not that it's a hardship for its far from that, what gives us all the trouble is to put things pat. Hence this care and caution like nothing ever seen, tis no trifling matter to be writing to *"Die Botschaft."* First you read it through yourself, then show it to your ma. Then to various other folks who don't know who you are. So take care and tear your hair and keep from being mean. You don't know who will read what you write to *"Die Botschaft."* So we spend an hour or two near a smoky lamp. Ask the family for a tip, and husband for a stamp. Sorry it's over for our joy was keen. Twas a thrilling pasttime writing to *"Die Botschaft."* Or was it?

• *The Church Community* •

Amish families living in their locally defined "East District" constitute the Fishers' church community of approximately one hundred people. Because the Old Order Amish have no church buildings, meeting in congregants' homes instead, and because of the limited distance a horse can pull a full buggy, geographic proximity determines to which congregation a family belongs. In the Fishers' rural area live enough Amish to constitute two districts, East and West; in Lancaster County there are dozens of districts, each identified in terms of location as well.

Held on alternate Sundays within each district, church services occupy most of the day. The location moves from home to home in geographical order to facilitate the movement of the church wagon, which is driven by each host to the home of the next, transporting the *Ausbund*s (hymnals), the specially built benches that convert from backless pews to tables, and the dishes and silverware that go on the tables for the traditional postservice meal, all owned jointly by the congregation. At each location, the benches are set up in the house, which, if built by an Amish family like the Fishers, has a specially designed floor plan to accommodate them; or, in warm weather they are set up in the barn. After the three-to-four-hour service, some of the benches are converted into tables so the women of the extended host family can begin serving the traditional "dinner" to the first of the several seatings necessary to accommodate the entire congregation. The people who began arriving early in the morning for the 8:00 A.M. service may begin leaving for home by 2:00 or 3:00 in the afternoon.

READING (AND WRITING) Reading and writing in this community are in some ways markedly different from any of the others, yet this is the context in which an individual's relationship to text is most important and in which the fundamental Amish attitude toward text is established. Little writing is done by the church community; the primary texts were written long ago and need no supplement from modern man. Extended text production becomes moot, therefore, and writing becomes useful only to conduct mundane church-related business: to produce the annual list matching Scripture portions with particular Sundays and to list nominees for the minister selection process, which is described later in this section.

In addition, the women of the church community sometimes use writing to organize each postservice meal. The host family is responsible for the food, but other women in the congregation volunteer to help. "We talk about it after church," Anna explained, "and if we forget to talk about it, we send the host family notes telling what we'll bring." Usually, Anna says, the host family bakes the pies, others volunteer for the rest, and the meal is always the same: cup cheese, sharp cheese, peanut butter and molasses, bologna, pickles, pickled beets, homemade bread (and sometimes rolls), butter, jelly, snitz (dried apple) pies, apple pies, coffee, tea, and water. Volunteers not only choose what to bring but how much to bring. (It takes between twenty-two and twenty-five loaves of bread to feed Anna's district each Sunday.) Does the host ever ask people to bring things? "Never, never, never!" Anna responded emphatically. "If no one offered, I would make everything myself. I would never ask, and I hope I would never have to."

Most church literacy activities, therefore, involve some form of reading, not writing. Individual congregants all have prayer books and Bibles at home, but they take no books to church despite the use of *Ausbund* hymnals, prayer books, and the New Testament during the service. ("The world does that," Anna pointedly noted. "We are supposed to carry our books in our heads.") The congregation supplies *Ausbund*s for everyone, but only the three ministers and the deacon, who conduct the service, actually use the other two texts. A small pamphlet that congregants also keep at home, *Ein Register von Leider un Schriften die in der Amischen Gemeinde* (A register of songs and scripture for the Amish church), lists the New Testament portions to be considered each week of the year and their appropriate *Ausbund* corollaries, often citing more than one hymn from among which to choose. Hymn choice is made during the service and is usually reserved for visitors to the district, or, if no visitors attend, falls to the adult male song leaders, the group with whom Eli attends practice singings.

The church service itself follows the same format across weeks and across districts. The service begins and ends with hymns, called for and started by a single male voice rising from among those gathered. The opening hymn leads to the *anfang* (the opening sermon) delivered by one of the three ministers and based on one of the assigned Scriptures. ("It's usually short," Anna explained, "no more than a half hour. It's really preparation for prayer.")

At the end of the anfang, the minister reminds the congregation to pray for him and his fellow preachers as all kneel for the first prayer. Conducted silently, this prayer requests guidance for leaders both religious and secular, ministers and presidents. Although congregants are free to pray silently in any way they choose, Anna believes most recite from memory the prayer that appears in their prayer books and that they learned as children or some personal variation on the same theme.

When the prayer concludes and the congregation sits down on its backless wooden benches, the deacon reads the second assigned Scripture directly from the New Testament. (In a conversation when I mentioned the deacon reading from the Bible, Anna corrected me at once. "It's the Testament, not the Bible," she said. "We never use the Bible in church." The Bible, to her, is the King James Version of both the Old and New Testaments. The "Testament" is the New Testament.) This reading establishes the focus for the *merre dale*, or main sermon, delivered by the second minister. Often lasting for nearly an hour, the merre dale usually explains what the deacon read and what it means to the community. Sometimes, however, the minister may feel moved to speak on another topic, one he senses as immediately important to the community, and he may change his mind at the last moment, as he sits before the congregation and watches them pray. (The same freedom exists for the anfang speaker, too.) This never results in the physical disposal of an unused sermon, however, because ministers do not write their sermons on paper; they prepare them mentally instead.

(Though unable to understand the German, I clearly understood the exhortative nature of the anfang and the merre dale in the service I attended. The impassioned delivery of each minister, his voice, his facial expressions, and his body movements, communicated considerable information. One minister, in fact, was so intent and intense that as the tears rolled from his eyes and his voice cracked, a young man in the congregation brought him a glass of water, the contents of which partially spilled onto the barn floor as the preacher's hand shook with the effort of containing himself. I asked Anna later if that minister usually grew so passionate, and she assured me that he did, that "that is his style.")

Testimonies follow the main sermon, the first given by that week's nonpreaching minister, followed by his two colleagues and sometimes by two or three men from the congregation. Testimony has a special focus in this context: each speaker "says how he felt about the sermon, whether it was upbuilding or not" and why. "Things can work two ways for the church," Anna explained. "They can build the church or they can destroy the church." The former is the major goal of the community, both as a group and as individuals, and the purpose of each sermon each week.

After the testimony, the merre dale preacher calls for the second prayer, which is always the same one and "touches a little bit of everything." It is a long prayer, lasting approximately fifteen minutes, which the minister reads from his prayer book while the congregants "follow in [their] minds," standing without instruction when they reach a certain line. Then the final hymn is sung, and the service concludes, three to four hours after it started.

Throughout the service, then, the congregation acts as one body, exemplifying in their actions the overriding importance of each individual's yielding to the unifying rites of the community. "The inward state [is] revealed by external behavior" (Cronk 1981, 30), so the hymns must rise from the congregation as one voice, prayers must be prayed in shared silence as the congregation mentally follows a single known text or a single minister's voice, and physical movement must occur on agreed-upon cues to demonstrate the unified wholeness of the church.

Another significant text used by the church community is the eighteen-article *Confession of Faith*, each article a statement of belief supported by Old and New Testament citations (the former from Genesis, Deuteronomy, Psalms, Numbers, Isaiah, and Daniel). Each church member has a copy printed in pamphlet form; the Fisher children received theirs as gifts from their grandparents. Like the Bible, the *Confes-*

sion of Faith text remains at home, but its content is the focus of the service held the week before each semiannual communion and of nine "instruction" Sundays for "young folks" (sixteen years old or older) preparing to join the church.

This pre-baptism instruction occurs during church over a period of eighteen summer weeks, but only during alternate summers. The young folks who've decided to "join church" and one minister leave the service during the first hymn and go to a separate room where the minister expands on each article of faith as the candidates sit and listen. The lesson involves no actual text; the minister speaks from memory as the students follow mentally. Study of the text itself occurs at home, before and after each instruction morning, preparing students to follow the minister's explanation and reinforcing what they heard.

The Saturday prior to their baptism, those taking instruction, their parents, grandparents, and any interested church members gather for a final reading of the articles by their ministers. Candidates sit in one row of seats facing a row of ministers, with their families seated behind the ministers. The process takes all afternoon, each minister reading several verses and explaining them, and it is followed by a shared supper.

The next day the candidates sit in the first row during the church service. When the time comes for baptism, the candidates are asked individually again, as they were asked at each previous gathering, whether they still want to receive Jesus Christ. If so, each candidate must answer "yes" to three baptismal promises—to accept Jesus Christ as God's son, to accept him as Lord and Saviour, and to accept the tripartite nature of Father, Son, and Holy Ghost. The bishop and deacon then conduct the actual baptism, their wives assisting with the removal and restoration of the girls' coverings. No text appears at any time during this process.

MEANING Though the Amish church service is completely text based, unless a minister is otherwise inspired, it seems to rest on the assumption that the physical text is largely unnecessary. Only the ministers who must share the assigned Scripture and the assigned prayer, verbatim, rely on texts during the service; other congregants follow their individual mental versions. In fact, the absence of text at regular services, instruction, and baptism suggests a priority of oral over written text. This may demonstrate both community knowledge and individual commitment and be a way of insuring the availability of the Word under any circumstances, but it is also a practice that reinforces the notion that meaning is in the words themselves, whether memorized or read.

As the primary church focus, the New Testament is taken personally and literally, an attitude extending to the Old Testament as well. "What's in the Bible is supposed to be the truth. We don't have second thoughts about what's in there, if that's what you mean," Anna said when I asked how she and her church believe it should be read and understood. Each year the same portions are read from Matthew, John, Peter, Luke, Romans, Hebrews, Apostles, Corinthians, and Galatians, and each year they directly instruct the Amish about their daily life as a church on earth.

While this application of the New Testament to life becomes explicit in ministers' sermons through explanation and parable, these ministers receive no special training for this purpose. Once chosen as ministers (through a process described later in this chapter), they "study the portion for each week" to discover what they must say, and week after week they find the "up-building" dimensions of assigned biblical portions. No matter what the text says, these ministers find it true, relevant, and good for the life of the church. This ministerial practice then becomes the model for how congregants approach text and what they bring to their own reading, not only in terms of particular biblical interpretation but in terms of attitude toward and expectations of text other than the Bible.

The Amish readers in my experience extend this approach to everything they read, finding personally applicable "up-building" meaning in both the positive and negative experiences of historical, fictional, and actual individuals, regardless of the text in which they're encountered. So what the church actually teaches is that meaning comes through scrupulous attention to words, but that the attitude toward and meaning of those words is often predetermined by the community in which they are read.

Reinforcing this model, the *Ausbund* hymnal is treated similarly as received text. Written by early church martyrs, its songs tell of suffering and faith, serving as an immediate connection between the Amish and their ancestors. Each hymn takes nearly an hour to sing correctly because of its slow tune, its length, and the complexity of the High German dialect involved. "They average 17.6 stanzas with as many as thirteen lines each, most with intricate rhyme schemes" (Schreiber 1962, 52). In addition, "very few changes have been made in the text in spite of the change which the language has undergone since the sixteenth century" (Schreiber 1962, 57). Grammar and syntax rules are often ignored to preserve rhyme schemes, spelling rules are often revised, and meaningless words often retained, but none of this matters to the congregation.

Appropriate reader response to these hymns involves personal and collective identification as it does to the Bible; "their appeal is rather to the heart than the head" (Schreiber 1962, 39). The martyrs were nonconformists persecuted for their faith; today's Amish are the same kind of nonconformists who cannot help but empathize with their predecessors. The way in which the songs are written, "lack[ing] concentration of language and expression . . . The formulation of the simple Christian faith protract[ing] through too many stanzas" (Schreiber 1962, 39), is irrelevant. Reader and writer purpose meld over the centuries, overriding any considerations of form, style, or mechanics.

Singing, then, becomes a supreme expression of the faithful community. The men in positions of power and authority, men like Eli and his friends who are heads of households and primary breadwinners, practice regularly to learn the difficult, complex tunes and to perfect their unified voice as the model for the larger congregation. Choral singing in church—the model for choral singing at "singings" and in school—expresses the total community commitment to unity in worship and in service of the Word perhaps even more so than unified prayer. An analogue of taking communion, *Ausbund* hymn singing is a corporate remembering of individual sacrifice and suffering.

The *Ausbund* also plays another role in the church, a special rather unique one that reinforces the unanalyzed power of religious text. When a ministerial vacancy occurs through relocation or death (usually the latter, ministers rarely moving from the districts they serve), the congregation nominates men to fill the position, this nominating procedure constituting the other use of writing by the church. The bishops and ministers sit in a room apart from the congregation, the bishop with pen and paper. Each baptized member of the church files past and whispers the name of a man who might be minister. The bishop records each name, putting a slash behind it for every repeated nomination; all names receiving three or more slashes then go into the lot.

When nominations close, the bishop selects the most similar-looking *Ausbunds* (those that look newest), taking one for every nominated man. He places a slip of paper inside one book and then puts all the books on a table before the congregation. As the list is read, nominees move to the table and sit down. After a communal prayer for guidance, each man is asked whether he still agrees to his baptismal promises and whether he would take the responsibility of minister should it be his lot. With full agreement, each nominee takes an *Ausbund* from the center of the table and places it before him. The bishop then opens one book at a time until the signifying paper is revealed. He addresses the man thus chosen, outlining the responsibilities of a minister, and repeats the question of willingness to serve. Assent brings a handshake and the "holy kiss."

From that moment on the new minister assumes an unpaid position he will hold—in addition to his secular occupation—for the rest of his life. Rather than seeing this process as a lottery with luck randomly choosing the winner, the Amish see it as divine lot falling to a man whose life will never again be the same. His becomes the awesome responsibility of doing God's special work on earth, so congratulations are tempered by tears and a sense of having witnessed divine intervention through the channel of the text.

The possibility of any man's selection by the lot highlights the implicit assumption that meaning is open to all men. The ministry is not accessible only to a corps of trained specialists, so meaning must not be the property of such an elite. If any individual who yields himself to God's will and serves God's community can be a minister, then any consenting individual can discern the meaning in even the most important text.

Baptismal instruction, too, confirms these notions of text as vehicle ` for truth and meaning as received. Baptismal candidates must be at least sixteen, old enough to understand the meaning of baptism and to choose it freely. They must be able to read the *Confession of Faith* and to comprehend related ministerial commentary, which involves not just statements of belief but the ways in which biblical text supports those beliefs. Yet the candidates need not make the connection explicit, need not analyze the *Confession* themselves. Instead they must accept and absorb ministerial interpretation without discussion and without question. During the weeks of instruction and during the baptismal service itself, candidates are not called on to respond to any but a few point-blank, yes-or-no questions. Passivity and yielding are the only proper responses to received truth.

Like the baptismal candidates, the ministers, must read and study text without benefit of any secondary-source interpretation other than ministers they've heard and may remember. Personal interpretation is believed to derive from the text itself, from attention to the words and any divine aid that inspires. Text brings truth to baptismal candidates and ministers alike, the latter sharing received meaning with the former.

It seems, then, that all Amish church members are personally responsible for knowing and accepting those texts that give them direction, those texts coming from a fixed unimpeachable source. Perceiving itself as a world of clear sources and competent readers, the Amish Church community significantly influences all other domains of Amish literacy.

• *The School Community* •

Meadow Brook School has two attending constituencies—the children and their parents. While the former attend five days a week, nine months a year with only one (or two) days off, the latter gather one afternoon each month for "school meetings," visit classes whenever they choose, and conduct fund-raising activities periodically. At these times they both read and write to accomplish their school-related purposes.

READING I attended several identically conducted school meetings during my research and was assured by Anna that they all begin the same way: Hymnals are distributed—a board member giving them to the men who sit on one side of the room, the teacher to the women on the other—and hymn singing follows. (Meadow Brook owns one set of hymnals used by the adults and the children, *Favorite Songs and Hymns: a complete church hymnal* [Dallas: Stamps Baxter Music, 1967]. This is not a specifically Old Order book, containing both modern popular hymns and musical notation neither of which the Amish use.) After books are distributed, a voice, usually male, calls out a number, and everyone turns to that page. The same voice then sings the first few words before everyone joins in, a procedure almost identical to that of church-service singing. Three or four hymns are chosen and sung this way, all without musical accompaniment of any kind. Though many participants appear to sing from memory—their eyes often raised from the hymnals and looking elsewhere in the room—book distribution and page turning are never omitted. The singing ends when at the conclusion of a song the three board members move from their seats among the men to positions in front of the group, indicating the beginning of the business portion of the meeting.

What seems to be the most significant business of the meeting is conducted in writing. Written on the blackboard in advance, a list of figures accounts for the month's expenses, including teacher salary, electric bill, coal bill, and "3 hours" (the teacher's eight-dollar allotment for working with the two fourteen-year-olds who attend school three hours a week until they are fifteen).[2] One month nothing else appeared on the board; other months—according to Anna, most months—each family's fee also appears there, total expenses divided by the nine families involved and weighted according to the number of schoolchildren per family. Therefore, when the president calls on the treasurer to conduct his portion of the meeting, the treasurer can just shrug and need not speak; all that he has to say appears on the board for everyone to read.

Election of school community officers also involves the blackboard. Although I did not attend that meeting, having been banned from the school several weeks earlier (an incident discussed in the "Meaning" portion of this section), Anna reported that the names of men nominated as chairman were written on the board, Eli's among them. Eli learned he had been elected when the president began erasing the name above his but carefully avoided erasing the top of the elaborate capital *E*.

Operation of Meadow Brook also involves other adult reading not done at meetings. Because it is responsible for school maintenance, both mechanically and financially, the parental community reads whatever is necessary to operate the building, much of which is similar to the operation of their homes and businesses. They deal with energy suppliers and tradesmen, buying coal and electricity; they do outdoor and indoor maintenance work, buying supplies necessary for those tasks as well.

In addition, the parents are asked to do education-related reading in the form of *Standards of the Old Order Amish and Old Order Mennonite Parochial and Vocational Schools of Pennsylvania*, the guiding document for Old Order schools that all receive when they enroll their children. For those elected as school directors, such reading is crucial since together they supervise all aspects of Meadow Brook and must do so in accordance with the rules of the system within which they operate.

Standards offers the parents some reading about reading and writing. Standard 7 outlines "The Education Program"; part "a—The language arts including reading, writing, spelling and english"—is explained this way:

> In this category are placed in order; reading, writing, spelling and english. Reading is recognized as one of the most important subjects in our schools today, and should be stressed as such in our parochial schools. Phonics should be used as an aid to the young child, and ability to pronounce words should be continued through the lower grades. Writing and spelling are also very important, and these three subjects should be a daily requirement. English is recommended as a requirement from grades four through eight.

Student report cards, sent home six times a year, also constitute parental reading. Small white cardboard folders, printed in black and adorned with a dove surmounting the Golden Rule, the report cards come from the Gordonville (Pennsylvania) Print Shop, the source of almost all school supplies (including *Standards*). On the front of the report card, below the decorations and individual student identification, is a note "TO THE PARENT":

> In return for the privilege of being granted our Parochial schools, let us have a record for our schools that will be respected by the state as well as having a feeling of satisfaction and sincerity for our own group.
> Before signing this card take some time to study it carefully. It is designed to help you better understand the relationship of your child with the school and their playmates. Take an interest in your childs school life, and if your child is worried or receives a mark that indicates a need of help, talk it over kindly with the pupil and also talk it over with your teacher.
> Absence or tardiness interferes with the progress of the pupil, and very seriously affects the efficiency of the school. In case of necessary absence or tardiness, please give the pupil a written excuse.
> Remember, your teacher is a person, same as you or I and appreciates your assistance. Your co-operation with your teacher also assists your pupil. You as a parent should visit the school.

And again, at the bottom of the front of the report card, in capital letters, "PARENTS ARE URGED TO VISIT THE SCHOOLS."

On the back of the card, another note to the parent says:

> You are requested to promptly sign, and return this report to your teacher. Should there be any question, kindly contact your teacher-POLITELY.

It is not just school business that requires parental reading. The annual school Christmas program does too. First comes the gift exchange. I saw Verna give gifts to all her students, including paint-by-number sets, tea sets, pick-up sticks, magic sets, and hand-held plastic pinball-type games. She also distributed "Silent Night" bookmarks, printed with the first verse of the song and a quotation from the Book of Luke. From her students, Verna received eggs, homemade cookies and doughnuts, cheese, and fruit. From their mothers she received a twelve-patch quilt, one square from each family embroidered with their children's first names and different decorations including flowers, butterflies, and mailboxes with the families' last names on them. A central patch read "Verna Burkholder, Meadow Brook School, 1982."

Then comes the program, during which all the children perform individually and/or in groups, singing songs, reciting poems, and reading from the Bible, all with texts in front of them. As they arrive, parents receive mimeographed copies of the "Meadow Brook Program," the outside of each decorated by a different child with crayoned candles, holly, stars, and the title on the front and *Welcome* with more seasonal designs on the back. Inside, in the ditto-master-duplicated handwriting of the eighth-grade boys, the program lists what will be performed and the names of all performers. In addition, parents receive "Christmas Songs," a booklet with twenty-one sets of lyrics set to half as many tunes, each indicated separately, including more than half a dozen set to "Jesus Loves Me," and others set to "Are You Sleeping?" "Twinkle, Twinkle Little Star," "How Great Thou Art" and other commonly known hymns. Each booklet has a green or red construction-paper cover crayon-decorated with a Christmas symbol, and each contains hand-printed, purple mimeographed pages. While the programs are souvenirs, the song books remain at school to be used for subsequent Christmases.

WRITING As noted in the previous section, the community of school adults uses writing to conduct business and to avoid speaking before the group. In addition, the school directors must file formal annual enrollment reports with the state. During this study, however, the women of the community also used writing to conduct activities more specifically their own.

At the December school meeting, someone raised a question about planned Christmas treats for the children: Would the mothers send a special meal on the last day of school before the vacation day? As discussion focused on what to serve, how to transport it, and who would be responsible for how much of what, the men's attention drifted away. Soon the two groups were two separate circles, the men facing each other and discussing their business (I overheard some conversation about *Hoard's Dairyman* and farm operation) while the women turned to each other, planning the Christmas party.

After a few minutes of random and tangential discussion about how much they disliked butchering for meat and whether poultry, beef, or pork killing is most distasteful, one mother, Emma Martin, brought the group back to planning the menu, and the teacher excused herself to get pencil and paper. When Verna returned, Emma took the tablet and listed the names of all mothers with children at Meadow Brook. She and the others then divided necessary chores, assigning tasks to those women not present.

I asked if I could take a message to the absent Anna since I was going to the farm after the meeting, and Emma gave me a note:

Anna,
     Enough Ice cream for 20 people. For Dec. 24. I will gather the food for Lunch. Also make drink. Each family makes 1 doz. cookies.

Written in pencil on the bottom portion of a piece of lined tablet paper, the note was physically written by Emma but composed by everyone. Emma's elicitations, "What else should I tell her?" "I'm sure I'm forgetting something," and "I can't spell," brought suggestions from the others. When one woman suggested she "ask the teacher" for a spelling, Emma replied, "No, I'll do it my way." Later, writing Anna's full name on the outside of the folded note, Emma remarked, "I can never spell Fisher. I always spell it the same way, the way I hear it when I say it." She used a variant spelling, one some families use, but not Anna's.

On a later occasion, The Meadow Brook women had another menu to write, one listing their offerings for potential customers. Emma's River Brethren family was moving to Lancaster County, where they would work at a tourist attraction, dressed and living as Amish, so they wanted to sell their farm equipment before leaving. The Meadow Brook mothers volunteered to operate the Martin sale lunch-stand to raise money for the school, an activity Anna organized "because no one else would. . . . Everyone wanted to help, but no one wanted to manage."

For Anna, managing involved both reading and writing. First she made a list of the women involved and matched each with a soup, sandwich, or dessert. Then she sent notes to the mothers through their children, telling them what to bring but not how much, leaving quantities to individual discretion. Responsible, herself, for bulk food and nonfood supplies, Anna comparison shopped for hot dogs, rolls, soda, gum, candy, and paper products until she found the merchant offering the best case-lot prices for what she needed.

On the day of the sale, Anna became the focus as the other mothers arrived to set up the stand. Price labels had to be written and affixed, and menu signs had to be made, but first someone had to decide how much each item would cost. Should individual slices of a pie bring a total greater than the whole pie would? How many Styrofoam cups of hot chocolate could be made from an eight-envelope package, and how much should each cost? Decisions were made communally after each woman did her own paper-and-pencil computations, some out loud and some accompanied by moans, comments, and laughter. Anna asked one woman's teenage daughter to make two menu signs, giving her two sides of a discarded cardboard carton and a red marking pen, but by 10:00 A.M. only customers were reading the signs, the Meadow Brook mothers having learned, through use, what each said.

MEANING It was in relation to the Meadow Brook adults that I experienced most dramatically what reading and writing mean in this community.

With only two weeks remaining in the school year, and only two weeks remaining for me to participate at Meadow Brook, the number of questions I wanted to ask seemed to increase as rapidly as the time available diminished. I worried daily about whether I could learn all that I wanted to know in the time remaining. My constant worrying became moot, however, with one unexpected 7:00 A.M. phone call.

"Did I wake you?" Anna's voice asked by way of greeting.

"Not exactly."

"Were you planning to come down today?"

"Yes, later this morning. Do you need something?" I asked, assuming that her reason for calling was to request my help in some way.

"No, I don't need anything," Anna replied, "but you can't come."

"I what?" The tone of Anna's voice made her message more than ominous. The ethnographer in me reached for pencil and paper while the rest of me just sat there, dreading her next words.

"You can't come to the school anymore," Anna continued. "The directors decided that this has gone far enough and it has to stop. The public is finding out too much."

"Did they have some kind of meeting or something about this?"

"No, there was no meeting. Just the directors and a few parents talked about it. They realized they don't know why you're here. All they know is you're writing a book."

"But I explained it all to them before I started!" I nearly yelled, remembering that initial meeting. "I really thought they understood!"

"They say now they never really understood," Anna explained. "They just didn't look into it enough and Verna didn't give them much satisfaction." She paused. "I tried to give the meaning I know, but I knew they weren't feeling too good about it. One lady really stressed it: 'You're just being used,' she said to me."

"Oh, Anna."

"It's my fault it happened in the first place," she continued. "I didn't ask enough questions, know enough about it . . ."

"You just trusted me," I interrupted.

"Anyway," she went on following her own train of thought, "since it was our fault this happened, I decided it was my place to explain to you why you can't come anymore, and I couldn't do that in a letter and let you come down before you got it. I told them that if you know about it, I know you won't come, so I figured I better call early."

"Is there anything I can do?" I asked with the optimism of a born outsider.

"I don't think so. They think there's too much information going out to the public. They even called the school committee in Lancaster to find out if they have to let you in, and the man there told them, 'We need the public when we need them, but this is too much.' They know it's not illegal to have the public in; we have to deal with them, but this has gone too far."

"Oh, Anna, I feel terrible," I moaned. "I wish there were something I could do."

"I know," she consoled me. "I can't tell you it's all right to go back no matter what they say, though. We have to support the directors now. We're part of the school." She paused before continuing. "When I got home, I told Eli what had happened and asked him what I should do. 'Tell her the truth,' he told me. I wanted to tell you myself because I can understand you better than they can. . . ."

"That's for sure," I concurred. "And you understand them better than I can. . . ."

"The only thing I can get down to is that they really believe too much is being carried out, and they're trying to protect their faith and avoid publicity," Anna concluded.

That the community perceives reading and writing as politically powerful seems clear from this experience. As Anna understood the issue, it was not one of my honesty or of the truthfulness of any text I produced; the issue was one of separation versus cooperation (as defined in chapter 7). I had brought the outside in, in some ways unavoidably disrupting the operation of Meadow Brook. Next, they knew, I would take the inside out through the "book" I planned to write, and that posed an unnamed threat to the community. Even if my intentions were honest and honorable, the parents could not risk the interpretations and intentions of other outsiders. After all, one mother reminded Anna, outsider investigation in Wisconsin had led to fines and imprisonment for Old Order parents whose children did not attend school as the compulsory age law there demanded. What else might investigation lead to? The community could not control the meaning others might find in what happens at Meadow Brook, so they chose to control what others might read and write about what happens, instead.

Frustrated, upset, and personally dismayed, I asked Anna if I could do or say anything to at least reassure the others if not to make them lift the ban. Though personally convinced I could not, Anna told the wife of one school director that I wanted to talk to them and try to explain.

"What for?" Etta asked Anna. "There's nothing to say," which Anna interpreted not as a slight but as a statement of fact.

Anna also told Etta I was concerned about hard feelings the school parents might have toward me.

"They don't," Etta responded.

Could I come to the school picnic with Anna's family?

"It's only for parents and scholars," Etta said. "That's the way Verna wants it."

The whole adult school community was of one mind about the outsider and her literacy activities; even Verna chose the most politically practical alignment.

(An interesting postscript: I asked Anna whether she thought the same fate would have befallen my research in a predominantly Amish school, Meadow Brook being predominantly Mennonite. "No, it never would have happened in an Amish school," she laughed. "They would have spoken to the Committee right away, and you never would have gotten in [to observe] in the first place.")

FOUR

The Family and the School

Not more than a five-minute drive, or a twenty-minute walk, from the Fisher farm, Meadow Brook School appears suddenly, at the crest of a gentle hill, a white rail fence separating school grounds from two-lane blacktop. Surrounded by farms, trees, and the meadows of its name, Meadow Brook's white clapboard exterior and rarely lit windows belie its daily activity. Only a half-dozen bicycles and some overturned scooters in the yard hint at the first-through-eighth-grade children who inhabit the building from 8:30 in the morning until 3:00 in the afternoon, five days a week, from mid-August through early May, with Christmas Day the only holiday. Although the children are clearly visible and audible during morning, lunchtime, and afternoon recesses, little else breaks the rural silence. Just the pair of children who bring water from the farm across the road each morning, the children who occasionally step out for wood stacked on the porch, and the children who, with permission, visit the white cinder-block outhouse behind the school itself signal the life within.

Like most elementary school classrooms, Meadow Brook's walls reflect the activity they contain. Middle grades studied Alaska: nine student-made igloos of white paper ice blocks glued mosaic-style on blue paper hang in rows, beside which two crayoned, cutout men drive separate dogsleds, each pulled by six, paired, cutout huskies. Lower grades had a health unit on nutrition: eight construction-paper "Mr. Breakfasts" with milk bottle bodies, bacon legs, egg feet, banana arms, orange heads, and inverted bowl hats stare from one wall at four more of their species hanging opposite.

Upper grades read Old Testament stories: eight crayoned illustrations, five apparently traced and three seemingly freehand copies, hang together, each identified by title—"David," "Joseph," "Jonathan," (two)

"Baby Moses," "The Great Flood," "Elijah is Fed," and "The Sheperd Boy's Fight with the Giant." (The latter had additional explanatory text: "Am I a dog that you come unto me with a few sticks and stone I will hang your flesh out for the birds.") Invisible to the casual observer, compositions hang beneath these illustrations, each telling the story of its picture, each copied verbatim from a book and bearing a student's name.

Beside the Bible pictures hang the products of art lessons. There is one group of twelve nearly identical pictures, each a crayoned cutout of a red house, barn, and silo surrounded by four green trees of gradually different sizes, fronted by a white rail fence and post-mounted mailbox. All twelve are glued on blue construction paper, only the arrangement of parts varying slightly. Next to those is another art-lesson set: five silhouette pictures each with two black figures, one bending over as though to pick something up, the other with one arm drawn back as though to throw something toward the first, set against broad horizontally striped crayoned backgrounds of Day-Glo pink, orange, and chartreuse, only the color choices and arrangements differing from picture to picture. A third set of nine identical cutout brown teddy bears, dressed for Christmas and holding candy canes, seems out of place on a late January day.

More immediately eye-catching than any of these is the near ceiling-level sign suspended from a rope stretched from one side wall to the other: "A man worthwhile is one that can sing and smile when all goes dead wrong," it reads, each word in black letters but the last two in red.

Also like most elementary school classrooms, Meadow Brook's walls wittingly or otherwise attest to the school's philosophy and priorities. Covered almost completely with work by all students in all grades, they celebrate universal achievement. That universal achievement is strikingly uniform, however, in groups unified not only by grade, lesson, or theme, but by content and form as well. Underlining this uniformity is the absence of student names on work displayed, suggesting that group achievement is more significant than individual achievers.

Without these defining displays, little would distinguish Meadow Brook from the popular conception of a one-room schoolhouse. Wooden slant-top desks on metal pedestals, with permanently affixed wooden swivel chairs, sit in six straight rows. A large wood stove, its flue ascending through the ceiling, dominates the front of the room, dwarfing the wooden teacher's desk beside it. Behind the stove and desk, a slanted blackboard protrudes on a slight angle from the front wall, print and cursive English alphabet charts above it, German alphabet chart to its right, wooden benches below. Two built-in closets flank the board, one housing the library, the other, supplies.

Along the back wall, behind a row of metal chairs available for visitors, are coat hooks for the children, and in the left corner a built-in wooden bookcase holds a few books and many lunchboxes. Pink flowered fabric suspended from curtain rods conceals bookshelves high on the rear side walls, protecting stored books of various kinds. The floor is bare wooden planks; the walls are brown-paneled to chair-rail height, beige-paneled above. In the right rear corner a hand-cranked ditto machine on a metal desk and a Coleman drink-dispensing cooler on a wooden dry sink strike the only discordant notes.

The most noticeable feature on first entering Meadow Brook, however, was none of the above for me, nor was it the twenty-some children usually present. Even when a lesson was in progress and even after months of observation, the feature most invariably striking was the silence. I could hear the teacher instructing or a student reciting, but surrounding those voices was the absence of others. On my first day, twenty-six pairs of eyes watched my uncomfortably loud entrance; on my last day, fewer noticed, but I still heard my own sounds distressingly distinct among theirs.

The twenty-six children enrolled at Meadow Brook represent nine families—six Old Order Mennonite, two Old Order Amish, and one River Brethen (an Old Order Mennonite denomination marked by its use of cars)—making Meadow Brook one of many so-called "Amish schools" that is not wholly Amish. In fact, because their similarities outweigh their differences in both number and degree, the Old Order Mennonite have joined with the Old Order Amish to operate a parochial school system governed by the *Standards of the Old Order Amish and Old Order Mennonite Parochial and Vocational Schools of Penna.*, none of which existed until well into this century.[1] Meadow Brook was built by the Mennonites as part of this system in 1979 and was joined by two Amish families (one of them the Fishers) in 1981 because of its geographic convenience, its low enrollment, and the overcrowded situation at Sunnyside School, the other local Old Order school which happens to be predominantly Amish.

As described in *Standards*, "The school district shall include the area within a radius of a distance of the school building where it is possible to establish a creditable attendance record without relying on tax-supported means of transportation" (Old Order Book Society 1973, 6). In addition:

> All children living within the school district shall be eligible to admittance provided the parents are willing to co-operate with the teacher and school officials in securing for it an adequate education; abide by its rules and do not cause a hindrance to the other pupils.

While Amish-Mennonite political problems do arise and the children are aware of these differences, the only visible distinction at Meadow Brook is in the children's clothing, which is most notable perhaps because they do work and play together so well. While the Amish children wear their traditional plain clothes, Mennonite boys wear denim pants more often than polyester with patterned and flannel shirts instead of solid synthetic ones beneath their suspenders. Mennonite girls wear identically patterned dresses (full skirts, bibbed bodices, and three-quarter length, bloused sleeves) in synthetic fabrics of various colors and small prints. Dark stockings, dark shoes or sneakers, and small, white net headcoverings also mark them as Mennonite. Neither the Amish nor the Mennonite make significant seasonal fabric adjustments. Instead, both boys and girls wear dark-colored cardigan sweaters for additional winter warmth.

Perhaps the most conspicuous feature of the children's attire is their footwear. While all Amish clothing is made at home, and all Mennonite female clothing is home-made, too, both groups buy shoes for both boys and girls. Although the Amish children represent only two families, those three girls consistently wore black laced oxfords, and those three boys wore generic running shoes in various dark colors. Among the Mennonite children, similar running shoes were the most popular, worn regularly by three boys and two girls, while low-cut basketball sneakers were favored by three more boys and one girl. Heavy brown work shoes were worn by five boys, black oxfords by two girls, blue oxfords by one, and black buckled shoes by another. Two children, one boy and one girl, wore tan, crepe-soled tied shoes. Brother and sister, they were two of the three River Brethren children.

Ignoring church differences, the seating arrangement was grade organized, rearranged at midyear, "just for a change." During this study, the children sat according to the plan shown in Figure 4–1 (grade levels indicated in numerals in parentheses). I sat in Arlene's seat, next to Daniel, when she was not present. When she was, she sat at the empty desk in front of hers.

The teacher's desk belongs to Verna Burkholder, an unmarried, twenty-seven-year-old Old Order Mennonite, who had moved from Lancaster County to teach at Meadow Brook. The year of this study was Verna's third and final one at the school, a year marked by considerable unhappiness among teacher, pupils, and parents, some of whom attributed the problems to Verna's standards and approach, possibly fostered by her education beyond the eighth grade. (Verna had attended a new order Mennonite high school after deciding to become a teacher, thinking it would better prepare her for the classroom; instead, it created serious problems, discussed at length later.) Her extended formal education exceeded the requirement set by *Standards* under "Teachers: Qualifications and Duties":

> It is recognized that the teacher is the hub on which the entire school revolves. Therefore it is highly essential great care and good judgment is exercised in selecting teachers. Realizing that the school teacher is very influential in molding the life of a child, it is of great importance that the teacher possess, first of all, good Christian character. Equal in importance is good education. Specifically the education shall consist of an eighth grade elementary education. Other characteristics a teacher should possess are: the ability to "get along" with children, willingness to cooperate with parents and school board and a sincere attachment to the teaching profession. (p. 10)

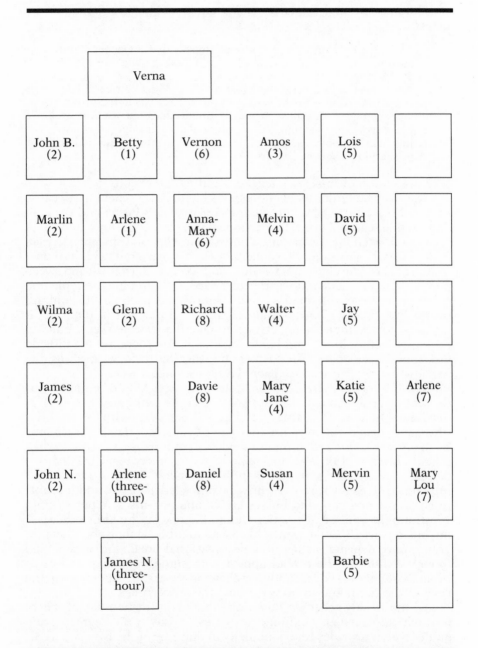

FIGURE 4–1 • *Seating Arrangement (Grade Levels in Parentheses)*

"Interpretive and Explanatory Material" included in *Standards* explains:

> It is the opinion of Amish school officials that a teacher should have natural talent, and be able to teach, with no other obligations to interfere with teaching.
>
> A teacher would be well advised to use the vacation period as an opportune time to give further study to the subjects included in the graded course of study of the school. While the formal education of a teacher should not be carried further than the eighth grade, a self-imposed course of research in the school's accepted subjects is necessary to provide and maintain that "margin of knowledge." (p. 17)

(For discussion of in-service teacher training see chapter 5.)

Nor are Old Order teachers responsible only for teaching. Because no support staff exists, school maintenance falls to Verna and the children. While seasonal tasks, like raking leaves, shoveling snow, and chopping wood, often involve parents along with teacher and students, Verna's "Chore Chart" allots daily responsibilities to upper-grade children on a rotating basis. The chart lists five duties: "Sweep," "Burn trash and sweep porch," "Clap erasers and wash blackboard each evening," "Staple first grade papers and pull shades," and "Fetch water each day 15 minutes before first recess." Lower-grade children help as Verna requests or requires, for example, being chosen to take the wastebasket around to each desk before lunch and before dismissal. And upper-grade girls do tasks not on the chart, like dusting and washing surfaces and washing windows, some chores once each day, some once a week.

The school year itself demonstrates the same kind of regularity as the seating arrangement and the chore chart. As mentioned earlier, only one school holiday, Christmas Day, occurs each year (with the day after Christmas, called Second Christmas, and Easter Monday observed only by the Amish). Once each month students get a half-day holiday when school closes at 1:00 P.M. to facilitate school meetings (like the one discussed in chapter 3). Other than that, Meadow Brook students have little time off. Snow rarely requires closing (sleds, horses, and feet able to go even when cars and busses can't), and parents or older siblings substitute on a moment's notice should the teacher be ill or otherwise unable to work. Special events, like visits to other schools, holiday programs, and a spring picnic, provide occasional breaks in routine, and though visitors to the school appear with some frequency and often bring treats like cookies, candy, or chewing gum, they sit quietly in the back of the room and in no way affect the proceedings.

So the weekly schedule Verna distributed on the first day of school is rarely superceded. Outlining activities by day, time segment, and grade level, it provides for spontaneity in only one of the twenty periods each week. (See Figure 4–2.) The last part of Wednesday afternoon serves miscellaneous functions, including art, egg hunts, and baseball. Each horizontal line represents a twenty-minute recess except the mid-

M	Tu	W	Th	F
1–8 Arith	1–8 Arith	1–8 Arith	1–8 Arith	1–8 Arith
2–4 Health	1–4 Eng	1–4 Read	1–4 Read	5–8 Test, Pen, Voc
5–8 Spell and Voc	5–8 Spell	5–8 Spell and Voc	5–8 Spell and Voc	1–4 Read
2–4 Spell	5–8 Ger and Voc	5–8 Ger	5–8 Eng & B.V.*	5–8 Health
4–8 Read	1–4 Spell	1–4 Spell	1–4 Spell	1–4 Test, Pen Phonics
2–3 Read	1–4 Read	Misc**	5–8 Geo	1–4 Phonics
4–8 Geo	5–8 Eng		1–4 Eng	5–8 Geo

*Bible Verse.
**Art, egg hunts, baseball and other assorted activities.

FIGURE 4–2 • *Weekly Schedule*

dle one, which represents the hour between 11:30 and 12:30 shared by lunch, recess, and fifteen minutes of oral reading by the teacher. A rope-pulled bell above the back door, sometimes rung by Verna, sometimes by a child who has requested the task, signals the end of each recess as well as the end of free time before school begins for the day.

• *Reading* •

According to *Standards*, "Reading is recognized as one of the most important subjects in our schools today" (p. 23), making it a primary reason for Meadow Brook School's existence. In addition, reading allows Meadow Brook to both conduct its business and construct its leisure. Students study "Reading," listen to reading, read aloud, read for information, read for enjoyment, and talk about books, just as their parents, relatives, and friends do outside the school. While some of the books and some of the activities found in Meadow Brook do not exist in the adult world, home and community adults sanction their use in school, making them acceptable to if not favorites of the children.

READING TEXTS Meadow Brook textbooks and workbooks come from three sources: the reading series comes from Pathway Publishing Corporation in Aylmer, Ontario, and LaGrange, Indiana; most other books and workbooks come from the Old Order Book Society through the Gordonville Print Shop in Gordonville, Pennsylvania; and a few come from local school districts when they discard what they no longer use.

Books from the local schools, discarded and stamped as such inside the front covers, generally fill gaps in the curriculum, that is, they provide a text in one subject for one grade rather than function as part of a series used across grades, and they provide free-time reading material for students, as well.

The Gordonville Print Shop, on the other hand, provides books not to mainstream schools but to Old Order ones. They either reprint mainstream textbooks after revising them (marking those books "Reprinted and Revised by Permission—[date]—Gordonville Penna. Print Shop"), or they write/compile books of their own. The revised books bear their original titles and publishers' names; the original books say "Gordonville" and have more functionally descriptive names, for example, *Plain and Fitting English, Starter History, Georgraphy Workbook*.

Like Gordonville, the Pathway Corporation is a primary supplier of Old Order schools. Pathway also compiles their own texts—in this case, basal readers—finding material in other publications including mainstream textbooks, religious publications, and other literary sources, and they write some of their own material, as well. The table of contents in the eighth-grade reader, for example, explains, "All stories not otherwise credited have been written as text for this reader by the editors. See acknowledgements on page 477," where two pages of acknowledgements begin.

Pathway readers for first through sixth grades, with such titles as *New Friends* (third grade) and *Building Our Lives* (fourth grade), contain stories about children the same ages as their intended readers involved with people and situations to which those students can relate. Each story for the early grades deals with primarily external behavior, like lying, and easily understood feelings, like sadness, concluding with an explicit moral. While fifth- and sixth-grade stories consider more complex feelings and motives—like guilt and responsibility—they remain overtly moralistic, too.

The seventh-grade reader, *Seeking True Values*, and the eighth-grade reader, *Our Heritage*, contain historically based and biographical stories instead of fictional ones. Both Old Order and other American heroes and history are recounted, the emphasis on people and events illustrating moral lessons. Colonial settlements and the Underground Railroad, the *Martyrs Mirror* and the Old and New Testaments, William Penn and Martin Luther provide material for these books; Henry Wadsworth Longfellow, Alfred Tennyson, and Edgar Guest provide poems.

One chapter read at Meadow Brook serves to illustrate these more advanced readers. From the unit "People Who Served," the story "Schoolmaster on the Skippack," in the eight-grade book, tells of Christopher Dock, an early eighteenth-century Germantown, Pennsylvania, resident, who was "a devout Mennonite and a lover of children." Preferring teaching to farming, Dock gave up the latter to teach at two schools, three days a week at each.

> For composition class the children in each school would write letters to those in the other; Christopher was the mailman from pupil to pupil. The letters were not filled with nonsense, but told about the pupils' progress at school and asked for answers to Bible questions.

In addition to teaching, Dock wrote "a teacher's guidebook" and a pamphlet called *"A Hundred Necessary Rules For Children,"* of which the story lists ten, ranging from being pleasant to parents and siblings first thing in the morning and eating breakfast at home (rather than on the way to school) to keeping promises and telling the truth.

The story concludes:

> The last years of this humble school teacher's life were spent in the home of Heinrich Kassel, a German farmer near Skippack. Christopher continued to teach, but one evening in the autumn of 1771 he did not come home. It had been his custom to remain at the school after the pupils were gone home, and there to pray alone. A search was made and he was found in the school house on his knees, dead.

A black-and-white illustration of the schoolmaster on his knees in the schoolroom faces the final page of text. In addition to such details as a broad-brimmed hat hanging on the wall and an open book (possibly a Bible) lying on the desk, a hand-printed sign hanging on the wall reads *Betet ohne unter-lasz.* When teaching this story, Verna asked if anyone knew what the sign meant. A seventh-grade girl responded correctly, "Pray without ceasing."

When Verna taught this story, she followed a set of procedures I came to recognize as her definition of a "class," be it a reading class, a geography class, a health class, or a class in any subject involving extended expository or narrative text. First, after the eighth graders lined up across the front of the room and she seated herself in the back, Verna called for oral reading of the story in a page-by-page rotation down the line. Next she asked a series of yes-and-no and straight recall questions, to which students called out answers without being specifically recognized and in no particular speaker order. Below are the questions Verna asked during this class with student responses in parentheses:

Who was Christopher Dock? (no response)
Was he basically a farmer? (Yes)

What did he become when he stopped being a farmer? (A teacher)
What did his pupils have to do for composition class? (Write letters)
Who was the mailman? (He was)
Did he write "A Hundred Necessary Rules for Children?" (Yes)
Was one of those rules to keep your books clean and neat and not to fight with each other? (Yes)
Where did he die? (In the school)

Verna then assigned the questions at the end of the story, requiring written responses. While this is a use of writing that will be discussed further in the next section, it exemplifies the kinds of content and kinds of thinking emphasized by and associated with reading at Meadow Brook. Under the heading "Thinking it Over," five questions follow the Christopher Dock story.

1. Locate on a map of Pennsylvania the area in which Christopher Dock taught. What large city is close to Germantown?

2. What differences can you think of between being a teacher in the 1700's and today? What was the length of the school term? How many days a week was school held?

3. Why do you think Christopher didn't want his "teachers' guidebook" printed? Name three places where you feel the story shows that Christopher was truly not selfish or self-centered.

4. Do you agree with Christopher's method of disciplining a student who didn't know his lesson? In what way?

5. Which of the rules quoted in the story mean the most to you? Which are followed by pupils in your school? Choose one rule and write a paragraph showing how a student in your school kept it or broke it.

Two noticeable similarities exist between these questions and Verna's, both in this and other lessons. First is the way follow-up questions suggest answers to initial questions. Items two and three clearly imply the answers to their first questions in their second ones. Number four theoretically asks for a yes or a no, but in order to answer the second part as phrased, only yes can comfortably answer the first.

The second similarity is the focus on facts offered in the text rather than on student analysis or interpretation of those facts. Even when students are asked to make connections with their own experience, the question directs them to supposedly objective rather than subjective aspects of that experience. Question five comes closest to trusting student-based response, but there the rules quoted in the story and the already established emphasis on moral behavior seem to preclude inappropriate evaluation of personal experience.

TEXT-BASED LESSONS Text-based history and geography lessons, involving the fifth and sixth grades and the seventh and eighth grades, respectively, not only follow the same format as reading but share the same general foci and require the same skills. By the time they reach these upper grades, students are sufficiently adept (or as Hymes would say, sufficiently competent) to help conduct their lessons without pause. In fact, Verna's questions alone facilitate reconstruction of both the lesson and the text chapter, demonstrating the practiced and collaborative nature of the exercise, as a history lesson on Woodrow Wilson illustrates. Before this class, the students read a chapter in *Great Names in American History: An Interdisciplinary Approach*, a Laidlow text, revised and printed by Gordonville for Old Order schools. Parenthetical responses below were those actually given by the students but appear in parentheses to emphasize the questions eliciting them. Two questions in a row indicate no response to the first.

Who was he? (president)

Can anybody tell me anything about his childhood? What did his family call him? (Tommy)

What happened to the word *Tommy* when he grew older? (stopped using it)

What did he believe was the very best job? (being president)

When his dad teased him about being president, how did he act? What did he say? (that he would be president)

What was his father? (a minister)

Were there any more people in the family who were ministers? (yes)

Did Tommy want to be a minister like his father? (no)

Who was his teacher when he was nearly nine? (his father)

Would you like your Dad for a teacher? (yes. [To this answer, Verna responded, "Then you tell him that next time we need a substitute."])

What did his father teach him was the most important thing in life? (doing what you believe is right)

If a man thinks what he's doing is right, should he do it no matter what others think? (yes)

Was his father a good public speaker? (yes)

What school did he go to after he was 17? (college)

Did he love baseball? (yes)

Did he love school? (yes)

Was he ever a lawyer? (yes)

Was he ever a teacher? (yes)

Did the pupils think he was an interesting teacher? (yes)

Do you know who he got married to? [the name is lost to my notes]

Did he meet his girl in college? (yes)

Were they in a war when he was president? (yes)

What war happened when he was president? (World War I)

In 1914 the war broke out where? (in Europe)

Did Wilson love war? (no)

Can you tell me anything about his ship? What kind of ship was the Lusitania? What country belonged to that ship? (Britain)

How many people were drowned? (1,198)

Did this make the United States angry? (yes)

Did they make war right then and there, or did he get them to agree not to do it again? (he got them to agree)

Why did the war start later on? Why did they decide to help in the war? [lost to my notes]

Was this World War II? (no)

When did they stop fighting? [After receiving the answer, Verna commented, "That's easy for me to remember. That's the year my father was born."]

Can you tell me anything about his death? Do you know when he died? (1924)

As this exchange demonstrates, these children know how to read a text to prepare for class. They know Verna will sit in the back just as she does during reading lessons with the textbook open on her lap, and she will formulate questions while looking at the text, turning the pages from the beginning to the end of the assignment. They know her questions will be predominantly text bound, so they know their answers must be, also. They attend to names, dates, and other facts exactly as printed, so they can respond to questions demanding such statements. They do not respond when asked to generalize, conclude, or interpret and need not develop these skills since such requests occur only occasionally and Verna will always rephrase them to facilitate student response.

A seventh- and eighth-grade geography lesson demonstrates the same emphasis, its only difference a procedural one; the children and Verna sat at their desks instead of moving to standard class arrangement. Verna still addressed her questions to the group; individuals still responded anonymously.

Who can tell me what the Sahara is? (a desert)

Does it get more or less than ten inches of rain? (less)

Does it have some [word lost], too? (yes)

What part is covered with sand dunes? (three quarters)

They have three important sources of water. What three places do they go for water or where does their water come from? (wells, oases, [lost])

What do they use to get water out of their wells? (pulleys)

How deep are their wells about? (200 feet)

Is that average for around here or are they deeper? Anybody know how deep their own well is? [Davie replied "275 or 285 feet." "Yes, and that's deeper," Verna commented.]

Now I want you to tell me about the lives of the people. Where do they live and what is their work? (in tents; herding goats)

Why don't they build houses? (They move a lot.)

Why do they have to move? Because it gets too dry? (yes)

Does the grass get all? [This regional colloquialism abbreviates *all gone*. The answer was yes.]

What other animals do they have in the Sahara besides goats? (camels)

Why is a camel a good animal to have in a desert? (It can go without water for a long time.)

What are *oases*? How does an oasis work? If we're in the desert and we get to an oasis, how do we know we've gotten to one? (see trees and water)

What is the greatest oasis in the Sahara? [answer lost]

What kind of tree do they grow for fruit? [answer lost]

Do they export it? Send it out to other people? ["No," Daniel said. "I think they do," Verna replied, and she read the appropriate text sentences aloud.]

What kinds of grain can they grow in an oasis? [answer lost]

What works against them when they try to grow these things? (sand storms)

What does it look like after these sandstorms? (like it snowed)

Do they have to get a shovel? (yes)

What happens to the crops? (They're ruined.)

Must everybody move away then? (yes)

At this point Verna addressed a particular student for disciplinary reasons. "Davie, are you reading a book?" she asked the eighth grader with a biography open on his lap. Davie nodded. "Turn it upside-down while we have questions," Verna instructed. "You may turn it back when we're done." And she returned to "questions," asking one more: "Do they often have sand-laden winds?" (yes). That ended the lesson, Verna turning without pause or comment to paperwork on her desk, the children turning to other work on theirs, and Davie turning his book right-side up on his.

Unlike the history lesson discussed earlier, in this lesson Verna confronted a wrong answer. By going directly to the text and reading from it, she reinforced the importance of accurately recalling what is read. Knowing text is all-important, even the teacher would not correct Daniel without textual certainty. Verna's literal and figurative matter-of-fact attitude in this case exemplified her usual approach to student error. Correction is purely objective; being correct is the only object.

In this lesson, too, Verna encountered an instance of student inattention and misbehavior. Though she considered Davie's inappropriate reading serious enough to require immediate public attention, the question addressed to him varied from the others only in its direct address with accompanying pause and emphasis. Verna's demeanor remained constant; Davie responded accordingly, with the facts, and the lesson continued without further ado.

In this geography lesson as in the history one, it seems important to note that Verna made two isolated attempts to connect student lives and imaginations to what they read. That they, too, have wells and that they could go to the Sahara and see an oasis are ideas she voiced that drew no greater response than any other. They prompted no discussion, received no additional attention from students or teacher. In the history lesson, Verna's more personal comments about fathers as teachers and about her father's birthday passed equally unmarked. Looking across observed lessons, a pattern—or perhaps a habit—emerges, with Verna sometimes asking one, but rarely asking more than two, personally linked questions, or making similar comments during most lessons (the greatest frequency occurring in lower-grade reading and preschool activities). In no observed instance did discussion result from such questions or was particular attention given them. The emphasis never shifted to individuals or to individual ideas. The emphasis never left the text.

German lessons, too, are text-based and conducted like reading and other such classes. Verna sits in the back of the room asking questions and following reading; students stand in front answering questions and taking turns reading. The German reader resembles the English reader, containing stories about children and their families, each with a moral lesson. One distinction marks German lessons, however; students alternately read and translate the pages of German text, instead of only reading what appears in the book.

A final variety of student reading-recitation lessons appears once on the weekly schedule as "Eng & B. V.," abbreviating "Bible verse." Verna assigns two Bible verses each week, one from Psalms for the second through fourth graders, and one from the New Testament for the upper grades, choosing those that focus on "behavior toward others." Students find their assigned verses in the black Gideon Bibles each received on entering Meadow Brook. (This edition of the King James Version includes a picture of the American flag facing the title page, with Proverbs 14:34 beneath it: "Righteousness exalteth a nation: but sin is a reproach to any people.") When class time comes, Verna calls for "poems," and students recite their verses in voluntary order. Standing beside their desks, each recites, gives the citation, and sits down. I never saw a student earn less than 100% for this lesson. (It should be noted here that this memorization/recitation and the copying/illustrating of Bible stories mentioned earlier are the only Bible "lessons" at Meadow Brook. Though established for religious reasons, parents do not want the school teaching religion, believing such instruction belongs at home and in church.)

ORAL READING Most of these text-focused lessons have a recitation or oral-reading component, and combined with singing (which will be discussed later), they place considerable emphasis on oral performance. What counts as good oral reading or recitation at Meadow Brook, however, differs considerably from mainstream standards and differs in terms of performance and instruction within the school itself.

Good reading, according to performance, is rapid, uninflected, nasal, and pitched slightly higher than speech in a somewhat strident minor key. Pauses fall as necessary to breathe, unrelated to meaning or text signal other than the end of a page, which may or may not be particularly punctuated. Meadow Brook's most diligent, most serious, most intense students, the seventh-grade girls, read so rapidly and so monotonously that even with a text, I was unable to follow most of what they read. Conversely, the first graders read more slowly and with more expression than any other group, while the grades between create a continuum of increasing speed and decreasing inflection.

The characteristic speed of Meadow Brook reading became particularly evident one summer night when the five Fisher children, their two Fresh Air Fund children, and my son played hide-and-seek outside the house. Sitting in the living area, we could hear sounds of the game in progress. "That's someone who goes to Meadow Brook," Anna remarked as we heard rapid-fire counting from one to twenty; "That's someone who doesn't," she said as we heard a voice declare each number distinctly.

The fifth grade, however, was notably out of step. Though more fluent than the younger children, fifth graders were also more expressive than any of the others. Not only was their dialogue reading inflected appropriately by mainstream standards (that being the last expressive feature to disappear in the other groups), but expository punctuation was observed and significant words were emphasized, not to a mainstream extent, perhaps, but to an unusual degree for Meadow Brook. Fifth-grade faces and bodies did not reflect this difference; only voices did.

While hesitant to speculate on reasons for this difference, I should note that Katie Fisher was one of these fifth-grade children, and her personal exuberance exceeds self-control in many contexts. Katie's best friend, Barbie Blank, was another fifth-grade girl, and two of the fifth-grade boys, David and Jay, were among the first to smile at me and were two I had difficulty telling apart initially, thinking of them as "the two friendly ones." I suspect, therefore, that individual personalities, coincidentally grade-level grouped, promoted this observed difference in reading behavior.

As suggested earlier, desirable reading as demonstrated by the children does not necessarily correspond to desirable reading as described by their teacher. In one seventh-grade lesson, for example, Verna interrupted with, "You go too fast and too quiet," making the student begin again. She frequently stopped younger children for insufficient expression, modeling appropriate inflection herself. "That's not how you read it," she told a second grader who had read the line, " 'That's mine,' he fairly shouted. 'Give it to me'!" without exclamation or near shouting. Later she instructed a fifth grader saying, "Melvin, you must read it this way. 'A SURPRISE!?' " Verna exclaimed, raising her eyebrows and furrowing her forehead.

In fact, reading to be understood and reading with expression seemed to be Verna's primary concerns. Yet the seventh grader mentioned above reread her passage only slightly more slowly and no less quietly (after the first few words) than she had initially. The second grader improved notably on his second reading of the sentences in question but resumed his monotone for the remainder. And Melvin changed his reading only by widening his eyes.

Why did her instructions have so little impact? Possibly because Verna's own reading reflects the same discrepancy, her modeled examples during reading class not matching her oral reading at other times. Verna's morning Bible reading and lunchtime story reading are nearly as uninflected as the children's. Though Verna never reads quite as rapidly as the older girls, pausing to recognize end punctuation, her reading voice bears the same relationship to her speaking voice as theirs, slightly higher and more nasal, and she inflects dialogue only but not always to the same degree. Otherwise, her one consistent emphasis while reading remains on replicating words as they appear rather than expressing meaning or feeling as they may be inferred, perhaps thereby rendering moot the comparatively fewer expression-related corrections she makes when students read to her.

Like her oral reading, Verna's grading procedures also conflict with her stated standards. Each student's daily reading score begins as 100% and drops 5% for every error, that is, for every misread word; expression, enunciation, speed, and volume make no difference in their grades. Although she interrupts students for these things occasionally, most interruptions focus on getting individual words right, and since that seems to be all Verna really wants—since that's all that affects their grades—students respond accordingly.

Apparently related to oral and other reading, hymn singing occurs each morning while all students stand in front of the room, and singing in rounds occurs periodically with all students sitting at their desks. Book distribution always precedes hymn singing (the same book school parents were noted to use), and hymn selection, called out by individuals, relies on page numbers, not titles. Students hold open hymnals as they sing, though their eyes do not always remain on the text. For singing in rounds, Verna writes the lyrics on the blackboard, identifying the song by the tune to which it is sung. (For example, "Are You Sleeping?" was the tune named for this round: "Love one another/As thyself/ This is his Commandment/Jesus says.")

The sounds of hymn singing and round singing seem similar, both to each other and to other oral work. Singing, like reading, is nasal and in a minor key. Though songs have tunes, students do not clearly sing each note but seem to slide between high and low, resulting in some monotony as their inflection follows these minimal distinctions. One notable difference does separate singing from reading, however. Singing is very slow while reading is very rapid. In school as in church, Amish children prolong every song, holding each syllable of each word, ignoring any musical notation. Though church clearly influences school in this way, I saw no evidence that school influenced home or church in terms of reading speed, for nowhere but in school did I hear readers orally zoom through texts.

Just as each grade's reading seems more polished than the one before, each grade's experience with reading reinforces the last and prepares for the next. Such in-school preparation actually begins during "preschool days," the orientation for five- and six-year-olds conducted the spring before they enter first grade. The number of these days depends on the teacher; I saw Verna conduct two, during which her two preschoolers, Mary and Eli (Fisher, Jr.), sat in the first-grade seats, had "classes," and did seat work like all the other children. They seemed to know they were expected to follow the rules, to do what they saw others doing, and to practice being "scholars" (as all Old Order schoolchildren are called), and Verna reinforced that notion, treating the preschoolers little differently than she treated the others. Though her tone with them was less strident, her movements less abrupt, and her language sometimes Dutch (which is the private language of Amish homes), Verna conducted markedly similar lessons, focusing on what could be called reading- and writing-readiness.

To begin one lesson, "Let's talk about bunnies," she instructed, nodding her head toward the two little children, indicating that they should stand beside her desk. She showed them pictures of rabbits, with the word *bunnies* and the number depicted appearing in word and numeral on each. After going through the pictures, saying "three bunnies," "four bunnies," and having the children repeat, she asked three questions about the texts of their lives (Friere 1983) and got three choral answers.

Q: Do bunnies like carrots?

A: Yes.

Q: Do they like lettuce?

A: Yes.

Q: Do they sometimes get in mother's garden?

A: Yes.

Were it not for some enthusiastic head shaking, Eli and Mary could have been fully matriculated students.

When she was ready to assign seat work, Verna gave the preschoolers pictures of bunnies to color and asked, "What do we do first? Color or write our names?"—the latter a skill they had been practicing by copying printed models Verna prepared.

"Write our names," the pair chorused.

"Yes, we always write our names first. Go back to your desk, write your name, then color the picture. Do nothing on the back of the paper." And the children did exactly that, doing "what we do" precisely "the way we do it."

Verna also conducted what she called a reading class for the two preschoolers during which they sat and she held an open picture book facing them. Talking about the picture, Verna made simple statements identifying different aspects of and actions in the illustration. After each statement, she paused and the children repeated exactly what she had said. The oral text accompanying one picture said:

Sally is eating chips and watching TV.

Sally has a red fish.
Sally has spilled the chips.

After reading the text this way, the children answered questions about it, in unison unless Verna called on one by name.

Q: What does Sally have?

A: A fish.

Q: What color is her fish?

A: Red.

Q: Did Sally spill the chips?

A: Yes.

Q: Did the cat eat the chips?

A: Yes.

While the content of this lesson seems incongruous, the form and conduct fit the Meadow Brook model quite well. Precise recall is all the questions demand. Even the last question, while not covered in the reading, requires recognition of only what happens in the picture.

FREE READING For many Meadow Brook children reading is a favorite free-time activity that sometimes constitutes a problem. As Davie demonstrated during geography class, the students enjoy reading on their own and frequently do so. Even when their assigned work is finished, and they are permitted to do as they please, however, Verna wishes they would read less: "Grades were falling lately because they were reading books instead of looking up vocabulary words," she sighed one day.

The school library, a closet in front of the room to which children may go when their work is done, holds several shelves of books, mostly paperbacks, given to the school by its families and purchased by the teacher, usually at yard sales. None look new; faded and worn, most look well used. Several series stand out, including the Sugar Creek Gang books (stories about the adventures of young teenage boys in the Midwest, which were the children's and Verna's favorite for her lunchtime oral reading) and the Little House on the Prairie series. Most are children's fiction published by companies recognized by the Old Order, like Rod and Staff, and Pathway; those not fiction are biographies.

Verna also borrows books from the local public library each month, making those equally available to the students. Public library books rarely stay on the shelves, however; students borrow them almost as soon as Verna gets them and keep them circulating until their due dates arrive.

"Does anybody have books from the public library?" Verna asked one due day. "We've lost the list. I know I'm missing *Davy Crockett*. . . . Do you have *Stephen Foster? The Bobbsey Twins*?"

Students scrambled to search for the missing books, someone finding *Davy Crockett* in the desk of an absentee. Though no others appeared, Verna seemed unperturbed.

"They have a list in there I can check," she concluded, turning to the next lesson.

Interestingly, as I looked around the classroom day after day, I saw boys reading more often than girls. Most upper-grade girls worked on embroidery during their free time; many lower-grade girls drew pictures, turned pages, or gazed around the room. The eighth-grade boys, who were clearly the school's social focus, read whenever possible, usually biographies. One day when Davie was reading *Jed Smith* and Daniel, *Zebulon Pike*, I was able to see inside Davie's desk when he propped open the lid to straighten things before lunch. Inside were copies of *Black Beauty, Jim Thorpe,* and *Dan Beard,* the biographies both with the same orange cover, part of a series written especially for boys.

At lunchtime that day I heard part of a conversation among a group of upper-grade boys. One, looking at the list of published titles inside Davie's copy of *Jim Thorpe,* asked "When are you gonna get *Buffalo Bill*? That's a good one!"

"I read *Jim Thorpe*," another boy said. "That's a good one, too."

Later that afternoon, while Verna was busy with a group up front, members of that lunchtime circle surreptitiously exchanged books, some sliding them across the floor to avoid leaving their seats, which was forbidden without permission. (More than a year later, Daniel remembered "the day [they] slid the books.")

On other occasions I watched these same boys take books from the rear shelves on which Verna stored basal readers donated to Meadow Brook by public schools. They would flip through the pages until they found interesting stories, sometimes returning for additional titles two or three times in an afternoon.

• *Writing* •

Writing is used at Meadow Brook for many of the same reasons it is at other schools—to study, to learn, to test and reinforce learning, to record, to report, and to communicate.

While studying and learning may be synonymous, both either acquiring knowledge or memorizing facts, studying often means intensive review of what has been learned, usually in preparation for a test. At Meadow Brook, Verna allows students to study at the blackboard, that is, to write their spelling words repeatedly on the board, either from their lists or as dictated by each other. Writing on the board is a treat, reserved for times when no assigned work remains undone, and is particularly favored by lower- and middle-grade students.

Arlene and Betty, the two first graders, spent as much time as they could at the board but never seemed to attract Verna's attention. Several older boys lost their board privileges, however, when Verna questioned what they were doing. "Melvin and Amos [grades four and three], in your seats! That doesn't look like spelling words," she said when the boys appeared to be playing a game of write-words-alternately-as-fast-as-you-can. While I could not see the tiny words they had written, conduct of the game was obvious and obviously not "spelling words" in the approved sense. A second grader lost his privilege temporarily, too. "James, in your seat. That's not spelling words," Verna instructed the child who, spelling book in one hand, was drawing chalk designs with the other. So while Melvin, Amos, and James enjoyed writing, their varieties were not kinds that "count" in school.

WORKBOOKS AND REPORT WRITING On the other hand, in-school learning often means encountering information for the first time, finding out what must be known. At Meadow Brook, this type of learning involves two significant forms of writing—workbooks and reports. While neither of these tasks could be accomplished without reading, they focus on what students write and what that writing represents. (In fact, workbooks are all the students read in some subjects, including lower-grade phonics, upper-grade vocabulary, and all-grade English.)

What do students write in workbooks? Primarily single letters, words, or phrases, sometimes only marks such as lines or circles, older children doing the former, all doing the latter. The first-grade phonics workbook, *Learning Through Sound*, requires matching sounds to pictures by choosing one sound from among three or four accompanying each picture, and children must only circle the right answer. In contrast, the eighth-grade vocabulary workbook accompanies the reading text and asks questions whose answers are found in that text, couched there as statements rather than interrogatives. When doing these exercises, Daniel, Davie, and Richard flipped back and forth, between text and workbook, copying words from one to the other. Other vocabulary lessons present lists of words and lists of definitions students must match. Instead of the textbook, this demands a supplementary dictionary in which to find meanings, but students write only the correct answer's identifying letter in the space next to the word.

One day when I asked Davie to show me the vocabulary lesson he was working on, the word list included *cinnabar, exaltation, abhor, chagrin, auxilliary, jocund, intermittent*, and *veritable*.

"Is this hard work?" I asked, receiving only a shrug in response. "They look like tough words," I continued. "Do you use these words after you learn them?"

A slow smile spread across Davie's face. "No," he almost laughed.

Workbook producers and client schools seem to assume these kinds of writing represent student learning of the information written or marked, which may, to some extent, be true. But workbooks seem to be teaching other, less subject-related, more Old-Order-appropriate lessons, as well. Both Betty in the first grade and Davie in the eighth are learning to look for the single right answer, choosing it from among others, all wrong. Davie must use an outside source to find his answer, adding complexity to his task, but his focus is the same as hers: find the right answer and mark it the right way.

Remarkably similar in such underlying lessons are reports, the other significant Meadow Brook use of writing as learning. Not considered compositions, report assignments accompany individual subjects and topics. Nature study, a separate subject that is studied each Monday instead of vocabulary, has no text other than student-produced reports. History and geography, while primarily text-book focused, have supplementary student reports. (All of these subjects are for the upper grades only.)

Katie Fisher gave me two of her nature-study reports "to help [me] with [my] work." One was called "Nature Study Book," the other "My Nature Study Book." Both had white paper covers on which she had crayon-printed titles and crayon-drawn flowers, colorful borders, and background lines—the latter a Meadow Brook trademark started by Daniel. Both reports contained six pages, a purple ditto-master flower on one side of each page and Katie's writing on the other. The flowers were prelabeled with names and numbers by Verna, and brightly crayon-colored by Katie, who gave some of them freehand background clouds or shadows.

Katie's writing was always in pencil, sometimes on pencil-ruled lines. Each written page had a capitalized, sometimes quotation-marked title identifying its flower, and most ended with the word *DONE* or the words *THE END*, appearing variously as

Katie's FORGET-ME-NOT report exemplifies all twelve of her Nature Study reports and is reprinted here exactly as it appeared in her booklet, though without her round upright cursive script:

Forget me knot, name given to plants of the genus Myosotis, belonging to the family Boraginaceae (q.v.) They are found in temperate zones in all parts of the world. A number of species are common in ditches and damp meadows of the U.S. The true forget-me-not, M. scorpioides, has creeping perennial roots with ascending stems bearing small sky blue flowers. The most Popular horticultural forget-Me-nots are varieties of M. sylvatica, admired especially for the brilliancy of their blue flowers. They are used extensively for ground cover in gardens and borders, and beside pools and strems. A dark blue species, the Azores forget-me-not, M. azorica, requires greenhouse cultivation in temperate regions. The romantic name is derived

from the last words of a legendary German knight drowned while attempting
to retrieve the flower for his lady.

The
End

Like this one, every report was copied verbatim from an encyclopedia
(the classroom set of *Funk and Wagnall's Standard Reference Encyclopedia*, 1961), complete with botanical names and vocabulary, making
fifth-grade Katie's report markedly similar to eighth-grade Daniel's. Their
primary difference was only one of penmanship, with secondary decorative distinctions.

As an eighth grader, though, Daniel also studied geography, a subject
supplemented by report writing. Each seventh and eighth grader was
assigned a country about which to write, Daniel getting Japan. His
report, between blue construction-paper covers, had seventeen lined
loose-leaf pages, almost all with traced illustrations, a few with no text
other than labels. The first page offered a map of the country marked
with six major cities. The second page, headed "Weather," had one line
of text—"Here is the weather in Japan."—and was divided in quarters,
each containing an outline map color-coded to illustrate "Average precipitation in August," "Average Yearly Precipitation," "Average temperatures in August," and "Average Precipitation in Feb."

The written text appeared on pages separated by topic and labeled
with headings: "People," "Lands," "Work," "Education," "Minerals and
Energy," "Masao Kitamura," "Factories and Cities," "Sports," "Phonetic
Syllables," "Judo," and "Japan and America at War–1941." Most were
illustrated, for example, a circle graph showing "Land Use" on the "Work"
page and two traced men in traditional Japanese garb Karate-kicking
each other on "Sports." The text itself, like that of other reports, came
directly from published sources, which Daniel cited at the bottom of
some pages but not others. Each of the last eight pages said "Old World
Lands" (his geography book), with a page number. Only the last of the
first six pages cited a source, "Encyclopedia," with one page number.
Another page, a map showing three major Japanese rivers, fell between
the encyclopedia and text-book-referenced pages, not clearly belonging
to either group.

When Verna returned Daniel's report, red ink dotted most pages.
Inside the front cover, she wrote, "Weather chart is nice in the book on
the second page. Whole book shows hard work," suggesting that unlike
the nature-study reports, the geography reports were not predesigned.
Students could include all that they could find in any order they chose,
and while Daniel included a commendable amount of information, his
hard work seems most apparent in decoration, reflecting the bold, clear-colored style his classmates recognize and imitate. Most of his headings,
maps, and illustrations were colorfully outlined if not completely colored.
Even pencil drawings bore the zigzag shadows that are his trademark.

Verna's concluding comment suggests she did have particular expectations, however. On the last page, she wrote, "–Nowhere could I find anything about what Japan leads the world in—*shipbuilding* and *fishing*." Between first comment and last, red circles surround penmanship problems (capital *T*'s that look like lowercase letters; elaborately curled capital *J*'s); red corrections mark some spelling errors but ignore others; and red words spell out an ampersand and a numeral three. Otherwise, only two comments appear. "How many?" rises in red from the statement, "Japan is a country of islands lying off the east coast of Asia," and "very interesting" underlines the page about judo. No grade appears anywhere on the report.

Report writing, therefore, as exemplified by Katie's and Daniel's experiences, teaches lessons similar to workbook writing. Instead of finding and marking the right answers, report writers must find and appropriately copy the right information. Just as workbooks limit possible browsers by providing limited choices, report writers cannot wander too far, limited by teacher-distributed pages (in nature study) and school-supplied references (in both subjects). Daniel did put the weather chart in an original place and did work hard, but he omitted what Verna considered significant facts and made penmanship and spelling/copying errors. In other words, Verna's assignments and responses highlight what is important: staying within the lines, working hard, and getting things right.

A second-grade activity represents an interesting combination of workbook and report writing. Because there were no phonics workbooks for the second graders, Verna required a page of copied reading-book text as part of each reading lesson, instead. ("Write cursive like the upper grades write," she reminded the second graders one day when assigning the page to be copied, making it as much a penmanship lesson as anything else.) To check their work as part of reading class, one second grader had to read his copied text aloud while Verna followed in her book. If that student made an error, the next student read, and the process continued until the page was completed, either by an accurate copier or, more often, by each student, in turn. Just like workbook lessons that teach students to find the right answer and mark it the right way and report writing that teaches students to find the right information and copy it the right way, second-grade reading gives students the right information which they must copy the right way, teaching a lesson that prepares them for upper-grade writing.

At Meadow Brook, then, report writing, like workbook writing, is text bound. It is the written equivalent of text-bound oral classes. While students need not literally recall—remember or memorize—each specific fact they write, their writing amounts to an act of recalling. They must reproduce in their anonymous written voices what they have read, and must do so accurately and completely. They need not evaluate the text; they need not assess the relative significance of ideas or select which to include and which to omit. All the book says is important exactly as the book says it; no interpretation is necessary. The book's meaning is in its words, not in any student interaction with those words. From this perspective, questioning, extending, or comparing ideas becomes un-verifiable inappropriate speculation, no more evidence of competent writing than personal inference demonstrates competent reading.

What keeps this Meadow Brook report writing from being plagia-rism, from being illegal or immoral as the Old Orders see it? The fact that plagiarism does not exist as an issue for them. Consider: the prob-lem of plagiarism is not simply one of copying or reproducing but one of perspective and philosophy, instead. If a mainstream student submits a plagiarized paper, he claims someone else's words as his own. That is only possible—in fact, only desirable—however, because mainstream society has declared that words are property and, once written, are owned by the writer, be he student or professional. Writing something "in your own words" makes it "yours"; therefore, writing something in someone else's words means stealing what is his. Yet why try to steal words? Why try to pass off someone else's writing as your own? Perhaps because published writing is often offered as models in mainstream classrooms and because student writing is often unfavorably compared to that of such "real" writers. If students feel they must measure up to these published adult standards but fear they never will, incorporating published work into their own may seem a possible way to do to the impossible (and a way to get back at the impossible assignment, not to mention the person who assigned it).

In addition, not only are words mainstream personal property, but ideas can be personal property, too. In a society that values individual achievement and original thought, the more often an idea appears, the less value it has, so while stealing someone's ideas does not make them less valid, it does make them less valuable. Since truly original thought is rare, however, the manner in which accepted ideas are presented becomes a significant variable, making style something else an individ-ual can "own" and something else an individual may want to steal or, at least, borrow. For these reasons, too, plagiarism is a mainstream offense and a mainstream problem.

For the same reasons, though, plagiarism is not an Old Order con-cern. No Amish student would submit a copied paper intending to de-fraud, because no Amish student would want to claim published writing as his own. The ability to write like a professional (however that is defined) is not a skill valued by the Old Order. New ideas, unique pre-sentation, and fresh style conspire to make an individual noticeable, to separate him from other community language users. Not only is such visibility undesirable but it opposes the basic community value of group identification. Copying at Meadow Brook is a way to keep from standing out, a way to write like everyone else.

Copying also eliminates any need for an assessment continuum in-volving other than the most objective, superficial (that is, external to the individual) criteria. Being a good report writer means being a good Amishman: being accurate, being efficient, and being one of a group, not one of a kind.

In other words, plagiarism is neither a legal nor a moral problem for the Old Orders. Plagiarism is not their problem at all. Why, then, does Daniel's "Japan" report cite his sources? Because Verna said it should. Why does his "Bird Book" (a nature-study assignment) not do the same? Because no one said it should. What conclusions can be drawn from this seeming inconsistency? If more than one source is used, all must be cited. If only one, it need not be. Besides when there is only one "Encyclopedia" (as he refers to the classroom set in "Japan"), everyone knows what books he must have used.

Since plagiarism is not an issue, both the workbook-controlled and teacher-controlled writing situations make Old Order–appropriate evaluation possible. How well a report stays within appointed boundaries, how well it fulfills general expectations, and how similar it is to others of its kind are important community values foregrounded by these assignments. From an academic perspective, Meadow Brook grades reflect supposedly objective criteria: How legible is the penmanship? How wide are the margins? How correct are the spelling and punctuation? Adherence to such overt standards of content and form marks the competent writer. (Interestingly, this reliance on a single accepted, objective standard keeps Verna from teaching poetry, despite its appearance in textbooks, hymns, and out-of-school life. "I never teach it," she explained, "because I'm not smart enough to correct it. I know it doesn't have the same punctuation or sentences. . . .")

TESTING A third purpose for writing at Meadow Brook is to test and reinforce learning, both in reading and in other text-bound subjects. While students receive grades for this written work, Verna refers to it as subject work—as reading questions or geography questions—not as writing or as tests; tests occur every six weeks and are referred to as such. (Six-weeks tests have the same form as these exercises, however. In fact, Verna culls her test questions directly from them, and the students know that.)

As the Christopher Dock story illustrated earlier, students write the answers to questions printed after each story in their readers, and this writing procedure echoes their reading classes; students present answers to Verna (this time in writing), who marks the number wrong and supplies the correct answers.

A set of eighth-grade papers reveals standards for acceptable written responses and those for acceptable questions, as well. Perhaps the most noticeable shared characteristic of answers is brevity: the best answer is a brief one. This produces single word, phrase, and sentence-fragment responses. For example, in response to the question, "What was the joke that the boys played on Eddie Davis?" (asked about a story in which boarding-school boys learn a predictable lesson about practical jokes) came the following from the eighth graders:

- DANIEL: moved the furniture into Charlies room
- RICHARD: moved his furniture in another room
- DAVIE: hid his stuff

This concern for brevity complements a second characteristic, directness. Even when the question is actually two questions and seems intended to prompt more or more complex response, these boys come right to the point. Question two following the same story asked both "Why did they choose Eddie to play [the joke] on?" and "What does the word *gullible* mean?"

- DANIEL: they could make him believe things that aren't so, easily tricked
- RICHARD: He was afraid of Charlie easy to be tricked
- DAVIE: He didn't get mad at him, easily fooled

When questions explicitly call for lengthy, complex response, all three boys ignore those directions, implicitly marking them unacceptable. To "What type of person was Dennis Conron? Use parts of the story as evidence for what you say," they answered:

- DANIEL: short and cheerful,
- RICHARD: cheerful looking boy
- DAVIE: Short cheerful little boy

Daniel's final comma seems to denote awareness that the text expected more; the other boys use the same device when they know the first half but not the second half of an answer. The others completely ignored the second half of this question, however, as did Verna. While she usually either checkmarks an inappropriately empty space or supplies its missing information, in this case she did neither.

When the text asked, "Do you feel Dennis could be blamed for Eddie's accident? Write a paragraph explaining your feelings on this," the boys wrote:

- DANIEL: yes,
- RICHARD: yes,
- DAVIE: yes, because he did it

Verna checked the blank spaces on Daniel's and Richard's papers. She accepted Davie's answer as written.

All three boys missed the final question not for reasons of form, but for teacher understanding of its meaning: "Did Eddie ever understand the joke? Explain."

- DANIEL: yes, because the joker did it [The story referred to the boys as known "jokers."]

- RICHARD: yes, they told him all about it
- DAVIE: yes, because it says

Verna checked both answers on all three papers, writing *No* above or below each yes. On Daniel's and Richard's she also wrote, "He asked if Charlie got mad." On Davie's, however, she wrote "no, because he asked if Charlie got mad." The story implies that the boys explained and apologized to their victim, as two of the three boys indicated in their answers, so both the boys and Verna may be right.

Explanations and interpretations, it seems, are more difficult to supply than facts. What the story says is available to all three boys; their own thoughts about what it says seem less accessible. Verna seems to accept this, allowing students to substitute phrases for paragraphs, but she seems unable to allow more than one acceptable interpretation, always assuming hers is the right one. Writing in class, then, like speaking in class, sends students and teacher back to the story, back to the text, all relying on what they find there, with the teacher's findings used as the ultimate arbiter.

Because Verna recognizes her students' difficulty in answering text-supplied questions, she occasionally substitutes her own restatements to facilitate their response. For history and geography she circumvents this problem, however, by writing her own questions, recording them in separate composition books. The following are Verna's written questions for two seventh- and eighth-grade geography chapters; Daniel's written responses appear in parentheses:

PAGE 72–79

1. Where is the greatest coal field in Europe? (Northwestern Germany)
2. Where is the greatest industrial area in Europe? (Ruhr)
3. How long is this city? (40 miles)
4. From where does this city import iron ore? (France [to which Verna added "Spain, Sweden, Africa"])
5. What are the leading field crops in East and West Germany? (grain and potatoes)
6. There are more _____ and _____ in Germany than any other country in Europe? (cattle and hogs)
7. Why do Germans have large yields of crops per acre? (farms are little [marked wrong])
8. Name two products as a result of forest farming? (lumber, paper pulp)
9. Where does cotton and silk come from? (silk from Japan, cotton from U.S.)
10. Where does wool come from? (Argentina, Austrailia)

PAGE 80–84

1. Name four ways of transportation in Germany? (highways, canels, air routes and railroads)
2. How have the main Rivers been improved? (dredging deeper channels 4 larger boats)
3. What are two leading seaports in Germany? (Bremen and Hamburg)
4. Name six things Berlin produced? (electric equipment, machinery, scientific instruments, chemicals, clothing, paper books)

5. What is the capital of Austria? (Vienna)
6. What part of Austria is Mountainous? (⅘)
7. On what river was Vienna built? (Danube)
8. What four things was Vienna famous for throughout the world? (music, art, science, education)
9. Name three kinds of trees found in Austrias forest. (pine, fir, and larch)
10. Name four crops farmed at the floors of the Mountains. (rye, oats, hay, and vegetables)

The physical act of writing seems to be the most substantial difference between this activity and the oral Woodrow Wilson and Sahara Desert activities described earlier. Such writing requires no greater personal investment than the oral work did (with formal classes perhaps more personally demanding because of the public display involved). So it seems that writing intended to reinforce subject-area reading, like writing to study and writing to learn, is another text-bound activity.

RECORDING AND REPORTING Writing serves several non–text-bound purposes at Meadow Brook, however, two of which are recording and reporting, the former sometimes in preparation for the latter. One instance of recording involves the three-hour pupils, each of whom must keep a daily diary. In 1981–82, Sarah, the eldest Fisher child, was a three-hour pupil, and her diary was a composition book shared with Linda, another "ninth-grader." One girl wrote from front to back, the other from back to front. Sarah wrote two lines each day, labeling each entry with day and date. Her entries for three consecutive days in February exemplify those for the year.

| 2/15/82 | AM: Did morning work |
| Mon | PM: Washed |

| 2/16/82 | AM: Went to the dentist |
| Tues | PM: Attended class |

| 2/17/82 | AM: Went visiting schools |
| Wed | PM: "   "   " |

Verbs dominate, as Sarah "cleaned," "baked," and "washed," not always at home (for instance, in March, "Helped my aunt house-clean").

Since Sarah's three-hour tenure, the diary rule has changed. Fearing that two-word entries would be insufficient if someone from "outside" checked, the school directors established a fifteen-word minimum. The two diary keepers I observed kept separate books, Arlene's a tan-covered, black-bound composition book with her name curlicued across the front in black ink, and James's, the same kind of book with a black crayoned name outlined in red, outlined in yellow, outlined in green, with blue lightninglike zigzags crossing the background.

Arlene recorded day and date, weekend events as well as weekday. James labeled only by date and skipped weekends. The following are Arlene's entries for a week in September:

MON   SEPT 6 • Labor Day Packed lunches. Washed the milkers then finished to wash. Went to Ed Zimmerman's for deisel fuel. Fed cows and calves.

TUE   SEPT 7 • Milked. Picked lima beans and string beans. Went to Lawrence Nolts for fruit then to Ike's Grocery. Trimmed yard Made supper.

WED   SEPT 8 • Milked. Cleaned upstairs. Fixed dinner Baked cookies and pies. Made supper Cleaned parlor Fed calves then helped bag potatoes

THURS.   SEPT 9 • Milked washed milkers. Cleaned refrigerator. Raked yard and trimmed yard Baked 2 batches of cookies. Canned several qts nectarines and pears

FRI   SEPT 10 • Norma's birthday. Milked Did milkers. Attended class Mowed lawn. Washed raked a little leaves. Mom baked bread and cleaned Had another fresh hieffer

And James's for the same week:

SEPT.   6. • David Sauder came to open up the fields. Got ready to fill silo. P.M. John Shirk came and filled 10 × 50, 10 × 40, and 12 × 50 silos. Had to drive wagons.

SEPT.   7 • refilled 12 × 50 silo. Got ready to fill trench put 16 loads in A.M. and 25 in P.M. one of the wagons has a cracked Beam.

SEPT.   8. • Finished up the barn. attended class. Had reading. In afternoon covered trench with black plastic, put tires on and put a fence around it.

SEPT.   9 • Finished up in the barn. Cleaned off roofs of the silage wagons. Went hunting for doves. John Shirk came to fill silo.

SEPT.   10 • Capped 12 × 50 silo. lime man was here. Mom and Dad went to town. Worked ground and sowed wheat. did chores in eve.

While Arlene's and James's entries were longer than Sarah's, their emphasis remained on verbs—what they did or what was done. Neither explanation, description, nor complete sentences mattered, for the context required only an account of their vocational training, evidence that they are needed at home and learn necessary skills there. Though no state-related outsiders have come to Meadow Brook in Verna's memory, that they might come and that they might ask to see these diaries makes such writing mandatory. Students record external, verifiable facts, without evaluation or interpretation, for the purpose of a potential report, not for self-exploration, self-discovery, or even personal-history reasons.

Another recording activity, this one always intended for subsequent reporting, involves the *Meadow Brook Gazette*, a school newspaper started by Verna. Produced on the hand-cranked duplicating machine and student-carried to each household, the school monthly underwent a major reorganization during this study, yet the format change affected neither content nor production procedure.

Throughout the year a single notebook rotated daily among upper-grade students; each one's task was to record a dated entry of that day's news, including absentees, visitors, interesting occurrences, changes in routine, disciplinary proceedings, and anything else the individual writer considered newsworthy. Once each month, the eighth graders used their scheduled English lesson to transcribe the notebook entries onto ditto masters. No revision marked this transcription, nor did bylines or other credits mark these pages.

In the issues between October 1 and December 1, the "News Page," as the first of three or four pages of notebook news was labeled, preceded student-written stories, headed "Something to laugh at." In October the story was "Camping Trip (fiction)"; in November, an untitled one "(fiction)" and "She Learned a Lesson (fiction)"—with the footnoted "NOTICE: Two fictious stories are printed this month, because there are fewer news pages"; and in December, "Anna Mary's Awful Day (fiction)." The identification of fiction as such seems coherent with the school and community focus on text as truth, yet these stories are not entirely fictitious. While none recount actual events, all involve only actual people—members of the Meadow Brook community. Similarly, while all are headed "Something to laugh at," all focus on mishap or misbehavior, subordinating humor to the moral lessons involved.

Another feature of this section sets it apart from the news: each story concludes with a byline. To identify the writers, however, readers must unscramble the names, which include "Chidarr" (Richard), "Earl Netirman" (Arlene Martin), "Roaly Om," (Mary Lou, misspelled), and "Norene Tall" (Arlene Nolt). These anagrams also connect stories to the single poem printed during the year and to the student-drawn cover of each issue. The poem is signed "Author Unknown," though it was student- or teacher-written; the covers bear the hidden initials of the artist, more as puzzle than display; and both attribute responsibility, without promoting acclaim.

All these newspaper features teach at least three implicit lessons. First, writing in the first-person plural is preferable to writing in the first-person singular. Even when the writer experienced the described activity, we includes him without undue personal attention. (This applies in fiction, too, though there third-person replaces first, as in "Chidarr's" story, which begins, "Daniel, Davie, and Richard wanted to go on a camping trip.") Second, products of individual rather than group effort require different treatment. Poems, stories, and drawings derived from single minds single out those minds. Yet no individual should attract disproportionate attention, so third, identification must be submerged or masked in some way. A creative writer must stand behind his work (as many *Botschaft* writers insist), but he should never stand in front of it.

In December, Verna decided to reorganize the newspaper. Thinking it "looked like something the children threw together," she wanted a more "formal," more "finished product." Additionally, she wanted easier access, "to be able to find something [she's] looking for" without having to read the entire paper. For both these reasons, Verna established news categories—"Unusual Things," "Recess," "Visitors," "Attendance," and

"Behavior"—and used them to head separate pages in the *Gazette* note-book. Student writers recorded each day's news according to category, and the paper itself reflected those divisions.

After one month's operation this way, Verna added a category—"Winners"—and rearranged the others, beginning with "Visitors," "At-tendance," and "Winners," then moving to "Recess," "Unusual Things," and "Behavior." Coincidentally, the decision of how to categorize fiction never arose. A school-board member objected to the stories as "silly . . . useless . . . and worthless. The pupils don't learn anything from them," he told Verna. "They're a waste of time." So "Something to laugh at" disappeared from the paper.

Individual student writing continued to appear, however, in two of the last three issues. In February, following "Behavior" on the last page, set off by a zigzag line, an anonymous poem entitled "How I Feel About Christmas" appeared, headed "This Composition was handed in before Christmas." In March, "Unusual Things" included the following:

Tonight the teacher made us write one sentence saying what we think love is. Here are the answers the pupils gave.
— Love is by behaving well.
— I think love is when everyone is happy.
— Love is obeying parents.
— Love is obeying the rules.
— Love is to obey.
— Love is recess.
— Love is to behave.
— I think love is when everybody loves one another.
— Love is if you like everybody. Love is sharing and and being kind to other people.
— Love is that you (the teacher) brought food.
— I think love is obeying our parents.
— Love is to behave.
— I think love is parents giving beautiful things to children.

That the intended audience for the *Gazette* extends beyond the stu-dents and teacher becomes evident in the remaining two kinds of writing printed during the year. In April, between "Recess" and "Behavior," appeared "An Invatation", the heading set off by fifteen asterisks on the left, ten on the right:

All the parents are invited to our school picnic held May 5th. Mrs. Levi Nolt is in charge of planning the food. A pet show will be held at 10:00 A.M. Next we will have poems, and songs also some German classes then lunch. After lunch voting for a new chairman of the board will be held. Then we will play base ball pupils and fathers mixed together. School will not be dismissed formally when parents are ready to leave pupils are to ask teacher for report cards.

In case of rain pet show will be cancelled. Be sure to put pets in proper cages, boxes or on leashes so that they don't fight when they meet other animals. If you don't have a pet you can bring something else.

P.S. Pre scholars and last years 8th grade are also invited to our picnic.

Verna also communicated with her students' parents through generally or specifically directed footnotes in all but the first issue. Each note appeared at the bottom of a page, and all but the longest, reprinted here, were separated from other text by a horizontal line. (This note was typed entirely in capital letters, and some words were run together. Because these features were probably "experimentally" produced on the newly acquired typewriter, I have omitted them here.)

A HURRIED NOTE FROM THE TEACHER: We are busy memerizing Christmas poems, practicing Christmas songs and coloring Christmas pictures. So we are going to take a break from news paper printing. There will not be any paper coming out Jan., 1, 1983 but the following month, February. We are looking forward to seeing the parents at our Christmas program Dec. 24; 1982. We are experimenting with our type writer. I wasn't watching Richard but it looked like he hit the keys too hard sometimes and punched holes in the masters. I expect him to become more skillful when he gets more experience. Merry Christmas to all and a happy new year.

The *Meadow Brook Gazette*'s appearance more closely resembles a mainstream newsletter than newspaper (despite volume and issue numbers on each cover), and looks more like a rough draft than a polished product. Before the typewriter arrived, penmanship changed from page to page (Daniel's, Davie's, and Richard's printing easily distinguished), and some pages retained guiding lines the writers had drawn. After the typewriter, each issue still had at least one handwritten section, and the March issue was not typed at all. Sporadic editing overlooked some spelling, punctuation, and typographical errrors in every issue. All corrections made, however, remained visible: words and letters were crossed out rather than scraped off; new ones were inserted next to or above the blocked spaces; typewritten text was corrected by hand. Whether student- or teacher-written, discarded ideas were often as visible as their replacements, providing evidence of the writer's process not usually found in final drafts.

The concept of multiple drafts does not seem to exist anywhere at Meadow Brook, however. Diaries, reports, newspapers, letters, and compositions (the latter two yet to be discussed) are written once, the newspaper requiring compilation but not revision. That no one writes perfectly all the time is as much a fact at Meadow Brook as elsewhere, but that fact both explains and excuses the visible corrections there. If time spent writing and reading "Something to laugh at" is wasted, time spent rewriting anything may be similarly condemned, especially if the unrevised version serves the intended purpose, which, in this case, is to record and report information for a clearly defined, assumed appreciative audience that demands no more.

COMMUNICATING While recording and reporting may be forms of communication, I choose to distinguish among them, defining communication as a function of writing involving individuals rather than groups. In the *Gazette*, Meadow Brook as a school reports to its parental community. While this communicates information in the sense of moving news from one place to another, it does not simultaneously share more personal feelings or thoughts, connecting one individual to another—or others, Verna's footnotes excepted. It is not the newspaper format, per se, that precludes communication (as George Will, Ellen Goodman, and any *Botschaft* scribe can testify), but rather the implicitly identified function of the *Gazette* in its context. Meadow Brook students do communicate, that is, express themselves in writing, but not through their newspaper—they do it through letters, instead.

The letter-writing lesson idea came not from Verna but from an unidentified source in Monroe, Indiana. One day Verna received nine letters, all written on tablet paper and mailed in the same envelope addressed to her in care of Meadow Brook School, the only return address a box number in Monroe. Each letter began "Dear Girls," but each was signed by an individual. One, written in green ink, exemplifies all:

Dear Girls,   Feb. 1983
    Greating's from Indiana. Wonder how it finds you? Here were fine. I am in the eight grade age fourteen. There are five in my grade with me. I am the only girl. What do you play in school? Yestered most of us went out for a snow battle! The snow is about all gone already, We play ping-pong to. We got two ping-pong tables in school. We live about two and half miles from school so we ride on a bus. We are going to have a Valentine party next Mon. The teacher put all the parents names in a box than every Fri someone picks a name than the parents have to come visit school the next week. 4,5,6,7,8 graders had to draw a picture to hang on the wall. Then we're going to vote who has the nicest. Well I have to get my spelling studied for a test. Write Back!

OUR FAMILY RECORD

	Barbara Martin	
Dad Joe L. Martin	Morrow, Ind	
Mom Maryann (Nickey)	Victor	Mandy
Roseann	Lisa	Lucy
Walter	Enos	Jonathan
Miriam	Barbara	Marvin

Assuming the letters came from an Old Order school whose teacher chose Meadow Brook as a pen-pal source from the list of all such schools that appears each November in *Blackboard Bulletin* (a monthly Pathway publication for Old Order teachers discussed in chapter 5), Verna distributed the nine letters to her oldest girls, involving all those in grades seven, six, five, and four. That Wednesday, letter writing replaced vocabulary study, and Katie Fisher wrote to Emma Schwartz:

Dear Emma Schwartz,
    Hi, Greetings from far and near. How are you hope fine thats how you would find me. I'm in the fifth grade and eleven years old. I go to Meadow Brook School. My teachers name is Verna Burkholder. I have a cat and a dog of my own. We live on a farm. We have forty-five cows to milk. I

sometimes help milk evenings not always mornings. What do you always do at your place? My Birthday is Feb—twenty eighth. You did not write when your birthday is?! Write Back and tell me. I have a friend Emma in Lancaster. She went to my school when we still lived in Lancaster. We have seven in our family with Mom and Dad. Well am about out of news. Write Back!!!

HERE IS OUR FAMILY

		Age
Dad	Eli B.	38
Mom	Anna S.	34
	Sarah Ann	15
	Daniel Jay	14
Me	Katie Mae	11
	Amos Elson	9
	Eli F. Jr.	5

Here's my address Write me then and give me your address then i will write you back.

> Katie Fisher
> c/o Eli B. Fisher
> ___Town___, STATE Box 345
> [zip code]
> I will be looking for your
> letter!!

Loads of Love
Katie M. Fisher

Verna's only comment on collecting the girls' letters was "Some of you girls don't have dates on your letters. Right across from the greeting you should have the month, day, and year."

Similarities between these letters and those in *"Die Botschaft"* are unmistakable. Formulaic openings and closings—the former *Botschaft*-appropriate, the latter more exuberantly preadolescent—mark most. All emphasize facts such as name, age, grade, activities, and family, and several even include recent weather (a *Botschaft* staple). Older students' letters are longer and/or more personal in content while younger ones personalize primarily through decoration instead. Perhaps the most consistent feature and the most culturally revealing one, however, is each writer's self-identification in terms of the groups to which she belongs. Without compromising individual indentity, each writer contextualizes herself completely, making these letters acts of affiliation as much as acts of identification and differentiation.

When Verna distributed the Indiana letters to her girls, she noticed "the eighth grade boys were smirking because they knew [she] would never make them write to a girl." Instead, Verna devised a similar lesson for them: the eighth-, sixth-, and fifth-grade boys would write letters to James, the "three-hour boy," instead. Curiously, Verna taped the boys' instructions to her desk, making each boy come forward to read it silently instead of telling the whole group at once. The message read: "NOTE: You are to write a letter to James Martin and don't tell anyone. So that he will be surprised when he receives a fat letter in the mail." (One boy's letter actually asked James if he was "surprised to receive a fat letter.")

"I don't know what to write," Daniel complained after everyone had settled down to work.

"Write about what you do after school," Verna suggested.

"Do we have to write our names down?" Davie asked.

"Yes," Verna replied, "Unless you want to make him guess. You can think about that yourself."

Davie finally signed his letter "From Guess Who" (a task made easier by the alternating red and green letters of his trademark signature). Daniel wrote,

> Dear James,   2/16/83
> Greetings. We have to do this instead of vocabulary. Did you start plowing yet? We plowed about 3 or 4 acres this spring. Norman's children are lucky to move to Lanc. Are you going to the sale on Friday? After a while we can work in the fields. I can't wait till I'm out of school. I'll work in the fields and have fun.
> You are lucky you are out of school already and you can farm with tractors.
>
> > from
> > Daniel

The biggest differences between the boys' and girls' letters seem to stem from their differing immediate contexts. The girls wrote to strangers while the boys wrote to a friend, but the girls had clear models in the letters they received while the boys had only Verna's instructions. This first distinction demanded that the girls introduce themselves while the boys could build on existing relationships and mutual knowledge. The girls' situation was simplified, however, by guidelines the Indiana letters established. The girls knew what kinds of things to write about; the boys had to make those decisions themselves. Interestingly, despite their greater latitude and lack of instruction, the boys produced letters remarkably similar to each other, as though following some implicit guidelines. School and home, recess and chores, likes and dislikes marked them all.

Several boys, however, found ways to make their letters different from the others', to mark them as their own. Davie, who wrote his letter in pencil, wrote the salutation and closing in his usual alternating red and green letters. Richard, another eighth grader, included a joke in dialogue form, writing speakers' lines alternately in pencil and in black ink. David and Jay, both sixth graders, featured their signatures, David with a zigzagging circle, Jay with similar underlining. Vernon, the youngest boy to write, drew an envelope around his signature and added a stamp with a smiling face in the appropriate corner. Curiously, Daniel, who hates to write but loves to draw, submitted his letter unadorned.

COMPOSITION Just as the letter-writing activity was an unattached, one-time-only event with no explicit lesson component, composition has the same discontinuous nearly uninstructed nature. With no assigned place in the schedule, composition is a relatively minor concern, occurring irregularly (". . . when I have an inspiration," according to Verna), approximately once every two weeks, most often replacing vocabulary. Composition is a strictly upper-grade subject, one Verna assigns in advance of the actual writing day. ("I always tell them two or three days ahead so they can think about it," she told me. "They write compositions that are okay if you don't give them time, but they write much better if they have time to think it through.")

Yet composition is never taught; no explicit lesson precedes, accompanies, or follows the writing. Verna's assignments either model her expectations, point to appropriate models, or so structure the task as to create an almost unavoidable model. Sometimes her modeling is elaborate, as it was for the "Embarrassing Moment" assignment. To demonstrate what she wanted, Verna wrote two complete first-person compositions, "God Took Care of Me" and "I Had Six Big Brothers," which she read aloud as part of the assignment. Offering her own religious and family experience, each with a clear moral, Verna wrote about embarrassment as a student that was mitigated by God and embarrassment she temporarily endured as a younger sister at the hands of her older brothers.

Student response to this assignment was wholly secular; most papers focused on home events, though two students wrote fictitious stories, and one retold a story Verna had recounted earlier about herself. Student compositions were markedly shorter than Verna's three- and four-page versions, written on 5½" by 8½" tablet paper. Only one student turned to a second side, and only one student wrote in more than a single paragraph, though all had titles (including "When I was embarrassed," "An Embarasing Thing," "An Emarressed Moment," "She was emarrassed" and "A composion"), and almost all marked conclusions with "The End," "done," or their signatures.

For this assignment, Daniel wrote a fictitious paragraph.

> Sally worked at market. One day she was pushing a cart up the alley. There were alot of people in his way. She went to far to one side and crash right into a window. Sonny came over and started teasing her. She was very embarrassed.

While "Sally" may be Daniel's sister Sarah, who works "at market," and "Sonny" may be her boss, Dan, according to Sarah this incident never actually occurred. Sarah often comes home with "I-was-so-embarrassed" stories, however, which may be what triggered Daniel's idea.

Katie Fisher, too, wrote a composition clearly her own, headed "Katie Mae 'SPOOKY NEWS' comisphion."

> One day mom told me to go
> to the basement to get fruit for

dinner. And i neaver wanted
to go alone. So i was grumbling and
     saying i don't know where the fruit
is. I just stood there grumbling till
     mom or dad told Sarah or one
of the boys to go with me. So mom told
     Sarah would you go with her and get that
fruit up hear? So she did and she made me
     go down first. You would not believe what
happened!! I went down first and looked down
and there was a father grandhog sitting
in a box. I *screamed* and *yelled* so as fast I
ran up to dad and Sarah just stood down
there saying what? What i don't see anything
so she was looking around and she saw it and was
screaming to. So Daniel went out to get
Lassie (our dog) to kill the thing. And so Lassie
killed it and i went up in my bedroom just
them domb things in my mind. And i neaver
went down alone.

At the top of her paper, Katie wrote "How would you feel about this??", to which Verna responded with "scared."

Though Verna did not read any of these compositions aloud, fear that she might prompted Vernon to write

                    NOTICE
              DO NOT read aloud
              it didn't happen to me although

on his paper. In fact, other than grades and her brief response to Katie's potential dialogue starter, no follow-up ensued from this "lesson."

A second kind of modeled composition assignment involves writing commonly encountered by the children. Just as the letter-writing lesson described earlier partially relied on such implicit models, so did Verna's "farm sale" assignment. Assuming the children were familiar with newspaper, poster, and handbill farm-sale announcements, Verna assigned compositions announcing the sale of their own homes. She briefly, orally reviewed the components of such advertisements—sale location, driving directions, buildings, stock, implements offered, and the auctioneer involved—but she offered no samples.

Two students had very specific models in mind, however; Katie and Daniel Fisher both wrote about "Eff Creek Farm" (though Katie called hers "Eff Creak"). Daniel wrote:

Located about three miles north of Smith's gas station. Go over Burds Run creek follow sign's. Sale will start at 7:00 a:m
     There are about one-hundred and twenty acres. About fourteen or fifteen acres of pasture land. There are eighty holstein heifers, and forty-six dairy cows. Most are vaccinated. The barn holds about one-hundred and

twenty-six cows and heifers. There will also be other little animals at the sale.

All the equipment is almost like new. One John Deere disk. One Bear Cat culipacker. Two Macormick cultivater's. Four horse drawn carts. One, two row New Idea corn picker. There are all kinds of other big equipment.
Actioneer: Kennth Upperman
Not responsible for accidents.
Lunch at sale.

Katie wrote:

At a farm located 3 miles from B—. Traving on [route] 11. Turn right at Kentucky friench fries. Turn right at smith gas sation look for sings in a long lane.

Tuesday April 26, 1983
at 10:00 Am.
Equitment and other things.

Have an 120 area farm and some wood lands.
Have place for 37 cows. All Jersey cows.

Have 1 big silo and 2 little silos. We have 6 pens for hiefers and 1 pen for freash cows. 6 big biuldings. A good herd of cows. 2 big woods. 3 meadows.

House
5 big rooms upstairs. 1 really big attic.

2 stairs to go upstairs. 1 big living room and a big kitchen to. 1 bathroom upstairs and downstairs also. A bathtub downstairs. 1 big wash house. 1 bedroom downstairs. Don't miss the big sale if needing cattle. Sale in a big tent.

Also lots of Equitment!!

Term: Don Ocker and luch as sale.
Aucts: Gary Stoltzfus, also Ralfh
Stoltzfus
No checks from out of state.
Ower (sic): Katie Mae, B—. [State] [Zip Code]
    in any information call: [her phone number]

These ads, combining truth and fantasy, reflect the different interests and ages of their writers, but they also represent more precise imitations of actual farm-sale advertisements than any of the other students' (perhaps because sale ads appear frequently on the Fisher family bulletin board). The current "Eff" farm has no creek—though their Lancaster farm did; in fact, it has no formal name at all. That both Daniel and Katie chose the same name may reflect discussion of the assignment at home, something Anna remembers them doing. That Daniel focused on the equipment while Katie focused on the house reflects their different daily orientations: Daniel works primarily with the equipment, Katie primarily in the house. Both can specifically describe the barn because both help milk once or twice each day. Their descriptive differences may be age specific, too: Daniel had a fourteen-year-old's awareness while Katie recently turned twelve. Daniel's exaggerated house size (there are six bedrooms but there are neither thirteen additional rooms nor thirteen rooms all tolled) seems more a matter of expedience than fantasy or unfamiliarity. He may simply have wanted to include appropriate information without bothering to count, the rest of his composition demonstrating the same no-nonsense, get-this-writing-over-with attitude characteristically his.

Katie, on the other hand, waxes enthusiastic in writing as she does in all other aspects of life. While Daniel's directions cite the gas station that actually marks the turn onto their road, Katie begins her directions two blocks earlier at a favorite place, the local Kentucky Fried Chicken outlet, whose "friench frieds" she particularly likes. Her facts are accurate; her enthusiasm produces "a big tent" to house the sale and directs potential buyers not to miss the opportunity to attend. She includes a lunch stand—an attractive and frequent feature of such sales that does appear in ads—and cautions that the owner is too smart to accept checks drawn outside her state, imagining herself as the owner who is available to counsel inquiring parties. Interestingly, Katie's ad, unlike her "Spooky News" composition, carefully follows established format rules, with appropriate headings, margins, paragraphing, and closing form.

The third kind of composition assignment, the unmodeled kind, does not give students more freedom than the modeled varieties; in fact, it constrains them more specifically, witness the "animal compositions." When Verna assigned a composition about an animal, it had to have three paragraphs—the first describing the animal, the second giving its good and bad habits, and the third "giving its future." The children had no difficulty finding topics (seven dogs, four horses, and one cow), but following directions was not as easy. Several wrote one paragraph; one wrote four. Some wrote the first two as assigned but omitted the third. Others wrote three, dividing the second assigned topic into two while also omitting the third. The most common characteristic, in fact, was omission of the third consideration, perhaps because students did not understand what "giving its future" meant or because they found that more complex and less familiar than following the more mechanical directions, per se.

Verna responded to the missing third topic with some consistency. In most cases she drew empty parentheses where the absent paragraph should have been and filled them with a large check mark. On one paper she asked, "Do you want to keep him?" instead of checking the space; on another she ignored the absence completely. Grading was erratic, some papers receiving percentages, others marked only with the number wrong. There was no correlation, however, between paragraph problems and grades.

Daniel's and Katie's compositions in this case represent the two most common kinds of responses.

REX [BY DANIEL]

He is brown and black mixed. He is about six feet tall. I have him around half a year.

His good habits are he doesn't kick and his bad habits are he tries to bite you. He doesn't follow me arround. I din't have him long enough to see how he got along with other horses.

The future of him is Rex and I are going to live together in an old shack.

"MY DOG" [BY KATIE]

My dog is little. He's mostly black but has a little white.

He's not to old yet. His name is Rover. He is a fat puppy.!!!!

His good habits are, he braks when people come, He does not run away, He is not scared of people He runs up to them and bits them.

His bad habits are, He runs after cars, trucks and other things. He follows us to school, He gets Moms things, He likes to chew on soft things, When I go out to milk He comes and likes to chew on my shoe strings.

"The End"

Not only may composition assignments be both modeled and/or understood, but they may require discontinuous writing not at all essaylike. One day before recess, Verna read two riddles to the class. (Riddles are a favorite Old Order kind of puzzle.) After recess, she announced, the upper grades would write similar riddles and then read them to the rest of the children who would try to guess the answers.

After recess, however, Daniel raised his hand to ask a question.

"How much do we have to write?" he asked.

"You read what you've written until someone guesses," Verna replied. "If they guess before you finish reading, you can stop. If you finish and no one's guessed, you have to say what you didn't write."

When she had finished conducting several lower-grade classes, Verna returned to upper-grade composition. "If you get ideas from other people's riddles, you may add something to your own composition," she said before asking who wanted to begin. When no one volunteered, Verna selected David. "Read one sentence at a time," she instructed. "Then pause. Look for hands. If there are none, go on."

David read three sentences before almost all the hands went up at once.

I am black and covered with dust.
The teacher is very mean to me.
She does not wash my face.

David called on Jay who answered "the blackboard," allowing David to sit down with evident relief.

Encouraged by this success, several students raised their hands, and Verna called on Mervin. A painfully shy boy, with buck teeth, thick glasses, and erratic hair, Mervin had been classified "special education" by Verna and his parents. Though he is chronologically a fifth grader, he takes some classes with the third grade and some with the fourth, keeping up with the fifth graders only in arithmetic. Mervin's reading is painfully slow, his penmanship tortured. When writing for me (an event discussed later), he negotiated his writing by drawing a picture after only a few sentences. On this occasion, Mervin strode to the front of the room but spoke almost too quietly to be heard.

"Three words that you use very much" was all he said.

When no one responded, Verna told him to continue. "That's all I have," he replied, looking puzzled.

"Make something up," Verna instructed.

Mervin thought for a moment. "Two of them have four letters and one has five," he said.

"When," someone called out.

"House," guessed another.

Mervin shook his head but appeared encouraged by the fact that the others were playing his game.

"They start with *T*," Mervin hinted.

"*That, they,* and *there*," Amos Fisher called out, too caught up in the game to wait for recognition of his raised hand.

"Right!" Mervin beamed at Amos.

Five more students participated, most at Verna's insistence, including Daniel, who had found writing his riddle difficult as his initial concern suggested. "I don't know what to write," he had told Verna during the process. "Do you have to write an answer?"

"Only if you think you'll forget," she replied.

After helping several lower-grade children at their desks, she moved to Daniel's, who had his hand raised again. He asked that she read what he had written. Verna did and suggested revisions, rearranging sentences, changing the beginning and the ending. Daniel read:

> This can go very far without stopping.
> This is black and gray.
> Dad got me this for a birthday present.

His brother and sister both raised their hands.

"Your pony cart," Katie "guessed" when called on.

What makes riddles an appropriate composition lesson? They are things written for no purpose other than writing practice and amusement, rather like fiction. What makes the riddle lesson most interesting, however, is its illustration of the children's thinking when given an assignment with little to constrain it, a format with implicit but unexplored subtleties, and teacher expectations without clear explanation. The riddle subjects chosen reflect the limited range of Meadow Brook student thought. Nearly all involved animals or school, those that didn't, like Mervin's and Daniel's, not going too far afield. Few of the riddles were intended to be funny or clever; those that were, restated commonly told examples, such as What's black and white and red all over? What has hands and a face but can't wave or see? Verna accepted all the riddles she heard with equal lack of enthusiasm. None were better or worse than others because all met two implicit criteria: they asked questions that hinted at their answers, and they asked about topics appropriate to Meadow Brook. In other words, the social and cultural dimensions of the lesson compensated for any academic or intellectual shortcomings.

One day I could no longer resist the urge and asked Verna if I might have the students write compositions for me. Though surprised by my request, she agreed that I could "some time." Perhaps ironically, however, my sometime came sooner than expected, and I was completely unprepared on the day Verna surreptitiously deposited a note on my desk which read, "After this class I want you to tell pupils their English assignments." "This class" was almost over when she passed my desk and dropped the note, leaving approximately five minutes in which to order my thoughts before she announced, "Put your pencils down. Now Andy has something to say to you."

Hoping to conceal my panic, I slowly stood up and looked around the room. All eyes were on me and the room was utterly silent until I heard myself tentatively begin, "Verna has given me permission to make your assignment for Thursday's English class." As I waited to hear what I'd say next, something unbidden clicked in my head. Suddenly, on some level, I realized that I had everyone's attention—that I had been given the floor—and I immediately forgot everything I had learned about Meadow Brook as I switched into some sort of mainstream "auto-teach": "Who knows why I'm here?" I asked, enthusiastically, expecting an immediate show of hands.

Silence and stillness answered me. Slowly, as the children exchanged unreadable glances, three hands went up—Katie and Daniel Fisher's and John Leid's. I called on John.

"You're making a book," John stated.

I smiled and said, "That's right, John," which made him smile, too. "What's the book about?" I asked, looking around.

Walter raised his hand. "About the school," he said.

I concurred, and Walter smiled back.

I began to explain in my best, most animated teacher voice that although I sat in their classroom every day and took lots of notes and talked to many of them individually, I could not talk to all of them enough. I wanted to know what each of them wanted me to know about the children and the teacher at Meadow Brook, about the books they read, what they do, and what they learn. "And I want to hear from everyone," I added emphatically, turning towards the smallest children. "That means upper *and* lower grades." At that, Betty and Wilma squealed and giggled, clapping their hands over their mouths and eliciting stifled laughter and grins from their schoolmates.

Two days later my "English class," as Verna repeatedly referred to what I thought of as a composition assignment, began with her abrupt announcement at the conclusion of another lesson: "And now you can have your English class, Andy." I stood up—still playing mainstream teacher—and began by asking who remembered what I had said two days earlier. Surprisingly, Mervin's hand shot up immediately, and when recognized, he repeated my words almost verbatim.

Before I could respond to Mervin, however, Verna, seated at her desk, began asking questions. "David, do you know when the schoolhouse was built?" she asked first. Getting that answer, she continued, "Richard, do you know the name of the schoolhouse you went to before you came here? Do you know how to spell it?" Several Meadow Brook–history questions later, she stopped asking and announced that she, too, would "write for Andy."

Not wanting to direct student thinking any more than Verna already had, I suggested everyone begin and said that I would answer any questions they had so they would not disturb Verna's writing. Periodically during the next half hour, children raised their hands and I responded by going to their seats, but most insisted they had to ask Verna their questions, not me. The few who didn't want Verna only asked me how to spell words.

Mervin, however, asked a different question using a different method. He came to my desk, handed me his paper, and said, "Read the last sentence." It read, "shall I draw picture." I said, "That would be lovely, Mervin," and the boy beamed, hurried back to his desk, took out his crayons, and drew with great intensity. Three other students—a first grader, a second grader, and a seventh grader—who may well have noticed Mervin's activity, also illustrated their papers, though without asking for permission.

Also after Mervin's foray to my desk, several other students came to me, and most asked versions of another question: would I let Verna read their papers? Wanting their honesty and not thinking far enough ahead, I said I would be the only reader, a reply that left me in an interesting situation when Verna asked to read papers like Anna Mary's, which said:

> I don't like school. I like the last day of school. On the last day of school we have a picnic. I don't like the teacher. At recess we play kickball. I like to play kickball. We don't get extra recess often. Sometimes we play baseball. Our teacher makes us write compositions. I don't like to write compositions. On Monday we are going to have show and tell. On the last day of school we are going to have a pet show.

In addition to Anna Mary, five children said they dislike school and one said he dislikes his teacher.

When Verna asked to see the compositions, she did so somewhat obliquely, asking for them only after I read them and only if I did not mind. I took them home, read them, and brought her what I called "the best ones." Knowing how sensitive Verna was, what a long memory she had for misbehavior, and what I had promised the children (whether or not I should have made that promise), I made the decision that seemed most fair to everyone involved.

The composition I asked the students to write differed in its assignment from those they were used to, providing neither model nor implicitly recognizable form, yet they managed to make it their own anyway. At first I but vaguely realized the complications my assignment involved. After considering it in the Meadow Brook context, however, I realized that I had asked for both content and form unlike the varieties they had experienced previously. They had never before been asked to consider what someone should (or should not) know about their school, nor had they read formal or informal essays either inside school or out. The most interesting aspect of the resulting compositions, therefore, is their marked similarities, which occurred despite the lack of explicit direction or prior experience. Though I referred to the assignment as "composition" while Verna called it "English," and neither of us modeled or specified format or content, half of the children turned writing *for* me into writing *to* me, producing letters complete with salutations and closings. Two who did not begin with a letter format closed with one, revealing a letter-appropriate mind-set beneath their composition surfaces. Only Verna herself, wrote a formal, third-person composition. The children all wrote in the first person, some using only the plural but most mixing it with the singular.

Content was remarkably similar, as well. Nearly all included some mention of planned end-of-school activities (picnic, pet show, fathers-and-children baseball game) scheduled for four weeks hence, and many mentioned show-and-tell planned for the following week. Another nearly universal topic was Verna's planned appearance as Clara Barton to supplement the girls' history report writing (Abraham Lincoln was the boys' topic). Having once worked in a nursing home, Verna had a white uniform and Red Cross pin she promised to wear while delivering a speech about Barton. (Katie Fisher's letter told me that Verna planned to do this on a day I could not come because "she don't want you to see her." True to Katie's word, Verna dressed up on a day I was not there.)

Other generally included topics were things enjoyed (recess, weekends, Christmas, and Easter), things disliked (school, different subjects), important school-related information (number of children enrolled, who's in what grade, number of families represented, subjects studied, Verna's planned retirement, and Meadow Brook history), and important personal information (names and ages of family members). None took Verna's hint to write about Meadow Brook's history, and only three children, besides the Fishers, wrote things that appeared nowhere else. First grader Betty said, "You should no that the teacher paddles us." Sixth grader Vernon told his favorite riddle—Q: "What did the Indians do when it rained?" Answer: "They let it rain"—and he listed the names of all the teachers he has ever had. Eighth grader Richard said his "Dad is school director till the end of this year then somebody else will have to take a turn for a while."

Again Daniel's and Katie's work accurately represents the group's while simultaneously demonstrating their individuality. Daniel wrote a three-paragraph composition, heading it only with his first name and "Grade 8."

DANIEL GRADE 8

We play kickball at recess. The name of the ball is "Big Kick" it is very light. Today, March 31, 1983 we played Amish against the Mennonite. I don't know who won yet because we didn't have last recess yet.

We give a newspaper out every first of the month. The name of the newspaper is "Meadow Brook Gazette". We each had to give a title to give to Verna J. Burkholder. She looked over each one to see which one was the best. A sixth grader won, Vernon Martin. And whoever had something to do with Meadow Brook got a prize.

There are two first graders, five second graders, one third grader, three fourth graders, five fifth graders, two sixth graders, two seventh graders, and three eighth graders. They average up to about twenty with the teacher. We have about four weeks of school left. And I'm the happiest boy alive!

His first paragraph combines shared and original information, no one else mentioning the name of the ball. The second paragraph is unique, and the third paragraph fairly common, with the exception of the final sentence.

Katie, on the other hand, wrote two full pages with her usual systematic indentation. She began "Hi Andy," and closed "Katie Fisher, Grade 5."

I'm glad we have to do this instead of English
Because I really don't like English. Well what
I think you should know is what Verna Martin
is going to dress up like an "Red Cross" women.
Because we have an book instead of our Geo.
And we have Clara Barton on Red Cross women. Next
week sometime, she said she is going to do it
when your not here She don't want you to see her.
Today she gave us each a Book-Marker for
Easter gift. For recess scheduled for frist
recess we have 15 min. and Lunch we let out at
11:30 and call in at 12:15 and for Last recess
we have 15 min. For our Voc we look up the
words if we don't know them.
We also have health its called *"Your Health"*
And someone copys the question's us and we write
our answers on table paper.
We do not read our Health out loud. English we
Singular and Plural Nouns, Capitalizing and
Punctuating Synonyms, Pronouns, Antonyms, and
we have to write letters, and storys.
We also have a flower book that we do every
Monday instead of Voc. We also have Great

name's in American History. We have reading
and also German. Would you believe this we are
going to have a pet show the last day of
school. I might bring my rabbit that
Daniel gave me for my birthday. I told Mom if
I could bring my dog alone she said
No way your not taking that big and dirty dog.
I'll tell you some things about the
school children. Some are poky others read
books befor they are done others are
fast and nice workers. At recess time we play
kick-ball and sometimes base ball. We (us
girls) bring something to sew when we don't have
anything to do. Verna Burkholder wants us sometimes
to read of Arithmetic Answers,
and other little things when she on behind.
We had all good report cards so we have 15
mi. more than we did before. Betty right
in Front of the teachers test has a habit of
turning around and doing her lessons. Barbie
Blank, David Leid, Jay Leid, Mervin Nolt are all in
my grade. Lois Martin moved to Lancaster
she was in my grade to. There were 3 boys
and 3 girls now there are 2 girls and 3 boys.
The Last time for art we had them cross's
up on the wall.
And before that we had them horse's and Buggy's.
This morning for arithmetic we had qt. gal. pt.
that is quart, gallon, pint. And Add Sub Mul.
Divide.

While Katie does include many of the common topics, her letter is
distinctly her own. Again Katie's writing is exuberant, telling secrets,
quoting her mother (with probable accuracy), describing her classmates,
and generally including more vibrant details than the other children.

To end my "class," Verna stood up and asked, "How many people
in this school would like me to read my composition so they can see if
it's true?" Most of the students raised their hands, so Verna read in the
same barely punctuated monotone used for all oral reading. Students
silently listened and remained silent when asked, "Does anyone think I
should change anything?" thereby confirming the truth of their teacher's
work.

By taking over my lesson—intentionally or unintentionally—Verna
made it consistent with her own. First, her oral reading provided the
model I had failed to provide and that she had attempted to offer through
her prewriting questions. Though reading her composition after the fact
could not direct student writing, it could implicitly contrast student
products with her own and, like all other composition and story reading,
contribute to the generally understood standard of what constitutes
"good" writing (and good reading). This oral reading also reinforces a

fact of Meadow Brook writing instruction in general. Verna never teaches composition; she just assigns and models it. I had done only the former, so she had to do the latter.

Verna's "takeover" also makes explicit another Meadow Brook priority, again, one usually unspoken. Verna's stated reason for reading aloud was to have students judge the truth of what she wrote. That what is written is true, that text does not lie, is assumed in text-based lessons. Any untrue text is a "story," something read aloud as part of recess or in a reading book. It takes a writer's perspective to make the issue of truth explicit, however. *Meadow Brook Gazette* stories, when permitted, were consistently labeled "Fiction." Without that label, a writer's obligation is to truth, even—or especially—when the writer is the teacher. In other words, published writing, not otherwise labeled, is true. Student writing, unless specifically indicated, must be also.

What can be said about the role of composition at Meadow Brook and its relation to writing? Composition, per se, is of minimal importance. Taught when Verna feels "inspired," it has no place in the regular schedule, nor does it have a place with other subjects on the report card, appearing in the second section between "Rank in Class" and "Neatness." Instead of having a positive identity, "Composition" is defined by omission; it becomes what report writing, story writing, letter writing, and all other writing are not. At best, it is a somewhat whimsical way to practice thinking and writing in socially approved ways. Composition resembles art, providing extra opportunities to transmit cultural lessons in palatable, change-of-pace ways. Both could be omitted from the curriculum, but while included, serve fundamental social purposes of the school.

Writing is considerably more important than composition, however, for the same reasons reading and arithmetic are important but not to the same conscious extent. Meadow Brook parents, according to Verna, demand emphasis on arithmetic and reading because those are the "things the children will need after school. The boys will have to buy feed and seed, and the girls will have to measure material and read garden catalogues and order from them." Because writing, too, serves "real" purposes, particularly using the mail for business and social communication, its curricular inclusion is assured by the *Standards*. Since *Standards* does not explain what constitutes "writing," however, the teacher decides, with parental approval, resulting in the Meadow Brook writing emphases described here.

All this Meadow Brook student writing, regardless of variety, reveals a unified notion of what is important, what counts in writing, regardless of kind. First of all, appearance matters more than form. Neatness and penmanship, the literal physical shape of the whole, greatly outweigh the less visible, organizational shape of introduction, body, or conclusion. Second, content matters more than form too. Appropriate ideas matter while organization and coherence may not. The presence of relevant, suitable, assigned, or text-bound ideas makes moot the absence of unity and coherence, of thesis statement, topic sentence, or transition. And third, mechanics matter more than form as well. Spelling, punctuation, and penmanship matter while sentence structure and paragraph construction do not.

This does not mean Meadow Brook children may be unconcerned about form. Rather it points to a definition of form different from that of many mainstream schools and composition teachers. Meadow Brook concern for appearance, content, and mechanics creates a culture-appropriate concept of form that has no need for focal, organizational, or stylistic considerations. Uniform appearance, appropriate content, and functional mechanics count. Student writing must look as it should, read as it should, and be accessible to an Old Order audience. Writing, including composition, must serve the group first, the individual second.

• *Meaning* •

Unlike the home and community contexts considered so far, the school does not directly address what meaning is, how it may be found, or how it may be created, assuming those ideas instead and implicitly modeling those assumptions. Based on the reading and writing observed at Meadow Brook, four notions of meaning seem to underlie school reading and writing.

First, at Meadow Brook meaning is believed to be in the text. It is explicit in reference-book facts and reading-book morals, accessible to anyone who can decode and define. What an individual brings to a text beyond those skills is apparently irrelevant; what happens when an individual interacts with text goes unconsidered.

Though the first part of this assumption seems well documented, the second becomes particularly apparent in a second-grade health class during which the unusual occurred: students gave several "wrong" answers based on individual interpretation. They were constructing the usual kind of question-and-answer lesson about a textbook section called "On the Farm," in which a child has an allergic reaction after eating too many strawberries.

Q: Are strawberries good for you?

A: Yes.

Q: What could happen if you ate nothing but strawberries?

A: [no response.]

Q: Does anybody know?

A: You would get as red as a strawberry.

Q: And would you itch too?

A: [No response.]

Q: What do we call that?

A: [No response.]

Q: Starts with an H.

A: Hyperactive.

Q: You'd get hives. That's what we call it when you get all red and itchy. What else were they working, besides picking strawberries?

A: [No response.]

Q: Were they working anything else, Wilma?

A: Yes.

Q: What were they working?

A: [No response.]

Q: Were they spraying trees?

A: Yes.

Q: What do we spray trees for?

A: [No response.]

Q: So the insects don't get at the fruit?

A: [No response.]

Q: Yes, that's why we spray . . . Look at the picture. What are they doing?

A: Picking apples.

Glen objected to this answer. "That's not farm work, picking apples," he said. Verna went right on:

Q: Look at the boy feeding cows in the picture. How many in second grade ever gave cows something to eat?

A: [All but James raised their hands.]

Several times in this exchange students gave answers that seem grounded in their personal experience or individual interaction with the text, but those were not answers Verna expected, not her "right" ones. Instead of reinforcing or dealing with those responses by recognizing them, however, Verna went on, using the student's answer to get to the one she wanted or ignoring the student's answer completely and giving the one she wanted without transition. Even Glen's honest objection, based on his experience as a dairy farmer's son, received no acknowledgement; his personal knowledge was subordinated to more universal understanding and to the need for a single meaning in the text.

The second notion of meaning at Meadow Brook goes on to refine the first one. Not only is meaning in the text, but meaning is in the words themselves, not in their display. Both readers and writers must get each word "right." A misread word tampers with meaning as may individual oral expression; a miswritten word obscures meaning as may a misselected one. With the reader responsible for knowing the words and the writer responsible for presenting them, the best way to read and write becomes taking each word exactly as it appears, saying it flatly or copying it accurately. Writing without a text focus—writing compositions or letters instead of reports or workbook exercises—requires adherence to instructions, format, and precedent to meet readers' expectations and to help insure communication of meaning.

Third, Meadow Brook teacher and students seem to assume that meaning can be expressed in few words and is best expressed that way. Encyclopedia, dictionaries, survey textbooks, workbooks, and basal readers dispatch whole subjects briefly as do all forms of student writing and oral response. Information, this suggests, need only be presented, not explained. Since readers need only recognize and recall it, writers need only present it in ways that facilitate their recognition and recall.

Fourth, at Meadow Brook meaning can and should be the same for everyone. If meaning is in the text, only one right answer exists. The differences among readers may complicate their extraction of meaning but should not be allowed to prevent it. Among writers, individual differences may be expressed in color or design but should not affect any text they produce. And just as text should not seem to come from too unique an individual, text is not directed at individuals; each reader is part of the larger audience and must read as one of the group, putting individual differences aside. Conversely, writing should address the group, each writer using easily read words in an easily read way on a readily apparent topic, selecting among personal choices according to universal criteria.

These notions of reading and writing underlying all such activity at Meadow Brook led to the school's implicit definitions of those terms. *Reading* becomes extracting meaning from text. *Writing* becomes transposing meaning into text. Neither involves any identifiable process; both are matters of product and both are coherent and congruent with definitions found in all other domains of Old Order life.

FIVE

The Teachers' Community

Although the community of Old Order teachers does not include any members of the Fisher family, some consideration of this group's literacy deserves attention here for two reasons. First of all, how teachers experience reading, writing, and meaning cannot help but influence their transmission of related skills and attitudes to the students and student families they encounter. Therefore, to understand the role and transmission of literacy among the Amish, I had to discover and understand something about its role and transmission among their teachers. Second, Old Order teachers' in-service training differs markedly in content, form, and atmosphere from that conducted by most mainstream schools. Those differences, I found, offer an interesting instructive contrast to the top-down, impersonal, sporadic nature of in-service days to which so many public school teachers are subjected.

Because their particular professional needs could be met neither outside nor inside the Old Orders, these teachers created their own occupational organization within their larger cultural framework. Though their network has neither formal name nor headquarters, officers, or letterhead, it serves a range of teacher needs and purposes both formally and informally. Informally, the organization helps teachers get to know and see each other frequently by encouraging and enabling individual and small-group visits to others' schools. Sometimes arranged in advance by mail, visits may or may not come as a surprise to the host teacher, but expected or not, visitors are always welcome both because visiting is a primary cultural ritual in schools as it is in other Amish contexts, and because visits remind teachers that they are not alone.

Formally, teachers gather with others in their geographic area for one afternoon every six weeks during the school year. Different schools serve as the sites for these meetings, those in the most distant or most

123

rural locations hosting fall or spring gatherings to minimize winter travel hazards. Each summer, a larger statewide meeting is held for several days in Lancaster County, featuring a tightly organized program covering pedagogical subject-area issues and other school-related topics ranging from disciplining students to dealing with parents and school boards. Experienced teachers run both kinds of gatherings, either sharing their accumulated knowledge or introducing outside specialists to instruct in areas for which they consider themselves unprepared. (In the summer of 1983, for instance, an English Lancaster woman spoke on teaching the mentally disabled.)

In all but these specialized areas, experienced teachers are considered the community's best resource for teacher education. In addition to their participation as meeting leaders, those with more than five years of experience are encouraged to invite new teachers to visit their schools and observe them at work. In some places, prospective teachers may even spend a term or a year as aides to experienced teachers before assuming full responsibility for their own schools. As in all other aspects of Old Order life, experience is believed to bring wisdom, and the experienced are considered wise.

Perhaps because of my presence, Verna did not leave Meadow Brook to visit other teachers while I was there, but she had taken the upper-grade students to visit a nearby Amish school earlier in the year. During my tenure, I saw Meadow Brook visited by three teachers from another county, who introduced themselves by name and school affiliation to the assembled Meadow Brook students before settling in for a day's observation.

I asked Verna how she felt about having the visitors in her classroom for a day, thinking how many teachers I knew would consider their presence an annoyance if not a voyeuristic, threatening, or intimidating act. "I like having other teachers visit and seeing other schools," Verna told me after she had compared notes with the visitors and they had left for home. "It gives me a chance to see how I'm doing and to get new ideas. Besides," she added, "that way I know I'm not the only one with problems," and she continued to explain how such visits support and encourage the visited teacher, whether she is experienced or not.

For the same reasons, Verna looks forward to the meetings held throughout the year, attending as many as she can as well as hosting one at Meadow Brook. Though she must request permission to attend or conduct these regularly scheduled gatherings, Verna's absence for half a day every six weeks seems expected and accepted by students, parents, and board members who allow her to find substitutes for those days. Because of the road-clogging wintry weather during this study, Verna and I could not travel to all the meetings planned, but we did go to the one in early April, held two hours away in a similarly rural area.

As Verna and I drove into the unpaved parking lot full of hired vans and black cars outside the white, siding-covered schoolhouse, we could hear the sound of singing from within. Entering silently, we hung our rain- and mud-spattered coats in the cloakroom, where a male greeter met us and directed us toward another man helping to seat late arrivals in the crowded classroom. We threaded our way among the seated singers to folding metal chairs set up between the last two rows of student desks and found our places in copies of the *Christian Hymnal* someone handed us just as a voice called out the next numbered selection. The setting may have been another school in another county and the people may have been strangers (to me, at least), but the procedures were identical to those at Meadow Brook, so we were both soon functioning as part of the group.

When the singing stopped, a woman moved to the front of the room and announced it was time to "number our teachers." The person seated nearest the door in the front row began with "one," and each teacher added a number until all sixty-two had counted. Then the program began, each portion conducted by a different teacher who had volunteered to participate under the direction of the moderator, another teacher who had volunteered to organize that month's meeting and who introduced each speaker by name and the topic "she has a talk about."

Because the meeting took place only a month before Old Order schools closed, two of the topics were end-of-school related, and those speakers distributed dittoed handouts outlining what they said. First Ruth spoke on "getting ready for summer" in terms of closing school and preparing to keep busy doing school-related work during vacation. She admitted "You have to get at it when the mood strikes, and let everything else lay because you may not be in the mood for long. . . . Get away from it for one week and you may never get back to it," she chuckled, which brought commiserating laughter from the audience.

Then Edna spoke about "Picnic Day," the last day of the term on which each school holds a picnic for "scholars and parents." Unlike Ruth's presentation, which had involved the speaker's expansion of the idea lists she gave her audience, Edna droned on in the silence of a group following her verbatim reading of "Indoor Games" and "Outdoor Games" as described on her handout. "I don't expect you to use all these," she finally concluded, "but I wanted you to have plenty of ideas."

Lydie spoke next, on a topic of recently past interest, "prefirst or preschool days." (See chapter 4 for a description of preschool days at Meadow Brook.) She distributed a sheet with illustrated sample worksheets and a list of other possible suggestions including scissor, clay, and chalk activities; counting; reciting short rhymes; and topics of conversation. "You don't just want to give them papers," she cautioned. "If you can, get them to talk." Lydie also posed questions her listeners should consider: How long will you have them? Where will they sit? She concluded by asking for other suggestions: "Any ideas I didn't have?" she smiled, "I could use some new ones." Only one person responded, suggesting that each child's name, clearly printed, be taped to his or her desk.

The greatest audience response came to Alta's presentation on teaching German during which she took several on-the-spot surveys. At least half of the teachers present raised their hands when asked who currently teaches the language, and most seemed to agree that their students enjoy those lessons because "it's fun," "it's easy," or "their parents encourage them." Only one teacher admitted having some pupils who do not like that subject, and none indicated they would voluntarily drop it from their curricula. Alta also raised pedagogy and textbook issues, addressing them herself and taking audience comments, questions, and suggestions. She then circulated a paper asking those interested in an eight-week summer course on teaching German to sign up and note the day and time most suitable. "A lot of you will have part-time summer jobs," she observed, "so we have to find a time when it would suit most people."

After Alta sat down, Barbara, the moderator, took over. She held two lists that had been circulating while the other presenters talked, lists on which the audience had been asked to write down "a composition title that takes a half hour for students to write." Not everyone had complied, so the lists were short enough for Barbara to read out loud, adding occasional comments of her own:

My Forefathers

A Baby Sister Has Arrived

Moving

A Bible Verse for Each Letter in Your Name

The Sense I'd Give Up ("When they hear each others' it makes them think again . . . should really have them write twice.")

A Quiet Evening Interrupted

Dad

How to Spend a Rainy Saturday

The Life of a Pencil

The Life of a Tree

I Am Happy/Sad

Journey ("That really goes over big with big boys.")

"Help Yourself" (to a topic from a posted list like the one in Pathway's *Tips for Teachers*)

When she finished reading and commenting on the lists and no one responded to her call for further comments, Barbara conducted another discussion through anonymous participation, this time based on questions audience members had dropped in two question boxes that had also been circulating among them. Barbara, assisted by Alice, read the questions submitted, answering those she could and referring others to the audience-at-large, so other teachers and the few school-board members present could share their knowledge with the group. The questions included:

How late must a student be before he is marked absent instead of tardy?

When you have a preschool day, is it permissible to let others go home when your school is too full?

How many *F*'s does a student have to get before you keep him back a year?

What should be done with K-8 report cards after a child completes eighth grade?

Is the Monday after Easter a legal absence?

What do you do with an eighth-grade girl who thinks everything wrong is your fault? I am up against it because her parents stand firmly behind her, which is the root of the problem.

Whenever applicable, answers referred to what the public schools do in similar situations, but respondents always noted the need to consider the parochial nature of their schools and their internal differences, as well. (The Amish and the Mennonites celebrate Easter differently, for example, the Amish considering Easter Monday a religious holiday, thus giving rise to the fifth question.)

Discussion of the last question, about the eighth-grade girl—and her parents—in constant conflict with the teacher, took more time than any of the others because many people offered a variety of comments. Someone suggested the problem could be a matter of "adolescent struggles, a personality clash, spite for a bygone incident, or just the girl's nature. She may be that way to her parents, too." Another seated voice said, "You have to treat [eighth graders] like adults but expect them to react like children." Barbara, herself, drew the most evident consensus, however, when she said, "Your biggest answer is love. When you get discouraged go to the love chapter, Corinthians 13, and read it and read it again." Heads nodded around the room as she wryly added, "You cannot go and change those parents . . . that's all there is to it. Might as well go out and run up against a tree."

The final meeting activity was "vocabulary class" conducted by Ruth. She distributed "Word Study—Lesson 7," two dittoed pages on which the teachers were to match sixteen words with their phonetically spelled equivalents and fill twenty-eight blanks in sentences with the appropriate listed words. A whisper-filled silence prevailed for the next half hour while participants cooperatively completed their work. When complete silence was restored, Ruth read the correct answers to the group, which then adjourned after a silent prayer.

Clearly, this meeting followed patterns established in other classrooms and at other meetings in the larger community. As in individual school communities, leadership came from a three-member committee elected the previous year, with help from additional willing volunteers. As in school meetings, church services, and baptism instruction, most of the agenda involved received instruction with followers listening while leaders talked, and response was minimal when leaders opened the floor in other than specifically designated "discussion" segments. As in school, "student" cooperation facilitated the vocabulary lesson, and anonymous participation in the composition and question segments kept the focus on issues, not individuals, so none received undue recognition for contributions or suffered undue embarrassment for lack of knowledge.

The greatest difference between this teachers' group and observed student and parent groups—besides the relative ease of teacher-leaders as they stood before an audience—was the immediate spontaneous response of many participants to the anonymously presented personal problems of others. Perhaps because theirs is a helping profession and they are accustomed to solving problems for others, perhaps because helping each other is their group's reason for being, and perhaps because they are used to modeling their culture's emphasis on selflessness and other-orientation, a palpable desire to help each other permeated the meeting, and even the faces of those not speaking showed empathy and commiseration as they listened. While a sober diffidence overcame the group each time a board member spoke, the mood switch was always rapid, both as the men began and as they concluded. (Interestingly, there was one other English woman present, one who teaches in an Old Order Mennonite school that could find no Old Order teacher. When she spoke, as she did frequently, her voice was louder and her manner more assertive than her colleagues', but their response to her was no different than to each other, though they seemed to respect her as a source of information about public schools.)

What seems the most significant unifying similarity between teacher, parent, school board, and student groups, then, is not the shared meeting format of singing, received instruction, and cooperative intent, but the undergirding philosophy evident in the fact of the meeting as well as its content and method. The identification of the teachers with each other—their coming together as a group that never forgets its differences from the larger society yet always remembers its need to cooperate with that society—and their conscious recognition of the biblical foundation on which they stand all follow the Old Order community model. And like parents, students, and school-board members, the teachers use literacy to foster literacy—to create, transmit, and maintain both it and their culture.

Like the larger Old Order community in which they operate, the teachers' community has a formal written medium through which they communicate. *Blackboard Bulletin* is the professional journal for these Old Order teachers.[1] With a circulation of 5,000 in 1971 (Hostetler and Huntington 1971, 66), the *Bulletin* reaches more than just current teachers. Former teachers, school-board members, and interested parents subscribe, too, and make their reader presence known, for like *"Die Botschaft"* in the larger community, *Blackboard Bulletin* is written primarily by its readers. Articles and stories are reader submitted; regular departments, including "Letters," "Frankly Speaking," "Reader Response," "Opinions Please," "Teacher Hints," "Bits and Pieces," and "Dear Readers," are all reader written, as well. Only the back-cover "From the Staff" column regularly inserts an editorial presence. But that presence, like most readers', remains anonymous, "the Staff" signing itself "E.M." each month (except when E.M. is on vacation and other initials take over). While some article and story writers sign their full names, most readers use first names, initials, state names, or descriptive signatures like "Needing Advice," "Just a Beginner," "An Ex-teacher and Parent of Nine," "Not Above Average, but Still Teaching," "Midwestern Father," or "Wanting to be Fair in Indiana."

Also like "Die Botschaft," a single Bulletin story, question, or comment can prompt an ongoing reader debate through subsequent issues. Each month, for example, the "Opinions, Please" column poses a question for reader consideration, and response to these queries often fills several pages of each issue, revealing through both questions and answers major Old Order education concerns. (In 1982 and 1983 these concerns included how poor parent attendance at school meetings could be improved; how many schools administer standardized achievement tests, why, and with what results; why parents oppose retention of a child who cannot keep up and how much authority parents should have in such cases; whether it is a good idea to convince reluctant individuals to teach school; and how second graders can learn to read and enjoy it.)

The articles in each issue also reveal community concerns, and, again like "Die Botschaft," a hot topic can promote lengthy discussion among readers, as illustrated by those about the roles of German and science in the schools, the importance of women in Old Order society (started by an article called "Why Men Cannot Be Equal"), and the nature of the parochial schools themselves. It is interesting to note that most of these expository articles begin with narratives about fictional parents, students, and teachers which introduce the problems and ideas the writer goes on to address. Implicitly or explicitly, these introductions seem to suggest that readers can and should empathize with the situations described and with their characters as though both were real, which makes reading this professional journal very much like reading other Amish-favored texts.

While at Meadow Brook, I discovered that Verna is an active Blackboard Bulletin subscriber. During the school year of this study she submitted a question, an answer, and an article, all of which were printed.

For "Opinions, Please!" she wrote:

How can I accept criticism from my school parents without despairing? When they correct me, I feel worthless and think I should just quit teaching, since I can't do it well anyway. I can accept suggestions when they are presented tactfully.

Does any other teacher ever experience feelings of complete failure when her school parents criticize her teaching methods, or her way of keeping things under control? If so, please share with us the secret of coping with such feelings. Is there a successful way to overcome this? I have been—

—Struggling For Years
(February, 1983)

In "Reader Response" to a question about poor attendance at and proper conduct of school meetings she reported:

Our parent-teacher meeting was a few days ago. Of all the fathers and mothers present, only one of them asked how the children are doing in lessons and behavior. it was the mother of my star pupils who always do their best, both in lessons and in obeying the school rules.

Also, during the past four weeks we have had very few visitors at school who are school parents. It seems outside people have a deeper interest in our school than the parents do.

What can be done about it? I complained to the directors and said school teaching would be more bearable if the parents cared about school. Their response was that the parents cared much, but they didn't take the time to discuss it and make their cares known. They talked of appointing parents to visit school once a week, taking turns. Then a plan entered my head. Why don't I dominate the conversation at the meetings? I could tell cute stories about the first graders. Maybe if I made the stories funny enough, the parents would be interested.

—Old Order Mennonite Teacher
(February 1983)

And in the fall, her full-length article appeared, including an essay by Daniel Fisher.

OUR READING BECAME ALIVE

—by Verna L. Burkholder

I was twisting and turning in bed. What could I do to inspire my second graders? Four of the six pupils did fairly well, but the other two were dragging their feet. Reading just wasn't interesting to them. It was dull, and they were not enjoying it.

An idea popped into my head. Maybe it would work. Maybe it wouldn't. I decided it would be worth a try. An eighth grader wrote a composition on what happened the day after the idea had come to me. Here it is:

THE CORN STORY

Last night the teacher called the seventh and eighth graders to her desk and showed them a note. The note said that we were to bring corn along to put into the second graders' lunch buckets, because of a story they were having in "More Days Go By."

In the story Peter was on his way to school, and passed a field that had a donkey in it. He gave the donkey apples. His mother found out about it, and told him to take corn along for the donkey, because they didn't have very many apples.

The next morning Peter got corn and put it into his lunch bucket. Levi came running out to meet him, and they went to school. A buggy came along, and the man in the buggy offered them a ride. Peter forgot all about the corn in his lunch bucket, because he was in the buggy and didn't see the donkey that morning. When it was lunch time Peter opened his lunch bucket and saw the corn. The other children laughed at Peter because he had corn in his lunch. Peter learned to laugh at himself that day.

The next morning at our school we seventh and eighth graders watched our chance and slipped the corn into the second graders' lunch buckets. They had the story "Peter Laughs at Himself" just before lunch. When it was time to eat, the first second grader to open his bucket stared in disbelief. "Look at this corn!" The second one opened his lunch bucket, and found corn in it, too. And so on until they had all opened their lunch buckets.

We all laughed and had a good time, but it was not over yet. When Teacher opened her lunch bucket, she had a surprise, too. There was an ear of corn in there, too!

–By Daniel Fisher

A fifth grader had put an ear of corn into my bucket, too. I laughed just as hard as the second graders did, because I thought it was a good joke on me. And best of all, I no longer have trouble with those two pupils who dragged their feet in reading class. They really look forward to reading now, because it has become alive for them.

(November, 1982)

These contributions of Verna's highlight an interesting difference between *"Die Botschaft"* and *Blackboard Bulletin* besides their different focal orientations. Unlike the editors of *"Die Botschaft"*, those at the *Bulletin* correct and to some extent even polish their readers' submissions. While it may be safe to assume that teacher-written text, in general, will be mechanically more accurate than most, the composition and letters Verna wrote for me contained a considerable number of mainstream-important errors, none of which appeared in her published pieces. Yet the *Bulletin* is as much an Old Order publication as the *Botschaft*, so what may account for the different editorial practices?

I suspect the *Bulletin*'s efforts are at least partially explained by the nature of its audience apart from their Old Order affiliation. Because teachers must teach grammar and mechanics, they are more aware of the myriad rules than most readers, and because they are accustomed to searching for infractions of those rules in students' papers, they are more likely to spot them in published text, as well. This then works two ways when teachers go to write for publication: they are more likely to observe more rules in their own writing, but they are also more likely to worry that readers like themselves may be aware of rules they inadvertently break. And as anyone who has ever taught English knows, it is much easier to correct other people's errors than your own, which makes writing for an audience of teachers risky business indeed.

In January of 1983, "E. M." addressed just this fear in a lengthy "From the Staff" intended to encourage more readers to write. Writing about the fear of not being good enough to write for public perusal, E.M. simultaneously revealed the editorial philosophy of the publication. Don't worry about whether you write well enough to appear in print, the editor told readers:

Let the editors decide whether you are a good writer or not, or whether your material is worth printing. Let them worry about getting the tenses exactly right, and the grammar proper. Let them polish your material, and decorate it with periods and commas and exclamation points. That is their work. Yours is to supply them with something to work with.

So it seems that while, for the most part, Old Order teachers read, write, and make meaning very much like the rest of the Old Order world, their occupation highlights different concerns and prompts different awareness of how reading, writing, and meaning are accomplished, creating a different definition of *literacy* in and for the community of teachers. It may be said, therefore, that Old Order teachers become professionals in their own right,

> [some professionalism] ... unavoidable, and in fact ... desirable, even within this small homogeneous subculture. As one Amishman put it, "It seems that after teaching school a while, a person gets a little hard to understand sometimes. And no wonder. Teaching is so far removed from farming or housekeeping that it takes just a little different kind of thinking, which is reflected in everyday living." (Hostetler and Huntington 1971, 67)

SIX

Literacy Defined

From the information and insights of the previous chapters, it might seem possible now to assess Amish literacy—to determine whether the Amish are, in fact, literate, or whether they are semiliterate, functionally literate, or literate to some other degree as measured against our common understanding of what literacy is. As suggested in chapter 1, however, "what literacy is" is impossible to determine, for literacy is neither a monolithic condition nor a decontextualized set of discrete skills transferrable across all contexts. Therefore, measuring Amish literacy against standards established by some other culture's definition—even those of academia—would be not only ethnocentric but pointless. The degree of literacy attained by an Amish individual can only be meaningfully assessed when measured against Amish literacy standards, against what counts as literacy for the Amish themselves.

As the data in this study reveal, certain things count as reading and writing in Amish culture while others do not, regardless of what outsiders may think. Though some might consider this an example of Old Order recalcitrance or myopia, in fact, the Amish are neither defiant nor nearsighted when it comes to their definition of literacy. Rather they are sufficiently observant and aware to discern and adopt those practices that will best serve their own way of life. Having gone to public schools and lived cooperatively with the larger society, many Amish adults may know little about alternative academic, social, and occupational literacies, but they do know these exist. They also recognize their contextualized and thereby limited viability, however, and consciously choose to avoid their influence just as they avoid their contexts. Making no claims of intrinsic superiority for their own practices, the Amish choose to count only literacies of proven value in their own culture. Like all else in their way of life, reading and writing are defined by the central religious themes of Amish life. The skills and texts promoted by their religious perspective "count"; abilities and forms that are irrelevant, counterproductive or potentially antagonistic to their Logos-centered view do not.

In the course of my research, I found six identifiable abilities that count as reading for the Amish both because they are useful to them as individuals and as members of the community and because they complement their relationship to biblical text, yet only some of these six are valued in more mainstream contexts. First, in terms of approaching text, is the ability to discriminate among print materials, to select from what is available and to manage what is selected. The ability to choose Amish-appropriate texts whether by choosing stores or stories, publishers or publications, reviewers or recommendations helps maintain the intercultural and intracultural balance of the community. Standard reference books and mainstream newspapers bought in mainstream stores and at Englishers' yard sales keep the Amish in touch with their neighbors and their neighbors' world in interculturally necessary and productive ways. Trusting only certain publishers and publications, however, and allowing trusted friends, both Amish and English, to preview, suggest, or censor material limits intercultural exposure and strengthens intracultural bonds through shared texts (and shared meaning—see chapter 9 for further exploration of this issue).

Once obtained, print material must be managed; readers must be able to find the desired portion of a dictionary, encyclopedia, the *Martyrs Mirror*, or the Bible and to locate relevant information, ignoring the irrelevant or inappropriate, as the Meadow Brook children located report information, as Eli found his devotional reading passages, and as Anna avoided certain kinds of magazine articles and book introductions. Similarly, published formats must be read and managed to locate newspaper sports or comics, to skip "Dear Abby" and automotive news, and to identify relevant information in texts like calendars, schedules, and bus and train timetables.

Another kind of reading, following written directions, is the second ability characteristic of Amish readers. Farm equipment and animal feed, recipes and canning procedures, road signs and business forms provide instructions necessary for successful use. As farmer and housewife, dairy operators, and frequent travelers, Eli and Anna rely on such printed material and teach their children to read such forms as well. Other Amish with other occupations rely similarly on written directions, the Kings, for example, following Department of Agriculture regulations on handling food sold to the public, and Anna's brother, reading labels on paints and solvents.

The ability to recall what is read is the third requisite reading skill for the Amish. In school, children practice recalling facts from their classroom textbooks and in church and home discussion, practice recalling stories from the Bible and *Martyrs Mirror*, whether read silently by individuals or aloud for others to hear. Adults and children share recalled facts and feelings drawn from personal reading, sometimes as part of community problem solving, sometimes as less goal-directed social activity. Like most Amish activities, reading is purposeful, implicitly if not explicitly so, and recalling text is both a reading skill and a reason for reading.

The community-recognized reading ability with the most limited application is memorization. The only formal memorizing I observed involved Bible verses at home and at school and occasional hymn verses at home. Other memorization of prayers and hymns seems to occur more naturally through their frequent repetition in home, community, and school contexts. Limited to the most important religious texts, memorization seems to manifest belief, the special relationship between man and God represented by this special relationship between reader and text.

The most complex reading ability, the ability to synthesize what is read in a single text with what is already known or to synthesize information across texts into an organized whole (that is, to draw conclusions) is a dangerous skill but a useful one when performed correctly, with a mind to the community. Based on the products of analysis, individual synthesis is potentially divisive and destructive, so group synthesis often literally or figuratively replaces it. When Anna and her sisters hold different opinions of the same issue or text, for example, they work toward a shared conclusion, successful synthesis bringing consensus within the group. When Anna reads alone and has no one with whom to confer, however, she may draw Amish-appropriate conclusions through consultation with her internalized sense of group norms, synthesizing her personal interpretation with that of the imagined group, again aiming for successful consensus.

Probably the most important and certainly the most characteristic reading ability that counts among the Amish is the ability to empathize with characters in a text and to apply the lessons discerned through such empathy. As noted earlier, the Amish do not use the term *characters* in discussing the population of fictional or nonfictional texts; instead they talk about the people in books and stories, be they historically authenticated fifteenth-century martyrs, hypothetical nineteenth-century pioneers, or supposed twentieth-century anti-Communists. Anything written about people—from basal readers to the Bible and the *Martyrs Mirror*, from *Journey of the Heart* and *Faith Despite the KGB* to Supreme Court decisions—requires vicariously experiencing the events recounted, appreciating the circumstances of the people involved, and applying the explicitly or implicitly drawn morals to one's own life.

Perhaps the most interesting example of this ability in action came not in response to some sort of narrative but in response to a Supreme Court case. Handed down in 1971, the *Wisconsin v. Yoder* decision resolved the decades-long Old Order struggle for the right to instruct their own children in their own parochial schools only to the age of fifteen. The Court explained its unanimous decision in favor of the Old Orders this way:

> Aided by a history of three centuries as an identifiable religious sect and a long history as a successful and self-sufficient segment of American society, the Amish in this case have convincingly demonstrated the sincerity of their religious beliefs, the interrelationship of belief with their way of life, the vital role which belief and daily conduct play in the continued survival of Old Order Amish communities and their religious organization, and the hazards presented by the State's enforcement of a statute generally valid as to others. Beyond this they have carried the even more difficult burden of demonstrating the adequacy of their alternative mode of continuing informal vocational education in terms of precisely those overall interests that the State advances in support of its program of compulsory high school education (Reutter and Hamilton 1976, 566–67).

At a Pennsylvania state Old Order school directors' meeting held soon after the decision came down, directors responded to what the Court had written:

> It made us feel humble to read through Chief Justice Burger's opinion. We were made to realize that our way of life is being looked upon and is better known to the outside world than we had ever thought likely. The principles stated, the ideals set forth, and the humble God-fearing people described by the judge in the opinion handed down, caused us to re-examine ourselves and wonder if we are really living up to these standards (Esh 1977, 75).

A characteristically Amish response to this "story" about people.

This leaves two mainstream-significant skills which do *not* count as reading among the Amish: literary appreciation and literary criticism. The first, reading to recognize or appreciate literary technique, is irrelevant in Amish society. Characterization or compression in a short story, point of view or irony in a novel, personification or alliteration in a poem may facilitate desirable empathy or recall, but recognizing such features is not necessary for empathizing or remembering. Amish readers need not analyze why they respond to a particular text or how the writer prompts them to respond as long as they respond appropriately. Although unlike many modern readers in this, the Amish resemble the ancients who saw language as action, not signification (Tompkins 1980). Those readers, too, focused on their response to a text and their need to ethically control the written word rather than on objectification and analysis of that word apart from the world in which it operates.

Similarly irrelevant is literary criticism. Because for them a text is not primarily an object, no Amish reader need analyze its objective components. Because it is, instead, "a unit of force whose power is exerted upon the world in a particular direction" (Tompkins 1980, 204), they need only determine whether it is a force for good or ill and respond accordingly. Doing this requires no independent text analysis; the "interpretive community" (Fish 1980a) manages such criticism itself, successfully precluding the need for individual critical skills, which could be divisive and destructive were they not irrelevant. (See chapter 9 for further discussion of this interpretive process.)

Although it might be said that ministers function as critics in Amish society, they do so not in the usual literary sense, but according to this view of text as power and as members of an ongoing interpretive community. Instead of seeing the Bible as an object for textual study and an end in itself, these churchmen see it as intending to produce results in the world beyond itself. This makes it their job to study the Bible not for its artistic or intrinsic merits but for its empathic and instructive power, to find the connection between what is written, what is felt or believed, and what should be done. In doing this, ministers both help maintain the interpretive community of the church and the culture at large and model how other literature should be read; the *Martyrs Mirror*, the *Ausbund*, or any narrative should be judged for its effect on people, its ability to evoke sympathy and to promote right living, not for its literary language, structure, or other mainstream critical concerns.

While the Amish definition of reading in some ways resembles that of other American groups and that found in other American classrooms, the Amish definition of writing is more characteristically their own (though it bears striking similarity to an earlier American definition discussed later). Usually aware of writer purpose and audience, Amish writers define their purposes and recognize their audiences as Amish first, individuals second. It might be said, in fact, that the Amish "generalized other" is Amish and that an individual Amish writer's purpose almost always serves the community as well as the individual.

I found five abilities that count as writing, publicly and privately, in the community: the abilities to copy, to encode, to list, to follow format, and to choose content. Before he started school, Eli, Jr., was copying his name as written by his sister and copying short notes he had dictated for her to write. On preschool day, Verna expected name copying from her two youngest students, and throughout their education, Meadow Brook students continue to copy their reports and Bible stories. Anna and other *Botschaft* contributors also copy; she, the closing saying in each letter and those she hangs on the family bulletin board, and they, the poems they submit, the sayings and verses they cite, and perhaps the recipes they contribute, too.

The second ability, encoding, also counts both in school and out. Legible penmanship, accurate spelling, and basic punctuation are fundamental to being understood by readers and mark the good Amish writer. They are among Verna's primary concerns in grading student papers and Anna's first observation in reading them. *Botschaft* scribes worry about their published equivalent in editorial and personal errors while Meadow Brook mothers "sound out" and ask the teacher to achieve accuracy.

Listing, the third ability, is also a personally and communally useful skill found both in school and out. The only two examples of writing in the church community involve making lists of nominees and Sunday Scripture readings. School parents, too, list nominees, as well as expenses, responsibilities, items, and prices, while school students include lists of family members, school activities, and personal preferences in their letters and compositions. *Botschaft* scribes, including Anna, list visitors at church, attendees at other functions, chores to be done, and almost anything listable in their letters. Mary and other business operators list products, services, and prices for their customers. Not surprisingly, Anna and her daughters make grocery lists before going shopping.

The fourth ability, following format, also works across contexts. Both in school and out, formats are modeled. *Botschaft* scribes receive no manuals or instructions to guide their writing; they have previous issues of the paper to guide them, instead. Elsewhere, too, letters written have letters read; notes sent have notes received; lists made have lists seen, and so on across recognized forms. In school format is modeled, and when not modeled, is clearly assigned—the paragraph-by-paragraph animal composition assignment, for example, and the *Gazette* recording notebook. When neither model nor assignment is forthcoming, however, Meadow Brook students adapt known forms to new circumstances, as they did when writing for me.

Such organizational modeling seems to extend even to sentence construction in some cases. Stylistic influence of text read sometimes appears in text written, as it does in Anna's apparent psalm and sermon phrasing in her *Botschaft* letters. While consciously done in some instances, modeling is so clearly a primary Amish method of teaching and learning that its unconscious application seems inevitable.

The fifth ability, choosing content, involves making audience-appropriate decisions about what to include in written text. Modeled or assigned in school, content receives little teacher attention there unless Verna's expectations are unclear or unmet, and then it is as often a matter of length as of substance. Content selection becomes an explicit issue for adult writers who criticize others' choices, however, and know their own will be scrutinized similarly. For these adults, context seems to be the guiding content consideration in some circumstances while purpose controls choices in others. *Botschaft* writers, for example, consciously select their topics for the newspaper and recognize that their weekly columns are not letters to their mothers or personal friends. Yet purpose rules more often in other circumstances; Mary, for example, decides what to include in her advertisements according to what she wants potential customers to know about The Stitchery, choosing item variety and "Closed Sundays" as more important than low prices or "Amish-made."

Of these five abilities, content selection seems to be the most problematic. Many Meadow Brook students find little to say even when given explicit instructions. Not knowing what to write was Daniel's biggest problem despite Verna's lengthy assignments, but his papers were not markedly shorter than those of his classmates (Katie excepted). Most *Botschaft* scribes, on the other hand, exhibit no difficulty writing at length but express concern about the appropriateness of what they have to say, instead. (That *Botschaft* writers may have been the Katies of their schools should be recognized, for *Botschaft* writing is voluntary and those like Daniel need not volunteer.)

Just as several mainstream concerns do not count as Amish community reading, four such concerns do not matter in Amish community writing, all four irrelevant or counterproductive. The first irrelevant ones, English grammar and punctuation, though taught in school are to a great extent unrelated to writing in school or out. Grammar affects writing in any Amish context only to the extent that word arrangement must make sense to readers, and punctuation matters for much the same reason. If a reader readily understands the intention of an adjective used as an adverb, a singular verb following a plural noun, a sentence fragment, or a compound verb containing a misplaced comma, the Amish do not see these as errors warranting attention, despite the fact that an English reader might. After all, though such an outsider might happen to read an Amish-written text, few such texts are intended for other than an Amish audience, and all of those readers share a similar sense of what counts and what doesn't. (I know it's difficult for a conscientious mainstream school graduate to imagine honestly believing mechanics don't count; I never thought I would be able to read *"Die Botschaft"* without involuntarily flinching. Over time, however, I found myself reading for meaning, not errors, and not only was that liberating but it had an important effect on my work in the classroom. See chapter 10 for further discussion of this point.)

Another writing concern important in mainstream schools but irrelevant to the Amish is the third-person formal essay. Not naturally existing in the Amish community, the essay entered Meadow Brook through high-school educated Verna but was never perceived or taken up as a model by most of the students. Not only is such a third-person-singular form foreign to this primarily first-person-plural society, but concepts like thesis statement, topic sentence, coherence, unity, and emphasis are equally unknown there. Mainstream journalism, also, seems similarly remote; third-person "objective" reporting and reporters, mainstream news-writing style and newspaper format bear little resemblance to *"Die Botschaft"* and have little bearing on reader expectations for the *Meadow Brook Gazette*. (These differences may well be acts of separation as discussed in the next chapter.)

Fourth, originality, highly prized in American schools and society, has no place in Meadow Brook or among the Amish. While community constraints sometimes explicitly limit the number of appropriate topics and forms a writer may use, original approaches to or applications of those topics and forms are implicitly discouraged by the similarity of models and assignments and by the absence of fiction as an appropriate genre for writers. In this community where all aspects of life reward uniformity, writing may provide an outlet for individual expression and identification, but singular creativity stays within community norms or, as in the case of Daniel and Davie's use of color and design, becomes a community norm.

All of this, from what counts as reading and writing to what does not, demonstrates how closely and consciously the Amish definition of literacy relates to Amish culture. While many Americans seem unaware of the connection between literacy and culture, perhaps assuming as I did that their literacy—and, therefore, their culture—are the only ones that count, the Amish cannot afford to lose sight of their society's historical and cultural roots or of the literacy traditions and tools that help maintain and protect those roots and their culture from extinction. Interestingly, what seems traditionally and characteristically Amish was once characteristically American, too. As described by Shirley Heath (1981), eighteenth-century Americans defined writing as current Amish do:

> Writing . . . was functional and even mundane. Three writing events were part of the social network of literate citizens: reports of opinions and events, how-to accounts related to nearly every imaginable aspect of daily living . . . and letters. Since most of the population had not studied English literature, they did not link the teaching of writing or the purposes of writing with literary appreciation. Instead in the practical school of daily living, they reflected on the utility of writing events in their culture and defended the emphasis on the practical. . . . (p. 27)

These early Americans were doing what the Amish still do—creating a society separate from all others, forging an identity, and attempting to survive.

Heath continues:

> The writing of reports of opinion and events and how-to accounts was viewed as the responsibility of all citizens across social classes and roles. Farmers, tradesmen, ministers, and artisans wrote about what they saw, did, or believed. . . . Societal needs for the exchange of information on a broad range of topics were met by sending articles to periodicals, posting broadsides, providing reports for local [groups]. (p. 28)

Amish men and women, married and single, farmers, tradesmen, ministers, and artisans write about what they see, do, and believe in *"Die Botschaft"* and in private correspondence. Their newspaper, their letters, their advertisements, their announcements, and their treasurers' reports all serve social as well as individual needs.

In eighteenth century America,

> A wide variety of content and form was acceptable for what may be termed "writing acts" published in the periodicals: simple questions, puzzles, word games and anecdotes. Any situation seemed appropriate to provoke a citizen to submit his thoughts in writing. . . . In most cases the first person was used throughout reports and instructional accounts. . . . The reader was

frequently invited by the writer to respond in the next issue, and numerous periodicals contained reports and counter-reports, how-to accounts which were debunked or praised in subsequent issues. . . . (p. 29)

"Die Botschaft"'s columns and letters, subscribers and scribes continue these practices today, as does *Blackboard Bulletin*.

When the American republic grew and became stronger, however, social needs could be subordinated to individual ones, so purposes and emphases in writing changed accordingly. Writing became associated with the development of individual "intelligence, morality, and industry" (Heath 1981, 36), and writing ability became a hallmark of social status and self-improvement rather than social interaction and community improvement.

But the conditions of Amish life continued (and continue) to more closely resemble eighteenth-century America than twentieth. Among the Amish, the community remains the focus—the object of greatest concern, the primary source of strength and direction, and the most significant reason for reading and writing. Individuals have yet to become more important than the group; their "intelligence, morality, and industry" still serve their community first, themselves second. As the larger society changed and its definitions of reading and writing changed with it, Amish society made no such adjustments, still seeing even newly created texts as "event[s] in the social world with social consequences" (Tompkins 1980, 215) to be judged according to their contribution to individuals as they strive to contribute to their society.

In sum, then, the Amish are literate as their culture and their lives define and require literacy, making the question of whether they are literate by any other standards effectively moot. If this is so, however, what does it portend for all the literacy tests, literacy teachers, literacy programs, and literacy politics proliferating so rapidly in anticipation of some universal literacy millennium? For these programs and people to be successful, must they take their good news to the Amish? Offer it to them? Foist it upon them by bureaucratic fiat? And if the Amish may be exempt, what other groups may be excused? Only those involved in private or parochial schools serving self-identified social or cultural groups? Are the rest of us generic, party to and, therefore, subject to public school homogenization? I don't think so. I think, instead, that just as the back-to-basics zealots might be wise to stop to define *basics* and decide which basics should be returned to by whom, so the literacy evangelists might be wise to stop crusading for reading and writing long enough to decide what those words mean to the people they consider the unconverted. We might all become more literate for the effort.

S E V E N

Literacy as a Cultural Imperative

As demonstrated in the previous chapter, there must be more to any definition of literacy than simply "the ability to read and write." Yet even a definition that describes the forms and features of Amish reading and writing (or any other variety) represents only one way of considering what literacy is. There is still another way to define literacy, one that goes beyond the forms and features of written language production and use to the social meaning of literacy as revealed by its larger social functions.

That becoming literate is a matter of becoming enculturated, that literacy is a matter of serving a culture's social needs may seem a grandiose claim at first. Illiteracy obviously creates social problems, but literacy seems more an individual than a social advantage; at least that was my perception before this study began. As my research progressed, however, and I was better able to mentally move between my participant's role and that of observer, I began to see the Fishers in their larger Amish context and to see their Old Order context in its larger American one. I began to see the family as individuals not only conducting their own lives but constructing the life of their society as well. It was then I began to understand how there could be more to literacy than the accuracy and appearance of the texts it created or the personal satisfaction (or frustration) it brought its participants. By looking at the Fishers and their relatively self-contained society, I was able to see literacy as tools they use to create, maintain, and preserve their society and culture instead of only as texts they produce or manage to serve their own purposes.

In fact, I discerned four identifiable functions literacy performs in Amish society: identification, affiliation, separation, and cooperation. The first two—identification and affiliation—occur intraculturally; the last two—separation and cooperation—occur interculturally. All four functions occur in all contexts, but each context foregrounds the function most coherent with its own nature: public contexts highlight affiliation while private contexts highlight identification, and formal institutions highlight separation while less formal organization highlights cooperation.

The intracultural functions, identification and affiliation, seem evident in all the communities to which the Fishers belong. At home, Daniel identifies himself through the Hardy Boys books he reads and the style in which he writes and draws. Anna is identified as primary arbiter of family reading and as a *Botschaft* scribe. Eli's reading and writing reveal a farmer, an Amishman, an American, and a grudging member of a letter-writing circle. Sarah's reading and writing identify one of the "young folks," an Amishwoman, a teenager, and the Fisher's serious daughter. Katie's points to a singer-turned-reader, her parents' exuberant middle child, and Sarah's younger sister. Amos's reveals a serious reader and a member of his extended family. And Eli Jr.'s shows that he is no longer a baby but a fully enfranchised Amish child.

One shared and perhaps most significant identifying and affiliating function remains: all of these people identify themselves as and affiliate themselves with their family through literacy. To be a Fisher, one must read and write, showing interest and taking part in family reading and writing. In the evenings and on Sunday mornings everyone reads and is read to from individually chosen or group-selected texts. Periodically everyone communicates with the immediate and larger communities, both as writers of their own texts and readers of others'. And in their spare time, everyone plays literacy-involved games, regardless of age or ability. Even when Eli, Jr., was too young to read, write, or play by himself, a sibling or parent helped him participate as part of the group, so he, too, could identify himself and affiliate with the family through literacy.

The same kinds of identification and affiliation occur in the immediate community. Susie reads James Michener and Lydie wants to read Emily Brontë, both personal, identifying choices. Mary writes advertisements for the Stitchery, identifying herself as its owner. Rebecca and Elam read books about others like themselves, and almost everyone reads *"Die Botschaft"* and the *Intelligencer*, all identifying and affiliating simultaneously. And Dad signs himself "D.B.," identifying himself to create an affiliating persona.

Members of the larger community identify themselves through literacy, too—some as writers, many more as readers—by creating and maintaining *"Die Botschaft."* Readers identify themselves as members of "Old Order Amish Communities Everywhere," and they affiliate by subscription. Scribes, like Anna and Dad, identify themselves as members of their districts as well as the larger community, making each letter a sign of affiliation, yet scribes also create more individual identities through personal content and style, making each letter a personal assertion, as well.

The church community, on the other hand, uses reading and writing to submerge individual identity and to highlight individual affiliation. To affiliate with the church, to act on one's personal identification with the group, an individual must read, memorize, and recite preselected texts precisely as everyone else does. Though literacy may seem to personally identify ministers and deacons who read the Bible and compose sermons apart from the congregation, it does so in terms of their leadership positions, not as individuals. In fact, it is in the church community that the singular Amish community identity is most often articulated as found in the words of a book: "But ye are a chosen generation, a royal priesthood, a holy nation, a peculiar people" (1 Pet. 2:9), ". . . a peculiar people, zealous of good works" (Titus 2:4).

The school community and the school students are also identified by books read and writing done. Special publishers and special publications define both groups' activities and actions. The adults read and write to maintain the identity of the school community (thus maintaining the school) and to identify individual responsibility for such maintenance. While the reading and writing done by students is constrained by adult decisions, Meadow Brook children still manage to identify themselves as individuals within those constraints by reading and writing in personally satisfying ways that also meet school expectations.

Adult school affiliation is both precipitated and marked by literacy, too. First parents join the school to promote literacy for their children and their community. Then parental reading and writing for school purposes continue to mark their sustained association. Student affiliation is more difficult to claim because the decision to attend Meadow Brook rests not with the children but with their parents. Student attendance and appropriate reading and writing may mark enforced affiliation rather than the voluntary kind considered thus far, yet their enthusiasm at Meadow Brook and their compliance with reading and writing constraints seem to indicate self-motivated student affiliation, especially when compared to the behavior of many mainstream children who attend school only at parental or legal insistence. Amish students' imitation of each other, at least, seems to represent voluntary affiliation with the student body, if not with other aspects of the institution.

Although these identified functions of literacy can be separated to highlight their individual differences, they frequently overlap. Individuals can identify themselves in two ways, first as different from all others of their kind, then as similar to some of those others. The first sort of identification leads to individuating activities, the second to affiliating activities, and such identification-by-affiliation seems to merge the two varieties. For example, Daniel Fisher identifies himself through the books he reads and the style in which he writes and draws. His personal interests also prompt him to read biographies as his friend Davie does, while Davie's signature and use of colors, his identifying marks, are modeled after Daniel's. So while the two boys use literacy to identify themselves as individuals, they also identify with each other, and this second kind of individual internal identification prompts demonstrable literate affiliation.

Another example, Anna's *Botschaft* letters identify her as an individual while simultaneously marking her affiliation with the larger community. Her letters actually demonstrate three identities: Anna, the writer, marked by style and content; Anna, the scribe, marked by observation of *Botschaft* "rules"; and Anna, the Amishwoman, marked by participation in the larger community. The first identification is individual, the second and third affiliating.

A third overlapping situation occurs when an individual chooses to read a community-significant text. Reading *Martyrs Mirror*, for example, helps the reader identify himself personally with individuals who have gone before. At the same time, however, reading *Martyrs Mirror* is a way of affiliating with the community, of expressing and reinforcing personal identification with the group. So affiliation may be a manifestation of identification, a way of actively extending and emphasizing personal identity. Identification may separate an individual from the group, but identification may bring the individual closer to the group as well.

Separation and cooperation, the two intercultural functions of literacy, do not overlap in the way identification and affiliation do, though they are closely related to both. Fundamental Old Order doctrine calls for separation from the world based on biblical injunctions (Rom. 12:2; 11 Cor. 6:14; 1 Pet. 2:9; and Titus 2:14), and literacy helps accomplish that task, as much by what is not read or written as by what is. The Fisher family and its various communities remain separate from mainstream America by reading very little of what that culture writes. Staying out of certain bookstores, staying away from certain publications, cancelling inappropriate subscriptions, and not buying English textbooks, all put greater distance between the Amish and the English. In addition, books and periodicals read as acts of affiliation further mark this separation. The *Ausbund, Martyrs Mirror*, Pathway books, and *"Die Botschaft"* generally are not read by other Americans, reinforcing Amish separateness. The fact that those texts with greatest significance—the Bible and the *Ausbund*—are often read in German serves to make that separation even more emphatic.

Similarly, the Amish do not write to or write according to many mainstream institutions or standards. Hiring intermediaries to communicate with most state and federal offices, they avoid doing that writing themselves. They do not communicate unnecessarily with mainstream concerns, writing no letters of complaint or praise, no letters to an editor. When they do write, personally, publicly, or scholastically, the Old Orders ignore certain matters of grammar, style, and form considered necessary by most public schools and publications and by many "literate" outsiders, thereby demonstrating their separate definition of what counts as literacy (as described in chapter 6).

Though not mandated by doctrine like separation, cooperation is equally necessary and requires crossing the separated boundary in and through written language for socioeconomic survival. Reading English newspapers, farmer-directed publications, and legal and government documents provides information necessary for dealing with and surviving within the larger culture. While reading English at all is a cooperative act, conducting school in English, as required by *Standards*, overtly acknowledges the need for such cooperation.

Conducting written business in English also facilitates cooperation and, thereby, survival. Filling out forms, writing checks, keeping records, giving receipts, and advertising products all enable the Amish to remain economically viable. Again, teaching English as a school subject and writing school assignments in English prepare students to cooperate with the English world as adults, so the schools created to reinforce separation and to promote affiliation and identification contribute significantly to cooperation as well.

Sometimes the decision to cooperate while remaining separate prompts interesting adaptations. Once, when Anna was working at the King family's meat and cheese stand at a local farmers' market, a state-bird quilt they displayed to advertise a school consignment sale attracted considerable attention. When Anna saw how many people stopped to examine the quilt, she thought the local newspaper might be interested and might help publicize the sale with an article about it. Instead of calling the newspaper, however, Anna called me to ask what I thought of her idea and to let me suggest that I call the newspaper. After contacting the paper, I went to the market and, coincidentally, was there when the reporter-photographer arrived. Instead of helping him collect facts and ideas for the article herself, Anna (and the Kings) stayed behind the counter, letting me answer his questions and suggest what he might write.

As Amish culture teaches individuals to meet their collective and individual needs of identification, affiliation, separation, and cooperation through literacy, it makes literacy a way to display appropriate individual functioning. Children in all societies learn "how to display their knowledge and skills in appropriate forms at appropriate times" (Cazden 1982, 210), which in some American subcultures may mean eschewing books and writing completely. For the Amish, however, involvement with literacy offers ways not only to identify, affiliate, separate, and cooperate, but to display one's identification, affiliation, separation, and cooperation as well. Participating in literacy activities and using literacy tools appropriately demonstrate an Amish individual's social competence.

Because learning these literacy lessons is crucial to Amish cultural survival, their transmission becomes a social necessity. Creation of contexts that will facilitate literacy socialization is a major community goal; the creation of situations in which appropriate identification and affiliation can occur, in which Amish culture is markedly separated from all others, and in which successful Amish-English cooperation can happen goes on all the time. While some situations—like regular visiting, church services, and quilt sales—seem to occur "naturally" as part of the Amish lifestyle, it should be remembered that the Amish lifestyle (like any other) has been consciously created to maintain and transmit the Amish way of life and is consciously chosen and re-created by each successive generation. The Amish school system may be the best recent example of such self-conscious effort that at different times on different levels both establishes and consistently reaffirms what seem to be "natural" patterns.

So while I may have been slow in recognizing the social meaning of literacy for the Amish, Amish adults have always known it well, and perhaps surprisingly, so have Amish children. In fact, for them, the social meaning of literacy may become evident long before more text-bound appreciation occurs (Chomsky 1971; Bissex 1980; DeFord 1980; Harste et al. 1981; Read 1981). In terms of literacy, Amish children "read the world" (Friere 1983) well enough to know that people are identified by what they read and write and that reading and writing connect people in various ways. They also learn to recognize places, people, and texts considered off-limits and those with which they may communicate. Eli, Jr., for example, knew which siblings liked which books and knew the Bible and the *Ausbund* drew his family and his community together before he could read any of those texts himself. He knew that everyone wrote sometimes, but his mother wrote most often. And he knew not to talk to me or read my books before I became an adopted member of the family. In other words, even as a preschooler, Eli, Jr., used literacy to both mark and maintain his cultural boundaries as did the other Amishmen he knew.

As Anderson and Teale (1981, 2–3) point out, all social groups use whatever resources they have available "to deal with the problems encountered in interaction with the environment," and the ways they use these resources characterize their cultures. Theoretically, the resources available to all Americans are available to Amish Americans, but the Amish, like other groups and individuals, have made certain decisions about which resources to employ, which to adapt, and which to eschew. They have dealt with literacy resources in all three of these ways, so that literacy now characterizes their culture and is characterized by their culture according to the ways it promotes and supports individual and group identification, affiliation, separation, and cooperation.

EIGHT

Literacy and Social Continuity

In addition to looking at the multiple definitions and functions existing for literacy, recent research also focuses on the continuity of these definitions and functions across home, school, and community contexts. To what extent are the literacy-related knowledge and skills acquired or expected in one context required or valued in another? What effect may the absence of such continuous definitions, practices, and goals have on the likelihood of children succeeding or failing to become effectively literate? The lack of such continuity, many researchers have found, almost inevitably prepares children to fail. (For relevant studies see Labov 1972; Rist 1973; Heath 1978b and 1980; Mehan 1979; Michaels and Cook-Gumperz 1979; Gilmore 1982; and Cazden, 1982.) And looking at Eli Fisher, Jr., for example, I can understand why.

Before he ever went to school, Eli had derived a rather extensive implicit understanding of what literacy is and whether literacy matters simply from "reading the world" in which he lived (Friere 1983). Imagine what might have happened next had Eli gone not to Meadow Brook but to a mainstream public school. Would he have been told, explicitly or through more powerful behaviors, that he really didn't know what counted as reading and writing, that his reading and writing were not real but other unknown or alien varieties were? What would have happened had his quiet imitative behavior made him invisible in the classroom, or worse yet, made his teacher assume he was withdrawn, problematic, or less than bright? What if his work were devalued because it was obviously copied or just unoriginal? What if he had been called on to perform individually in front of the class, to stand up and stand out? Or what if he had been asked to discuss private issues in public? Or to evaluate what he read?

Had any of these things happened, I suspect that Eli would have had to make some difficult choices, choices that would have amounted to choosing between what he had learned—and learned to value—at home and what he seemed expected to learn at school. To conform to his teacher's demands and values, he would have had to devalue or disavow his parents', and that would have been a worst case discontinuity scenario come true. Unfortunately, it would not have been an uncommon one; public schools seem to make such demands frequently on children from cultural or socio-economic groups different from their teachers' or their schools', demands that seems unfair, uncalled for, and unnecessary, not to mention counterproductive and destructive.

While most research focuses on such actual discontinuity, however, the Amish of this study provide an outstanding example of the opposite, allowing us to look at the kind of continuity, the kind of "positive transfer" across contexts that Cazden claims "we must eventually learn . . . to create" (1982, 211). Not only are the Amish school, home, and community of this study continuous, but their continuity is not a matter of home and community aligning themselves with school (as many public educators would require), but rather of home and school aligning themselves with community.

In fact, it may be the presence of a separately identifiable community that enables this group of homes to create one school and to remain continuous and/or enhancingly parallel with it. Instead of remaining potentially opposite poles, home and school become two sides of a three-sided relationship, their triangular equilibrium more stable than any two-sided interaction. Nor is the triangle equilateral; instead, the two sides of home and school depend on the third, community, to keep their balance. Unlike the "school community" in some recent studies (Heath 1980; Gilmore and Smith 1982), the larger Amish community is not created by home and school but is a preexisting entity from which home, school, and school community derive. This direct derivation seems to promote the observed continuity and parallelism and to support the efforts of all involved. (Which is not to say that a school community cannot offer such support and balance; there are instances in which just that has been accomplished successfully.)

It does seem, however, that the Amish chose to create such relationships—as Cazden suggests we all must do—only after realizing that public schools were becoming significantly discontinuous with their homes and community and posed a serious threat to both. The continuity observed in this study seems the result both of this realization and of subsequent decisions to control and insure their cultural survival by charging home, community, and school with the responsibility for Amish-appropriate literacy transmission.

To accomplish this, schools like Meadow Brook were created not as highly specialized organs but as direct reflections of Amish homes and communities in terms of their methods, expectations, and goals. As became evident in chapter 6, definitions of reading and writing do not change significantly from home to community to school. Based on this shared understanding of what it means to read and write, each context can comfortably assume some responsibility for fostering the literacy all find necessary. The school does not seem to be the primary vehicle for literacy transmission, however, nor does the focal community. Instead, the home seems to be the dominant educational institution, implicitly and explicitly teaching what the community requires, effecting positive transfer of goals and methods shared with the community and the school, and enhancing their parallelism with its own practices.

An instructive example, the Fisher home performs three literacy-related tasks. First, it introduces the children to almost all forms of reading and writing as natural and necessary aspects of life, not as discrete disconnected exercises. Reading and writing are work-, leisure-, and religion-relevant; books, magazines, and newspapers, notes, lists, and letters all become involved as part of life, not lessons. Reading is silent and shared, individual and choral; writing is public and private, lengthy and abbreviated at home just as they are outside. Only in terms of religion does direct teaching occur, parents believed responsible for the religious and moral instruction of their children (supplemented in both by the community, in the latter by the school). While Eli and Anna help their children, and older siblings aid younger ones in literacy activities beyond their immediate ability (working in Vygotsky's "zone of proximal development" [1962]), literacy transmission at home remains largely informal and implicit.

In addition to introducing literacy, the home provides primary motivation to become literate through modeling and reinforcement. The Fisher children see the necessity of reading and writing for full participation in the family. They see both of their parents reading and writing by necessity and by choice. They see siblings reading and writing for the same reasons, receiving parental praise and places in the family circle as a result. Wanting to be included equally, to be like their older siblings and ultimately like their same-sex parent, these children want to learn to read and write.

The third task of the home, one shared with the community and the school, is to provide literacy experiences at which children can succeed. The Fisher children handled text, pencil, and paper before they could actually recognize or reproduce letters and words, but they believed they were reading and writing because their behavior was treated as such. They read books and newspapers and listened to books and newspapers read aloud with the rest of the family, and they corresponded with Lancaster cousins, too. Eli, Jr., even participated in oral reading experiences, repeating the text as it was recited for him. "Real" reading and writing became a natural next step, one he wanted to take and one everyone expected him to take successfully.

Like the home, the community also teaches through modeling and reinforcement as well as through some direct instruction. With the exception of matters moral and religious, little is explicitly taught there. Instead, the community goes about its business, demonstrating the need for literacy as it does so. By almost never barring children from activities, the Amish insure that little ones observe what older ones do and come to recognize that they, too, must follow suit. As children begin to act appropriately—as they begin to sing with the group, write letters to relatives, or show interest in *"Die Botschaft"*—adults reward them with attention and sometimes with overt praise, making literate behavior even more desirable.

In addition, the community provides literacy experiences for children, simultaneously motivating them to learn. Children attend church almost literally from the time they are born, experiencing the reading, praying, and singing of the service. They attend extended family and community gatherings where they hear oral reading and discussion of texts read, see and hear text-based singing, and see signs others can read, all of which tell them that to participate fully they must read too. The less immediate but no less important larger community indirectly encourages reading as well; *"Die Botschaft"* becomes of considerable interest to children identifying and wanting to affiliate with the community. And of course, it is the community with whom writers want to communicate.

The community's unique contribution to literacy comes through the church as baptism instruction. While the home, the community, and the church read, write, talk about, and practice religion, direct teaching of the Confession of Faith as preparation for church membership is reserved for the ministers in the eighteen summer weeks prior to baptism. But ministerial instruction employs the same methods as some home and school teaching: learners sit quietly and listen while teachers read and explain, sometimes for several hours at a time. Students ask no questions, answering those asked of them with a yes or no. During the days between lessons, students study the Confession text to help them understand previous and future received instruction, but they never deal with it in any other way.

To the school falls responsibility for instruction neither the home nor the community has time for, the teaching of discrete skills believed necessary for successful reading and writing. Penmanship, spelling, and punctuation, decoding through sight and phonics, vocabulary and text manipulation are taught in school through the received instruction method established by home and community. The teacher instructs, asks questions, and gives directions; the children listen, respond in as few words as possible, and do what they're told, asking few questions of their own.

Some of these school-instructed skills, like completing forms and copying, have clear home and community models. But most of these skills, like writing reports, compositions, and workbook exercises, have neither outside applications nor corrolaries. Whether students recognize the presence or absence of such parallels makes little difference, however, because an overriding continuity makes all schoolwork acceptable even if not clearly relevant: home and community sanction school, legitimizing anything that regularly occurs there.

The school's second unique responsibility is providing practice literacy experiences involving both these discrete skills and more socially relevant ones (like oral and silent reading, hymn singing, and letter writing). School is the only place in which Amish children function away from the eyes of most adults, the place in which they prepare to function in the community without being in the community. At school, children practice Amish-appropriate reading and writing just as they practice other Amish-appropriate activities and relationships using Amish-appropriate methods. This does not imply that school is not "real life," for that suggests children are not really living seven hours a day, five days a week, nine months a year. Rather, school is real life but on a smaller, more protected scale, where real successes are significant but real mistakes less damaging.

All of this reveals the remarkable degree of continuity across Amish home, school, and community contexts. Yet no methods, content, or purposes are superimposed on home, school, or community to enhance transfer artificially. Instead, the methods, content, and purposes arise from a culturally unified world view that seems unable to produce or tolerate much that is not "official literacy" (Fiering, 1982).

What might account for this remarkable degree of continuity? Perhaps the nature of Amish philosophy and society itself. The Fisher home, the family's communities, and Meadow Brook School are components of the same basically authoritarian society in which received instruction from a dominant figure is an organizing fact of life. Authority is not sought in this society; its status derives from the awesome responsibility it entails that members believe they must assume. Parents are ultimately responsible for the souls of their children, ministers for the faith of their congregants, teachers for the schooling of their students. Parents, ministers, and teachers take on these roles because God directs them to do so through his commandments (to marry and have children), his blessing (with the ability and desire to teach), or his direct intervention (in minister selection) all for the greater communal good. Those chosen do not feel particularly able to lead or teach; in fact, they have no special skills or preparation. Instead they have faith, trusting God and each other, allowing themselves to be held accountable as they hold others. Therefore, what may appear to be blind obedience in parent-child, minister-congregant, or teacher-pupil relationships is actually a concept of cooperation, of how life is most successfully organized for individual and communal benefit.

This universal trust and accountability produces social organization equally consistent across contexts. As noted earlier, people are grouped according to naturally occurring, patently obvious categories of sex and age, not intelligence, ability, or any other humanly determined distinctions. When there are turns to be taken, everyone shares equally. When the group has a goal, anyone may—and everyone is expected to—help achieve that goal without regard to who volunteers most or least. This relates to literacy and its transmission because it produces the assumption that everyone is or will become literate, according to the community definition of that term. Adults and students have equal opportunity and obligation to participate in literacy events, none allowed to dominate or to demur completely. This does not deny the inclination of some family members, school parents, church members, or students to be more verbal than others, or of some to be less so, but in situations with clear, shared purposes—be they school meetings or history lessons— the most assertive must make way for the most reticent, who also must participate.

Such philosophical and social continuity readily yields purposes, methods, and activities that are equally coherent across contexts, as data presented here reveal. In addition, such continuity produces particularly appropriate individual relationships, too. As noted earlier, though Amish society is undeniably authoritarian, authorities are not considered significantly different from other people, their status accruing from without rather than merited or intentionally acquired. Like parents, relatives, and adult friends, ministers and teachers are community adults from whom children learn. They have the same credentials—the same training, the same beliefs, the same lifestyle—so they deserve the same attention and respect. Unlike public school teacher-student relationships in which mutual trust and accountability are "on the spot accomplishments" (McDermott 1977a, 166), Old Order trust and accountability are assumed before particular students and teachers even meet. This fundamental assumption allows students to call teachers by their given names (as they do all adults except their parents and grandparents), without any hint of disrespect, marking their basic shared humanity instead of their superficial superior-subordinate relationships.

This striking continuity should not be allowed to obscure some coexisting discontinuities, however, for not only do discontinuities exist across Amish contexts, but they suggest that seamless continuity is not necessary for literacy transmission to succeed. While all school activities and methods are shared or sanctioned by the home and the community, for example, the school does not employ all home and community methods. In fact, several seemingly important discontinuities exist in this regard, which highlight literacy considerations of the home not present in the school, instead of the more usual reverse situation. While the home does all the school may expect, the school does not do all the home does with literacy. Yet the children exhibit no difficulty adapting as they move from one context to another.

Perhaps the most important of these discontinuities involves discussion of meaning, an important home and immediate community activity that does not occur in school. The Fisher parents value their children's understanding of what they read, whether or not that understanding is coherent with their own. Though in most instances consensus seems almost automatic, occasional misunderstanding leads to open discussion between parent(s) and child(ren) until agreement is reached. Similarly, the extended family of aunts, uncles, cousins, and grandparents and the immediate community of close friends discuss contrasting views also to agreement, as the data demonstrate. Yet at no time were the children observably uncomfortable with Verna's dictated opinions or observably frustrated by the absence of opportunity to express their own.

Other important discontinuities exist from home to school, as well. At home the Fisher children receive individual attention and are valued as much for their differences as for their similarities while at school their identities remain submerged with others' in their grades. At home they freely express personal preferences and ask questions about anything that interests them while at school they almost never speak unless spoken to and then only on teacher-raised subjects.

These discontinuities highlight an important explanatory dichotomous continuity in the Fishers' lives, between home on one hand, and school and certain public communities on the other. Home is discontinuous with such contexts to the extent that home is the haven of individuals. Places away from home, public places, need not be continuous with home as long as they are continuous with each other. No negative transfer occurs because public and private places can coexist as parallel rather than conflicting situations as long as each domain remains continuous within itself. These children may feel little need to speak up (or act up) in school, therefore, because they have an outlet for such behavior at home. Just as they distinguish what is Caesar's from what is God's, so they distinguish what is appropriately public from what is appropriately private.

The rationale behind what is considered appropriately private and what public may have several bases. Perhaps certain aspects of child guidance are reserved to parents as teaching religion is, the teacher or the larger community not held responsible for such sensitive, potentially difficult kinds of instruction. Perhaps the school and the church are not considered appropriate forums for discussion of doubt or evidence of disagreement, reserved for displays of unity instead. Perhaps schoolchildren are not considered ready to share opinions publicly, requiring practice at home first. Or perhaps the relatively free discussion witnessed among the Fishers and their immediate community is uncommon in the larger community where private and public contexts may be more completely continuous. Whichever the case, this kind of culturally tolerable discontinuity points out the danger of assuming that any children's behavior in school reflects both their church and home experiences as some kind of monolithic "family background," or of assuming that homes must be as much like school as possible for children to become literate. Rather it suggests that the home-school-community relationship may be more complex than many of us imagine—or want—it to be; it suggests that children can become literate in honest, mutually supportive environments even if discontinuities exist and that we need not—or perhaps should not—hold a school-centered view of learning for our children to become effectively literate.

NINE

Literacy and Meaning

Before I became involved with literacy as a theoretical, philosophical, dissertation-research issue, I never thought about "meaning." I never wondered where meaning is found or how meaning is made; in fact, I never even knew those were things to wonder about. To me, the notion of meaning was simple: if I wanted to know what a book meant, I read it. If I didn't understand the meaning on first reading, I read it again. If I continued to miss the meaning on second reading, I knew I was not smart enough to understand that text, so I either asked someone smarter to explain what it meant or I gave up, leaving the meaning in that book for someone else to find. This process served me well all through school, for my teachers were usually both willing and able to tell me what books meant. Especially my English teachers. They always knew.

Then, when I became an English teacher, somehow I always seemed to know what books (and poems and stories and plays and essays) meant, too. I could tell my students when they had the right meaning and when their interpretations were wrong, and I could tell them what to think if they didn't know. If anyone asked me how I knew what a particular text meant—how I figured out a certain verse or passage—I pointed to the words themselves. There was the meaning, I said, in that word, that line, available to anyone who knew how to read. It never occurred to me that I was reading in one particular way, reading as my teachers had read. It never occurred to me that the academic community in which I grew up had taught me what meanings to ascribe to words and what views to take of different kinds of writers and different kinds of texts; so it also never occurred to me that there might be other meanings or other views. In other words, that I was putting the meaning in through what I brought to a text, not taking the meaning out only from what I found there, never crossed my mind. Instead, I believed in and perpetuated the myth that a single meaning is bound in every text and that a single way exists to discover and understand the meaning hidden there.

I no longer subscribe to that myth, however, for I no longer understand reading, writing, and meaning that way. My experiences with the Fishers and subsequently those in my own classroom revealed very different truths about the ways people make sense of text, and those revelations changed my perspective and my teaching significantly. How those changes affected my classroom practices is explored in the next chapter; here I want to introduce the issue of meaning for readers like me who never considered it an issue before, and point out what Amish reading, writing, and meaning suggest about the ways we all make sense of text. Though this may seem a theoretical or philosophical concern of limited intellectual interest and one with little direct bearing on how we teach reading and writing or how we may begin to solve the literacy-related problems confronting us every day, I believe the Fishers show us that considerably more is at stake.

First, I must admit that though I now view meaning making differently, the myth of text-bound meaning to which many people subscribe still seems eminently logical. The assumption that meaning resides in text still seems a plausible belief: dictionary definitions suggest that words have meanings apart from the people who use them, and common usage suggests that words have common meanings, for in no other apparent way could different people find the same meaning in the same text. If words did not have such inherent denotative meanings, it seems, English, or any other language, would create its own monolingual Tower of Babel.

Even were this not true, however (and multiple interpretations of Shakespeare, bureaucratic communications, and daily misunderstandings suggest it may not be), social reasons exist for assuming and promoting the myth of meaning in text. Any individual or group believing—or wanting to believe—that the world is not contingent, that there are overriding, universal absolutes, needs the assumption of a stable, objective, accessible source of evidence supporting their beliefs. Similarly, any group seeking unswerving unity and obedience among its members needs a focus consistent across time and individuals to serve as both bellwether and anchor. In literate societies, text can serve all these purposes, for as Louise Rosenblatt points out, to people in a shared context "the text as 'control' or 'norm' usually seems . . . paramount . . . [as they] take for granted their commonly held assumptions" (1978, 129). So it is not surprising to expect an assumption of text-bound meaning among mainstream Americans or among the Amish.

And I did find such an assumption operating in the Amish community in return for the stability and constancy, encouragement and reassurance it offers in this world of discomfiting flux and uncertainty. Yet while the Amish believe in most circumstances that meaning resides in the text, they clearly demonstrate the fact that meaning is culturally shaped by individuals and the community instead. And, perhaps surprisingly, many Amish readers and writers themselves realize this fact when it serves their personal and communal purposes to do so.

The assumption of text-bound meaning serves its most significant purpose for Amish individuals and communities in the most significant realm of Amish life—religion. The Amish church, society, and concomitant worldview all stem from the perception and acceptance of the Bible as the work of God. Though recognized as physically written by men, both Old and New Testaments bear His imprint, reified as the Word. Given this premise, biblical meaning must be extracted from the text, not imputed to it, for the Word is complete unto itself and as such never changes. The Bible's purpose in this context is didactic; the Amish reader's goal is to learn what the Word has to teach and to be identified as one of the instructed.

The displacement of this text-bound meaning approach from religious to secular reading happens perhaps automatically when religious faith directs secular activity as it does among the Amish. Then all other reading is modeled on the biblical, with lesser texts and authors similarly reified to serve similar didactic purposes for similarly identifying readers. Pervasive across home and community contexts, this perspective is conscientiously and institutionally promoted each time the Amish establish a school.

At Meadow Brook, for example, the assumption of text-bound meaning transfers to all kinds of reading and serves several important communitywide functions: it reinforces the faith of the church; it promotes the kind of consistent thinking, subordinate self-images, and supportive social relationships necessary to maintain the faithful community; and it prevents, forestalls, or at least blunts exposure to antithetical skills that could endanger belief.

Of course, this relationship to biblical text and this displacement of the biblical approach to meaning are not uniquely Amish. According to Zinsser (n.d.), Fundamentalist Christian churches reify texts and find meaning in similar ways for similar reasons. My own experience suggests the same holds true for many nonreligious communities, as well. Though its church and creed are secular, the faithful academic community, for example, perpetuates itself by requiring that doctrine be accepted as given and the status quo maintained. Academics, therefore, often reify texts and turn meaning into dogma to promote the consistent thinking (and subordinate student self-images) that strengthen their positions within the community and strengthen the community against outside influences.

This sense of textuality seems most easily promulgated, however, in group situations like church and school. Away from any human authoritarian presence with only the inert authority of the text, problems arise as individual readers are more likely to question what they read or at least to find meaning directed but not necessarily specified by any authority other than themselves. It is in such situations that Amish readers seem to sense that meaning is at least partially in the individual or the community and not solely in the text. When Anna or her sisters read books, for example, each knows that the meaning she derives may differ from other readers', so they frequently discuss what they've read with each other to be sure they understood it "correctly." Similarly, when Sarah reads *True Confessions*, she knows her understanding may be unique, so she, too, wants discussion. In other words, perhaps without conscious reflection, these readers seem to accept the fact that at times meaning is in themselves, not in their books.

Simultaneously, however, these readers are accepting the fact that meaning resides in the community as well. When they discuss individual interpretations, they do so to obtain consensus, to reach a shared understanding consistent with community beliefs. The sisters want each other's support for their individual interpretations. Sarah wants to know that she is reading as her mother would, as "we" would. And even before they read a particular text, these individuals know there is a way they should read. Anna, for example, can articulate how "we read" the Bible and tacitly knows how certain books should be understood, whether actually read or actively avoided.

This "we" of comprehension is so important and so pervasive that its consistent application is not surprising but can be problematic for individuals whose understanding differs significantly from that of the group. When I was banned from Meadow Brook, Anna agonized over her role in the situation. Her understanding of me, my work, and my purposes conflicted with that of the school community, yet she understood their interpretation too. She knew how she read the situation and the implications of my proposed text, but she also knew why the others read them as they did. In the end, Anna had to chose between her own and her community's meanings, and community meaning prevailed as Anna consciously chose it.

Deciding where meaning lies or which of multiple interpretations to accept is not always easy, as Anna's experience illustrates, and such decisions are not always consciously made. In the course of my research, I identified four factors that implicitly seem to determine the relationships among reader, writer, and text as well as the degree to which they are aware or unaware of their own interpretive processes. Sometimes operating simultaneously and sometimes independently, these factors that help determine where meaning should be imputed are (1) the nature of the text; (2) the reader's perception of the writer; (3) the reader's purpose for reading; and (4) the reader's perception of himself or herself in terms of the text and the writer.

With their special significance in Amish life, religious texts stand in special relationship to the reader. Amish faith is rooted in what they perceive as the written word of God, and as Anna explained, that word is not to be challenged or questioned, only received and accepted. Handed down in writing through the generations, read, recited, sung, and memorized in English and in German, biblical text is never debated; conflicting English and German translations or King James and Living Bible versions are assimilated instead. Interpreted publicly by ministerial sermons and baptismal instruction, interpreted privately by parents and elder relatives whose teaching remains coherent with that of the church, biblical texts are truisms that may be applied or explained but never questioned or argued. To avoid conflicting or even variant readings, the Bible is neither taught nor discussed in school, only memorized and recited. The text is sacred; the writer, almighty; and the reader, worshipful.

While nothing shares this sacred nature of the Bible or receives the same special literal and figurative handling, the *Ausbund* is another authoritative religious text believed, sung, and memorized without question. Instead of being the Word of God, the *Ausbund* is the words of early Amish martyrs and church fathers whose trials and faith stand as models for the community today. Instead of being in only ministerial hands during services, the *Ausbund* is in everyone's hands, offering opportunities for more direct, personal experience and identification. Again the text is not open to interpretation, but again the community sees no reason to interpret, not because the writers' power extends beyond human comprehension but because the writers' faith and experiences seem self-evidently instructive. This text is religion in action; these writers, exemplars; and these readers, disciples.

Martyrs Mirror, "compiled from various authentic chronicles, memorials, and testimonies" (front dust cover) including stories of songs, letters, prayers, and confessions, is another example of a religion-in-the-world text read as authoritative. Essentially a history book, the *Mirror*'s editor, translator, and several publishers wrote lengthy prefaces and introductions to assert the book's truthfulness and thereby win the reader's trust. If Anna is any example, however, Amish readers may trust without such scholarly reasons, accepting the content on faith, and never reading how the translator dealt with problems of obsolete language, "letters [originally] written by comparatively illiterate persons" (p. 4), or writers' references to different versions of the Bible or how the editor found the original accounts of "faithful and authentic authors" (p. 15). Not reading introductions may also mean not reading instructions on how to read the text ("Read it again and again, and with the same attention and emotion with which we have written and rewritten it" [p. 8]) or explanations of why to read it (as "incentives . . . to live a more consecrated life . . . and help us to appreciate more highly the privileges with which God has blessed us above our forefathers" [p. 2]). Knowing how and why to read the *Martyrs Mirror* comes "naturally" to those knowing how and why to read the *Ausbund*; not straying from the faith and example of their forefathers is implicit in Amish life, and no text need tell them that.

The *Ausbund* and the *Martyrs Mirror* share one remaining authoritative characteristic. Besides the significance of their content, both books were written during and immediately after the early struggle for Amish survival by those who had participated in or witnessed it. The earliest *Ausbund* hymns were composed in the fifteenth century; the original edition of the *Mirror* was published in 1660. Texts of both the hymns and the *Mirror* came to America with the first wave of European immigrants. This contemporaneous writing combined with the tradition of faithful use gives both texts special authenticity and power. It seems, therefore, that Amish religious texts have long histories, unparalleled origins, and singular authors. Reading such texts must then edify and strengthen the faith of readers who see themselves as unworthy disciples, needing help in their daily struggle for right living.

Though certainly not in the same category as the Bible, the *Ausbund* and the *Mirror*, some secular texts, reference books, and textbooks are taken at face value also, writer accuracy or motive never questioned, and this acceptance, too, seems more a function of the four factors listed earlier than of any inability to read another way. The Amish seem to assume, as do most people, that reference books are repositories of secular truth published on the presumption of their accuracy. Their writers are assumed to be trustworthy people doing their best to provide specific information for readers who need their assistance. Such texts are perceived as truthful, their writers as knowledgeable, and their readers as needing that knowledge. So reference books have their place and serve their purpose but represent no transcendent truth.

A similar belief seems to accompany the reading of most fiction and nonfiction narratives and may account for their acceptance as well. With narratives, acceptance seems based on the assumption that the narrators are people who have experiences and/or religious perspectives similar to those of the reader and who write to share what they think and do. These writers, too, are assumed to tell the truth, for that is their perceived purpose. The Amish read these books for reasons similar to those discussed earlier, to experience vicariously events that have morally edifying implications. They easily identify with the narrators, seeing themselves as fellow travelers, with disparate writing abilities. Again, acceptance of text is based not on the fact of text alone, but on assumptions about the people behind the texts, the reasons for reading the texts, and the reader's relationship to the texts and the writers.

Most open to question and debate among the Amish is journalistic text, a fact that seems related to the four factors directing acceptance in most other instances. Newspaper writers are fallible human beings whatever their outlet. English people who write for the *Lancaster Intelligencer* may be extensively educated and have great worldly knowledge, but they are not significantly different from Old Order *"Die Botschaft"* scribes, who also write for a newspaper and who also make mistakes. Reading any newspaper may be economically helpful and personally desirable, but it is neither necessary nor spiritually edifying for the reader in the way other texts may be. Newspaper readers are little different from newspaper writers; in fact, their roles are often interchangeable. This makes "journalists" seem more accessible and makes what they write not less truthful but more equivocal and open to question.

What appears to be a totally text-bound sense of meaning, therefore, is actually not a monolithic perspective at all but one modified through individual and community use according to individual and community perceptions and purposes. And just as this modification affects the understanding of texts read, so it affects the understanding of texts written. When a writer writes, the meaning is in the writer before it is in the text, a belief Anna and other *Botschaft* scribes share. Though writers may do all they can to put meaning into their texts, the possibility of being misread always exists. Who is responsible for such misreading? According to most, the writers themselves are responsible, for Amish writers say that it is not the text but they who are misunderstood. And because *"Die Botschaft"* or personal letter readers have a heightened sense of who wrote what they read, they too are more apt to blame the writer for any misunderstanding than the text or themselves.

On the other hand, writers who do not accept responsibility for misunderstanding in this context blame their readers instead, expecting them to bring sufficient applicable, community-based knowledge to any such text they read. *"Die Botschaft"* readers seem willing to accept this responsibility; they frequently read through writer errors and omissions, using what knowledge they have to make communally acceptable sense from idiosyncratic text, a feat I saw performed repeatedly by my Amish friends as they understood text I could not. So in the most immediately personal reader-writer contexts, text is not necessarily authoritative; meaning may lie elsewhere—notably in the community—and the text may be only its imperfect vehicle, a reality acceptable because of the readers' perceptions and purposes.

From all this, it seems that Amish readers and writers choose where meaning resides, their choices not always conscious but usually contingent on the particular context and purpose of each textual encounter and rooted in personal belief. From a broader cultural perspective, this choice like all others the Amish make depends on what serves the community best. If the community is best served by an authoritative text, that is where individuals willingly posit meaning. If the community is best served by vesting power in the reader or writer, readers or writers become authoritative figures. No contradictions exist here, for individual belief and community doctrine coincide, the latter serving as ultimate source and guide for the former. Conflicts arise only when an individual moves outside prescribed understandings and then, as Anna painfully demonstrated, the choice is not for or against an interpretation but for or against the community, a choice that is no choice for the Amish faithful.

Several theorists offer reasons why the Amish—or any readers—can posit meaning in the text and believe they are reading literally even when meaning is cultural rather than textual and even when they can, in other circumstances, be aware of text's tentative nature and their own cultural orientation.

As noted earlier, shared culture means shared assumptions which often operate beyond individual awareness. (In the case of the Amish these assumptions derive from their religious faith and its concomitant worldview. They seem to assume (1) that most texts are true, (2) that most writers are well informed and well intentioned, and (3) that moral lessons are textually available for readers willing to recognize them.) When members of the same culture discuss a text in their particular framework, therefore, "they bring a sufficiently similar experience to the text to be able to arrive at fairly homogeneous readings" (Rosenblatt 1978, 128), which they attribute to the text in question rather than to themselves or their implicit cultural understanding.

Stanley Fish explains this phenomenon through his notion of interpretive communities, an idea originally posited to describe literary critics but applicable to any group of readers.

> Interpretive communities are made up of those who share interpretive strategies not for reading (in the conventional sense) but for writing texts, for constituting their properties and assigning their intentions. In other words, these strategies exist prior to the act of reading and therefore determine the shape of what is read rather than . . . the other way around. (1980a, 182)

Members of any interpretive community are not necessarily aware of their interpretive process, however, both because interpretive ability "is constitutive of being human" (Fish 1980a, 183) and because their interpretive process is so much a part of their thinking process. Yet they can be more aware of it some times than others. "The choice is never between objectivity and interpretation but between an interpretation that is unacknowledged as such and an interpretation that is at least aware of itself" (Fish 1980a, 179). When the Amish believe they are being objective—that is, when they believe meaning is in the text—they are unaware of any interpretive process though, in fact, they are reading no differently than they do when they discuss individually variant meanings. In other words, attribution of meaning is actually a matter of cultural and circumstantial awareness, not a matter of text itself.

The idea of an interpretive community that determines how an individual reads (and writes) applies not only to obvious religious or cultural groups like the Amish but to any group of people with a shared perspective or set of beliefs whether created by occupation, geography, politics, or some other commonality. Traditionally trained mainstream schoolteachers, for example, represent an interpretive community and one with perhaps less awareness of its own existence and effect than the Amish. While in some situations the Amish recognize that they read and write as Amishmen even though they know that other equally viable ways exist, I remember few teachers of mine acknowledging that there is more than one way to read and write properly, and until recently I rarely did either. For the most part, they and I seemed to believe that the way our high school teachers, college professors, and teacher educators—and possibly our parents and friends as well—read words (and worlds; Friere 1983) was the right and only way to read them.

In other words, instead of encountering and appreciating different worldviews as I went through school, I learned to recognize the "best" one. I learned from art teachers that the sky is best seen as blue, the grass as green. I learned from social studies teachers that the American revolutionaries are best seen as patriots, George Washington as a hero, and the redcoats as villains. And I learned from science teachers that theirs are the most significant subjects, the only courses with "hard" facts, the only disciplines with objective methods.

Then, too, I learned from language arts and English teachers that sentence fragments, slang, and first-person pronouns are best seen as errors, that Eustacia Vye (or Hester Prynne or Lady Macbeth or Daisy Buchanan) is best seen as a villain, and that "To be or not to be" is best interpreted as a statement about suicide. Not only did I learn from those teachers; until recently, I taught as they did, too.

In effect, many of my colleagues and I, insisted, as did many of our predecessors, that our way of reading and understanding makes people literate while other ways clearly mark them otherwise. The problem was not that we believed such things; the problem was that we believed ours were the only legitimate beliefs. We were culture bound, which may be acceptable, but we were also culture blind, which is not. While we recognized the existence of other cultures as marked by their food, clothing, housing, and habits, and we granted other people their philosophies, their gods, and their rituals, we saw literacy as a monolithic universal. Cultures were oral or literate. People were illiterate or not. Especially within our own country, we brooked no subcultural excuses.

In recent years, however, as concern about American illiteracy grew, researchers began looking more closely at "high-risk" groups and communities. Urban blacks, rural whites, and burgeoning immigrant populations all came under closer mainstream scrutiny. Some of these researchers "discovered" exactly the kinds of cognitive and social deficiencies they expected to find among these culturally different people; others, willing to abandon the expectations of their own interpretive communities, allowed themselves to ask what might be there and began to understand the roles and kinds of literacy existing in those groups. These researchers found different definitions of literacy operating in different communities and saw different interpretive communities finding meaning in the world and in the word in different ways.

So what are the lessons to be learned from this notion of multiple worldviews and multiple interpretive communities making meaning in multiple ways? First is the lesson of consciousness-raising. Before mainstream teachers can effectively teach others, we must all learn what many of our students already know—that there are different literacies and different interpretive communities in this country, that each has a particular context in which it operates, and that our academic variety is only one of many. While recognizing others' reading and writing as different from our own is easy, recognizing our own for what it is seems much harder. We have a well-established, well-entrenched tradition that tells us how to read and write—one that reifies Shakespeare and the five-paragraph essay—and our kinds of reading and writing serve personal, social, and cultural purposes for us just as the Amish varieties do for them. Unlike the Amish, however, we have decided our varieties are not only advantageous but superior. Suddenly seeing our literacy as limited, contingent, and optional, therefore, cannot help but upset the comfortable, somewhat smug equilibrium we now enjoy. What we need to realize is that such a disturbance would not be fatal and would not destroy the networks and institutions to which we are related and on which we depend. Instead, seeing our literacy as one of many legitimate varieties would broaden our perspective; it would create more curricular and pedagogical options than are traditionally available and would thereby strengthen, not weaken, our academic communities and institutions.

This does not apply only to those who teach in urban or inner-city neighborhoods, however, for interpretive communities are not always racially, religiously, or geographically identifiable. Those of us working in apparently homogeneous mainstream schools, where students and faculty are predominantly white, middle-class, Christian Americans, need to recognize the variety of interpretive communities existing even in these places. How a thirty-year-old unmarried, feminist female teacher reads *The Scarlet Letter*, for example, may well differ from how her fifty-five-year-old married male colleague understands it. And how the sixteen-year-old son of divorced parents living with his working mother reads that book may differ from both of those teachers and from how his classmate, the daughter of a still-married Baptist minister and his homemaker wife, reads the same text.

Which of these readers is right about what that book means? Should we suspend all of their understandings and go to the literary critics or perhaps to the author himself? Even if Hawthorne had left an annotated explanatory version of his novel for us to use, his nineteenth-century understanding and intentions might seem less right for these twentieth-century readers than any of their own. For no matter how personal and idiosyncratic a reader's understanding, it is not necessarily more personal or more idiosyncratic than the critics' or the writer's, nor necessarily less valid either.

Our job as teachers, then, is not to decide what things should mean to our students but to help them deepen and strengthen their individual readings of texts and, at the same time, to show them that other equally valid readings exist. Conflicting interpretations neither refute nor negate each other; rather they send readers back to reread, rethink, and re-evaluate, to decide that they were even more right than they first thought or to modify their original understanding as they encounter and assimilate new perspectives and ideas.

The second lesson multiple realities teach is that we must recognize not everyone needs or wants to enter academe or academically oriented worlds, so not everyone needs to read and write as we do. While it was relatively easy for me to grant the Fishers their own literacy because of the large, successful, supportive community to which they belong, it is more difficult to grant the same right to my students whose circumstances and futures seem much less secure. But for me to assume that the ability to parse sentences, paraphrase sonnets, or produce essays provides some lifetime insurance would be worse than misguided; it would be counterproductive cultural bias and would cause more problems than it would solve. Students have important choices to make, and sometimes those choices involve choosing between school and family, teachers and friends. These choices are both life-threatening and life-affirming; they will affect students' present lives and their futures. We must allow them and their families to make those choices for themselves.

But we can help them choose, and that is the third lesson to be learned from all this. Teachers have an obligation to be honest with their students. Once we recognize academic literacy for what it is and acknowledge what it can and cannot do, we should tell those truths in the classroom. We should admit to our students that there is no inherent value in knowing grammar, reading literature, or writing essays, but there is personal, economic, and social value instead. Our students already understand that certain language skills make them feel good about themselves and give them access to certain social groups. The ability to write and perform a "rap," to write notes to each other in class, to decorate their notebooks and lockers, or to read *Thrasher, Car and Driver, Seventeen,* or *Ebony* marks them as literate in special, socially acceptable ways. We can point out that academic literacy may yield similar benefits. If they want to go to college, join the armed services, or enter certain occupations or professions, they must be able to read and write as people in those contexts do. If they do not want access to those domains, however, they do not need those kinds of literacies. Any kind of literacy empowers and identifies; our students and their families must decide for themselves what kinds of power they want and with whom they want to identify. They must recognize and accept the fact that they have choices and options and, at the same time, so must we.

As the Amish know and the rest of us must learn, meaning is in the minds of the beholders, and minds exist not in social or cultural vacuums but in interpretive communities. As a result, meaning becomes something cued by texts but created collaboratively by people. This suggests, particularly in a pluralistic culture like ours, that monolithic text-bound meaning is a myth. And like most myths, this one solves problems and fulfills wishes for those who choose to believe it but, at the same time, it obscures a reality more complex and problematic but much richer and more interesting, as well.

T E N

Ethnography on Monday Morning

To this point I've written primarily as a researcher, sharing my data and my findings, focusing on my informants and what they revealed about literacy in their lives. Now I'd like to change perspectives and write as the teacher I was before and have been since my research experience. I want to focus on what my research means to someone who spends five days a week, 180 days a year, dealing with literacy in a public school classroom, someone whose biggest recurring Sunday evening problem is what to do on Monday morning, and, curiously, someone who had no use for research or researchers until very recently.

For most of my teaching career, I thought research meant numbers—statistics and percentages, means and medians, sample sizes and regression analyses. Educational researchers seemed concerned only with nameless, faceless, disembodied composites that could be added, subtracted, divided, and multiplied to suit their preconceived purposes. None of the traditional school research I read seemed willing to admit that any school was more than "a school," any student other than typical, any teacher not just "the teacher." Yet I had never met a generic student, and I certainly did not consider myself a generic teacher, which made traditional quantitative research as insulting to me as it was irrelevant to my concerns.

Then I went back to graduate school and discovered something called qualitative research in the form of ethnography. I began reading about teachers, parents, and students in Pennsylvania and Hawaii, the Carolinas and Alaska, about situations with real teachers and real students in real classrooms facing real problems. Reading a well-written ethnography was like reading biography or recent historical fiction, or like watching a good dramatic film. It was fascinating, engrossing, and believable; it made me happy, sad, and angry; I could understand and

I could empathize. Of course, I could also put down the text and say "That's really interesting!" without making the slightest connection between "that" and my own situation.

In addition to ethnographies about schools, I read ethnographies about families, homes, and communities, about babies, toddlers, and preschoolers. These, too, were enthralling, as I shared meals with urban Italian families, bedtimes with Piedmont black families, and bureaucratic encounters with Asian refugees. I watched the development of language in one-year-old twins, bilingual two- and three-year-olds, and precocious nursery schoolers. Unlike the nameless, faceless populations of traditional research, these were living, thinking, feeling people, and I read everything I found about this ever-changing cast of characters. But no matter how much I read, I could still walk away without connecting these varied individuals and experiences to my own predominantly white, predominantly middle-class, small-town secondary school students. Uniqueness was the hallmark of this kind of research; its informants were as different as we were, and though that made them real, it didn't make them relevant. Ethnographic researchers would not generalize from their data, and for a long time, neither would I.

Then I became a fledgling ethnographer and entered the Old Order world and Meadow Brook School. I sat in that classroom feeling as though I had been transported to Laura Ingalls Wilder's Walnut Grove. The rows of wood and metal desk-and-chair combinations, the teacher's desk on its raised platform up front, the students peering at each other from under lowered eyes, the sounds of memorized recitation and choral singing, the whispered requests to go to the outhouse—surely this was a living anachronism, and certainly I was lucky to see something so different from my own professional situation.

But wait. If Meadow Brook were so different, why did it sometimes seem so familiar? Why did my own seating charts, showing the big desk facing the parallel rows of smaller ones, come to mind as I sat there? Why could I see my own students shooting looks at each other across the room? Why could I hear choral voices droning the Pledge of Allegiance and hear individual ones quietly asking to use the "lav pass"? And what about the aspects of Meadow Brook reminiscent of not only my teaching days but my own elementary education in the 1950s and my son's in the 1970s—the student artwork on the walls; the group configurations for reading lessons; the reports on the geography, climate, and major products of foreign countries; the student monitors in charge of different classroom duties? And why could Verna and I talk so easily about pop quizzes, unit tests, and report cards? Something strange was happening; I was making connections where I had assumed none existed.

And while those connections took a long time to develop, their power steadily increased. By the time I left Meadow Brook, those connections led me to question my long-held, subconsciously cherished notions of education and schooling, teaching and learning. I became aware of myself and my students in new and sometimes disconcerting ways. In other words, by doing ethnographic research, I had answered my own "So what?" response to other similar researchers. So what? So plenty.

While the initial fascination of looking at Meadow Brook and the Old Orders lay simply in their singularity, the long-term value of such research lay in how looking away from my own world toward Meadow Brook enabled me to see my own school and culture more clearly when I looked back. At first, I was overwhelmed by Meadow Brook's individual character, and I didn't look back too often. The Old Orders enthralled me, and since I knew how different Amish society was from my own, I dismissed apparent similarities as coincidental vestiges of our shared one-room-schoolhouse heritage. Over time, however, my focus exchanged background for foreground—like a clever figure-ground picture in a basic psychology textbook—and the differences receded, allowing the similarities to emerge and with them, their deeper shared roots. I discovered that I had been misled initially by the Old Order clothes and curricula; my new inverted focus revealed that classroom management and pedagogy so decked out were really little different from those in modern dress at my school. Neither the subjects in the curriculum, the contents of the basal readers, nor the topics of the reports were the core of education at Meadow Brook; those were the trappings, the vehicles for transmission of what really mattered—the schooling Meadow Brook children received. And it was only the trappings of Meadow Brook that were significantly different from those of my own school; I found the schooling strikingly the same.

As I came to realize that this very different culture with very different ideas about education (and life in general) schooled its children in ways similar to my own, I came to realize that my research had raised some important questions for me to answer, not just as a researcher but as a teacher. How could such different societies be equally well served by such similar schooling? How could we use the same means to achieve such supposedly different ends? How could I do what Verna did and consider my job well done?

Both Meadow Brook and my school offered teacher-dominated, arbitrarily organized educations. Both Meadow Brook and my school devoted most classroom time to direct instruction and isolated seat work, and both prided themselves on atmosphere conducive to learning—as close to silent as possible. Both Meadow Brook and my school conducted traditional initiation-response or initiation-response-evaluation based lessons, and both Meadow Brook and my school "objectively" tested and quizzed at regular intervals. If this kind of schooling were congruent with Old Order philosophy and practice, producing people who thought, believed, and behaved in Old Order–appropriate ways, how could it be congruent with more mainstream society? If this worked well for the Amish, in other words, how could it work well for us?

To answer these questions I had to reconsider education and schooling in light of the fundamental differences between Old Order society and my own. A single authoritative voice dominates Old Order life out-side school as well as in. For the Amish, authority and responsibility come from God, and all must heed His voice—embodied in His word, interpreted by His ministers and by parents, teachers, and tradition. In all realms of Amish life, such impersonal authority decides what is right and what is wrong, what is possible and what is not. It determines how people should relate to all creatures, creations, and events of this world. Men and women, boys and girls all have recognized places in society; they know what they must do and how it must be done; they know to what they must attend and what they must avoid. The younger watch the older who learn from their elders too. Authority is never sought, responsibility always assumed. The only acknowledged differences among people are the obvious distinctions of sex and age, and it is these distinctions and beliefs that operate inside school as well as outside.

But is Old Order life the kind for which my students prepare in school? Will they enter a world governed by a single unquestioned authority with a single moral and ethical code for measuring all behavior? Will they enter a world with places already prepared for them? Will they be told how to take those places, what to do and how to do it? Will all their decisions be made implicitly as much by their society as by them-selves?

To some degree, that may have been the case for public school students in the late nineteenth and early twentieth centuries in this country. Then public morality may have been more consistent and in-dividual choices more limited. Then schools trained the thousands of assembly-line workers American industry demanded, and those students may have been destined for factories in which an impersonal boss gave unquestioned orders and passive workers stood in their places perform-ing mindless isolated operations repeatedly for ten, twelve, or fourteen hours a day. Then, too, public schools trained the thousands of immi-grants who came to this country wanting only to be assimilated, Amer-icanized. Those students wanted only to be told what to do, how to act and how to speak like their new compatriots. They wanted to accept and be accepted; they wanted to blend in, not stand out.

Obviously, however, this is not the student body we face today nor is this the kind of world they confront. We no longer have the kind of industrial growth that automatically accommodates as many workers as the schools produce, nor do we have the kind of silent subordinate worker population those industries desired. We also no longer have even a superficially monolithic morality or culture. I don't have to enumerate the social changes or describe the social conditions of the late twentieth century to say that ours is a different world not only from that of the Amish, but from that of our parents as well.

Yet while I always recognized the relationship between these social changes and curriculum, until recently I saw no connection between such changes and schooling, nor, it seems, did most of my colleagues.

In fact, it seems to me now that few of us were even aware of schooling as a separate, distinct, potentially variable aspect of education. Curriculum could be changed and so, to some extent, could pedagogy, but school was school; as it had been for us, so it would be for our children.

It was not surprising, therefore, that when the Pennsylvania Department of Education established its "Ten Goals of Quality Education," we viewed them with the same jaundiced eye cast on any such pronouncement from on high. Helping all children develop positive self-concepts, maintain emotional well-being, discover their creativity, and "prepare for a world of rapid change and unforeseeable demands" (Seiverling 1976, 4) sounded wonderful, but to us it also sounded like the kind of ivory-tower thinking practiced by bureaucrats and philosophers who know nothing about the realities of school. Real schools are not about self-images, creativity and the unknown; they are about English, math, social studies, and science. Real schools are not about adapting to change; they are about maintaining the status quo, about keeping things from getting worse. Only the third and the ninth of the ten Pennsylvania goals seemed possible in real schools—"Helping every child acquire to the fullest possible extent, mastery of the basic skills in the use of words and numbers" and "Helping every child to understand and appreciate as much as possible of human achievement in the natural sciences, the social sciences and the humanities and the arts" (p. 4).

Not until after I left Meadow Brook did I realize that while the state's goals may seem idealistic, the problem lay not in the goals' ideals but in educators' perception and construction of reality. What the state had done was formulate goals theoretically appropriate to the society in which we live and the principles we espouse. They are goals that recognize the supposed differences between public school contexts and Old Order contexts and that could direct public schooling, yet they do not. Looking at the reality of our schools in the light of Meadow Brook, I realized that we are more likely to achieve Old Order goals than we are to achieve our own.

As articulated in the *Standards of the Old Order Amish and Old Order Mennonite Parochial and Vocational Schools of Penna.*, the few shared objectives we have are curricular. The Old Orders agree with the state about the need for certain academic subjects, mandating reading, writing, spelling, English, and math, and suggest that schools teach geography, history, health and safety rules, German, and vocal music, paralleling state curricular suggestions except for the natural and social sciences. Yet neither Pennsylvania's "Goals" nor Amish *Standards* focus primarily on curricula. Pennsylvania's public school goals emphasize the need for all children to develop their individual potential, to achieve individual physical and psychological well-being, and to find their individual niches in society; Pennsylvania's Old Order school goals focus on making every child an assimilated member of the larger social group.

Old Order children have no choices to make from the school's perspective.

The goal of the school shall be to prepare the child for the Amish or Mennonite way of living and the responsibilities of adulthood. In short, these standards are designed in an effort to establish the foundations of useful, God-fearing, and law-abiding citizens. (Old Order Book Society 1973, 5–6)

While these educators do recognize the need for school to be a place "where the child's God-given talents are encouraged to increase, and his or her intelligence developed" (p. 3), they also see school as

a place where the child will become fully aware of the essential underlaying concept of peace on earth good will toward men and a place where they are instructed, trained, and educated to earn an honest living and lead a christian life. (p. 3)

In other words, these schools teach children what to think and one way to think, the way they believe God intended.

Children are an heritage of the Lord, and the same Lord who gave us the children expects us to "train them in the way that they should go" and to bring them up in the "nurture and admonitian of the Lord." So that they may grow up to be a light to the world, a salt of the earth, and bring glory to God's kingdom. Amen. (p. 3)

Removing the specifically Christian components from these Old Order goals would leave passivity, conformity, and acceptance—community-oriented homogeneity—as the single goal of education, preparing children to enter a single preselected world, able to use their individual abilities in service of that world, believing good will toward men and a selfless existence are the greatest and only good. Going one step further and removing all particular philosophy from these goals would still call for passivity, conformity, and acceptance, this time creating hollow, unfocused homogeneity, the kind we seem best at producing in our current public schools. I'm not suggesting that we put religion or even a particular philosophy back into our schools or that we program our children in a certain positive way. Rather, I'm suggesting that we stop programming our children as a group to believe in anything or nothing, that we change our methods of schooling to conform not with Old Order goals of social universality but with our own goals of informed individuality, offering students both choices and the decision-making skills to choose effectively among them.

Of course, all of this highlights an interesting paradox: how can we have goals and not work toward them? Or, more frustratingly, how can we have goals and flagrantly ignore them, working toward opposite ends? One reason, as I've already suggested, is that too many of us do not realize what it is we are actually doing; too many do not see the distinctions between education and schooling or the possibility of addressing schooling as other than a preordained, unchangeable order. Another, more insidious reason—one easier to see but harder to admit—may be that when confronted by the constant, seemingly uncontrollable changes in the world, many of us yearn for something familiar and stable that we can manage and control. We yearn for the "good old days," when men were men and women were women, when children were to be seen but not heard, when minorities knew their places, and when everyone knew the hero by his white hat and the villain by his black one (all conditions that still obtain for the Amish). We know we can't bring back those days; we can't wish away the civil rights and women's movements, homogenize our pluralistic society, or hide from the questions of morality and ethics our technology has wrought. So we look for a place where we can both vent our frustrations and play out our fantasies, and what do we find? The schools.

Low-slung, glass-walled, sprawling structures. Multistoried, brick, graffiti-covered buildings. Students driving up in their own cars and trucks. Students strolling in to the sounds of "boxes" and Walkmen. Males wearing earrings; females wearing high-top sneakers; males and females with identical haircuts—sometimes you can't even tell them apart! It must be the modern methods, people say. It must be the modern curriculum. Counseling? What was wrong with paddling and detention hall? New math? What was wrong with old math? Computers? All we needed was pencils. "Back to the basics!" they order at their local school-board meetings and in letters to the editor of their local paper. What these people do not seem to realize, however, is how "basic" current schooling still is, how close it comes to their romantic notions of what school should be like regardless of how it is dressed. And that may be why our methods of schooling have gone unchanged and, for the most part, unchallenged; they come closer than anything else to the kind of schools we once had and claim to still want.

When I returned to my own classroom from Meadow Brook, a combination of reformer's zeal and middle-aged caution demanded significant changes made quietly and slowly. In my heart, I wanted to change my whole school, not to mention my school district—to raise everyone's consciousness and usher in the educational millennium—but I knew the fate awaiting prophets in their own lands and the scorn awaiting researchers in schools, so I kept my vision to myself and set about revolutionizing my own classroom world first. I had no clearly conceived or articulated plan; I only knew that if I wanted to be able to justify my teaching in terms of the society and institution I supposedly served, I would have to make the schooling I offered coherent with the social realities and goals they articulated and I perceived. I would have to abandon the methods of schooling appropriate to the Old Order and the old order. As it turned out, I made significant changes along four dimensions: I changed classroom management methods, organizational practices, relationship patterns, and testing procedures, all growing from my new awareness and new attitude.

The management changes came first, not because they were easiest but because of the chronology of the first days of school. In years past, when students entered my room in September, I would assign seats alphabetically. This helped me learn student names, I told myself, and it made taking roll easier, which legitimized such arbitrary procedure. Besides, the school ethos demanded it. Students sat alphabetically in homerooms, classes, and assemblies; that was one way teachers demonstrated control. Anyway, everyone knew that students sitting as they chose could only lead to chaos.

Or would it? What would happen, I wondered, if I allowed students to seat themselves? Would friends sitting next to friends be unable to learn? Would I be unable to teach? I decided to find out, so on the first day of school, I refrained from telling my eleventh and twelfth graders where to sit. As they came into my room, I smiled, asked their names, said "welcome," and watched. These sixteen-, seventeen-, and eighteen-year-old almost adults stood around, looking uncomfortably at each other, waiting to be told what to do. When no instructions came, some sat down but others asked me, "Where should we sit?"

"Anywhere you want to," I told them.

"Oh, you'll assign seats later," some replied, half to themselves, half to me.

The next day, the pattern repeated itself. They came in unsure of where to sit; they asked me what to do; I told them to decide for themselves. They looked at each other until unspoken decisions led them tentatively to seats. I was amazed. I had imagined glee or, at least, relief at the freedom to sit as they chose. I was unprepared for the insecurity stimulated by the simple task of choosing a seat. It was as though they anticipated a trick or a trap, as though they thought something negative would happen if they asserted themselves by sitting where and with whom they chose. They didn't want to make decisions; they wanted me to decide.

By the second week of school, choosing seats was no longer an issue as my students found a way to relieve their anxiety. Each day they sat where they had the day before. These well-schooled people imposed rigid organization on themselves, and seating never became a problem again until a few people in the back left corner could not see something written on the far right side of the blackboard. Then they strained forward, never lifting themselves quite off their seats, and when that failed, they looked at their neighbors' notebooks with panic in their eyes—what were they to do?

I always watched these scenes with combined amusement, frustration, and anger. They were silent comedies with tragic overtones. Why could these people not do what they needed to do? Why couldn't they get up and move to a place from which they could see? The schooled virtue of staying in their seats had more power than their need to see what I had written, so they stayed put and struggled, finally guessing at what I wrote or asking me to tell them what it said. It took months before my students learned to move around the room as their work required it—despite my repeated assurance that such sensible behavior was acceptable—and even in the spring I caught some of them straining to see the board but unable to give themselves permission to leave their self-assigned seats.

Although one year's flexibility in one classroom cannot counter years of rigidity, I have not returned to assigning seats. Instead, I make an issue of flexibility, trying to raise students' consciousness as mine was raised. Even if I cannot empower them to take control of this minor aspect of their lives, at least I can make them think about their willingness to yield control to someone else. Where they sit may seem too insignificant to worry about from some perspectives, but my students' inability to make even such small decisions for themselves reveals the paralyzing nature that years of traditional schooling can have on their ability to find places for themselves, both literally and figuratively.

As I changed the procedure for taking seats when I returned from Meadow Brook, so I changed their physical organization: the seats in my room are no longer in straight parallel rows. Though a double semicircle is hard to neatly maintain since the linoleum blocks on the floor create no useful, chair-placing pattern, I tolerate the lack of symmetry (which I rarely notice anymore) in favor of the open atmosphere and refocusing the arrangement permits. With students facing students, I am no longer the center of the classroom world. And with space in front of and behind them, students' minds seem less constrained as their bodies do. Now they are not only likelier to say what they think but to say it to each other instead of just to me. Real conversations develop, as the students attend to each others' ideas and opinions instead of only to mine.

"Ah, yes," some of my colleagues gloat. "That's precisely the problem with your classroom. Students talk and listen to each other instead of to you. Their minds relax as their posture does. No real teaching can go on in that kind of situation."

By "real teaching" I suspect these people mean lecturing, and their "relaxed minds" are the kinds not hanging on the teacher's every word or focused on taking notes. What these people want, it seems, is for my room to be more like theirs and more like Meadow Brook, a "temple to magical thinking" (Emig 1981, 21). Originally named by Piaget, magical thinking is the belief that students learn because teachers teach, and they only learn what the teachers believe they are teaching. But as I learned from my own student experience, tuning out a lecturer is easier than tuning in, and even lectures consciously attended leave minimal traces a semester later. And as I learned from Meadow Brook, traces of history or health lesson content are not what really matters; the ability to sit still, be quiet, wait for and follow directions does. That is the real teaching and learning my colleagues seem to be calling for, though I doubt that is what most would claim to want.

Finally in terms of classroom management is the matter of the "lav pass." Like assigning seats, keeping students from leaving the room traditionally demonstrates teachers' power. Finding ways to finagle passes, however, has traditionally given students a way to wrest some power into their own hands and given them a focus for their creativity. Deciding that my students should be empowered to control their own bodies and that we all had better uses for our energy and creativity, I made the pass available without my permission. (I would have eliminated the pass entirely were it not for school policy and the hall monitors who enforce it.) I both anticipated and dreaded the relay race that could materialize as students handed the pass one to the other, but it never happened. Students started using the lav before they came to class so they wouldn't miss anything, or they left and returned with dispatch, relieved to be allowed to be relieved.

These classroom management matters could be addressed once and for all during the first week of school, and because of their visibility, they at least made my classroom look less like Meadow Brook at first glance. But another organizational issue—organizing activities—had to be addressed before my classes were unlike Meadow Brook's in more significant ways.

At Meadow Brook I had seen students spend most of their time in silent individual seat work. Whether listening to Verna "teach" math, German, or English; using textbooks, workbooks, or worksheets; or writing reports or compositions, students sat and worked in isolation. Occasionally, older children helped younger ones, or two worked side by side at the blackboard or phonics chart, but for the most part, when not in "class," students were on their own.

When they were in class, however, learning and its display became anonymously social. Then all students in a particular grade were expected to contribute to the lesson in progress; none were excused, none ignored, and none featured, regardless of individual ability or knowledge. In other words, these children spent their solitary time preparing to contribute to a group effort, and even their test results were spoken of in terms of how well or how poorly an individual grade group or the school as a whole performed.

I, too, had habitually kept students in their seats, kept them passive and isolated, either listening to me or doing seat work of one kind or another. In my room, however, students could not help or seek help from anyone but me. Peer conversation, at best, seemed distracting or irrelevant; at worst, it was cheating. I was preeminently the teacher, and if students needed to know anything, I was the one they had to ask. Of course, this made me centrally important; I became the individual around whom classroom life revolved. I was also the busiest person in the room, the one doing the most talking, the most thinking, and probably the most learning. Yet this seemed logical to me. It seemed logical to assume I knew more than anyone else because in some ways I did. The problem with this perspective, however, was that it implied such a negative view of the other people in the classroom world. It implied that students knew nothing important, nothing of interest or value, that they had nothing to offer me or each other. It implied that students learn only from teachers and they really cannot learn without them. And it implied, too, that student collaboration can only be defined in the worst sense of that word, meaning something sneaky and subversive, working against the established regime. To a greater extent than even Verna, I had established myself as the authoritative voice and my students as the passive audience.

When the individual work in my room was done, display was neither anonymous nor collaborative. Students performed when called on by name, and envious glances met the name of the brightest student as sneers and groans met the name of the slowest. And just as everyone else knew who would have the right answer and who would have the wrong one, the brightest and the slowest knew who they were as well. Of course, there was also the majority of students in the middle, those at neither extreme who rarely volunteered responses and were rarely called on to respond. Those people could sit back and disappear if they so chose. Their voices rarely heard, their writing rarely "published," those students soon became as invisible to themselves as they were to everyone else. Unlike their Meadow Brook counterparts, my students not only learned alone but they displayed their learning alone, choosing to risk their images and their selves by competing with their peers or choosing not to.

If I were to bring these practices more in line with my state's goals and with my own understanding of what would help my students prepare for mainstream society, I would have to stop outdoing Verna as an authoritative voice and learn something from her when it came to collaboration. I had to give students more control of and responsibility for their own learning, and I had to help them value themselves and their peers as learners and as people. I had to help them learn to budget their time, organize their work, trust themselves, and trust each other without relying too heavily on adult support, but I had to do it without withdrawing that support entirely.

So I established groups in all my classes for both reading and writing, not based on ability but on proximity or student preference. (Both of these methods work and may be the only ones feasible in September when students and teacher are new to each other. Later, different criteria—like putting quiet students together so they cannot hide behind their more outgoing classmates—work as well.) The groups did not meet every day, and in the beginning they rarely had full responsibility for choosing, structuring, and carrying out a task. But they met frequently and at different points in the writing or reading process to discuss, analyze, synthesize, hypothesize, or apply the material at hand. Since none of these are cognitively easy tasks or thinking skills with which high school students have had much practice, at first I never turned them loose without specific guiding instructions. I gave directions, provided questions to answer or issues to address, set time limits, and required a written or oral product, but then they were on their own. Organizing, directing, and accomplishing the assigned tasks fell to them.

Not only did each group of three, four, or five students have to deal with the literature or writing at hand and what I told them to accomplish, but they had to decide how they would approach it, who would lead and who would follow, how decisions could be reached and disagreements resolved. And almost never did they allow one person to dominate or one to abdicate responsibility.

As the semester wore on, however, and students began to internalize the kinds of questions that could be brought to whatever they were reading or writing, explicit directions from me became less necessary —even unnecessary in writing classes. There, because I began allowing writers to own their own texts—to discover and develop their own meanings instead of mine—students became readers for others and for themselves, eliminating my position as ultimate arbiter. Instead, my role quickly became that of coach-collaborator, my job to raise issues for the whole group to consider and to consult with individuals as they needed such consultation. (A great deal has been written recently about the conduct of writing workshops, a format that, for me, seemed to grow unbidden from my Amish experience. Rather than describe that approach in great detail here, I refer interested readers to those who have already done so, notably, Calkins in *The Art of Teaching Writing* and Atwell in *In the Middle*.)

People walking past my classroom while group work was in progress voiced a number of doubts, questions, and objections to such proceedings. It's too noisy, they told me, for any real work to be done. The kids probably talk about their past and future weekends more than the subject at hand, they were sure. And groups probably came up with the wrong answer when they did give five minutes' attention to their work, these cynics concluded.

I know these people are right about students occasionally going off on personal tangents, but I know they are wrong about the time and effort spent and the results obtained. When group work is structured so students have a frame of reference, when it becomes a regular learning opportunity integrated into a course, and when a product is required so they know they must accomplish something reportable, group work works. I could explain why groups work by discussing the theories and research supporting such practices, but I leave that to Bruffee, Brannon and Knoblach, Goodlad, Calkins, and so many others who have already offered eloquent statements on the subject. Instead, I offer the comments of students who experienced my classes in the spring of 1986.

During the last week of school, my department's policy suggests that English teachers have students evaluate their just-completed courses. Instead of creating an "evaluation instrument," however, I asked my juniors and seniors to imagine that they were going to teach the course they had just taken (either "Reading the Short Story" or "Highlights of British Literature") and to describe what they would change about content and method, what they would retain, and why. I did not direct or even suggest that they consider group work or any of my particular strategies or idiosyncracies. I wanted to know of what they were particularly aware as well as what they considered more or less effective. The following are comments from these student assessments:

> I would keep the group work because that gives students the chance to see if they think like everyone else. They are not embarrassed to express an idea either.

> I would keep the group work because it is good to know other students' opinions and group work also breaks up the monotony of lecturing.

> Group work is a plus when taking Brit. Lit. It was a help to work in groups and hear each interpretation of a reading.

> Another aspect of the course I enjoyed was the group discussions. These discussions helped us to better understand because sometimes conversing with friends to come up with a result is easier than trying to do it alone.

> I like group work. It's easier to tell Kristia and Julie my feelings than the whole class.

> Please retain your group work. It does add tremendously to this course. When we aren't presented with all the "flavors" of a writer (which is impossible to do anyway), group work brings more discoveries of such flavors to the student.

> You didn't simply have us read, answer questions, and take a test. We actually became "involved" in the literature and the authors.

> I think the individual group work on the poets was a good idea. It gives a student the chance to feel in charge.

> The students I was with had a great impact in helping me learn.

> The group work allowed me to hear all the interpretations of the poems, right and wrong, and I could see I wasn't the only one having trouble with it. . . . The group work allows the students to learn things by themselves and not sit there and take notes all period.

Of course, some students made less-than-positive comments about group work:

> The group work is another thing that I really liked about the course. Being in groups we had some not-so-relevant discussions, but we did have some good ideas generated when we were on track.

> I feel we spent too much time in groups rather than as a whole class. While this procedure is beneficial in some cases, it is not so in others. Perhaps that may be a feeling coming only because of the particular group I was in.

> I think a lot of the group work should be eliminated. It lets some of the people get out of doing their work.

I think the small groups are important, but they often fall apart because usually only a couple people in a group have read the assignment.

And others made suggestions as to how group work could be more effective:

Groups would work better if you assigned people in groups (keep friends apart), more boy/girl mix.

As a teacher of British literature, I would allow time for group work and discussion but would continue to change the groups so that students get to discuss ideas with a variety of people.

I think that the students should pick the people they want to be in their group. That way they would feel more comfortable discussing what they were supposed to be discussing. I really don't enjoy being put into a group in which every person is on my hate list.

Groups should switch partners every once in a while so that a variety of ideas, personalities, and beliefs are exposed to everyone.

. . . how about bigger groups? Our group sometimes had a hard time brainstorming due to lack of ideas.

All these comments, the negative ones and the suggestions along with the positive ones, tell me not to eliminate group work but to refine and vary the ways I structure and oversee it, and it seems infinitely more appropriate to refine my collaborative methods rather than return to more authoritative, Meadow Brook–like ways.

Some of the student comments about group work suggest the third dimension of schooling I chose to address when I returned to the classroom. Several students noted the value of sharing ideas in a supportive atmosphere, the value of recognizing more than one legitimate response to any text, and the value of students learning from students. Add to this the value I found in teacher learning from students, and you have the character of interpersonal relationships I wanted in my classroom.

Unlike Meadow Brook and the Old Order world in which the single authoritative voice of the Bible models how all texts should be read, my school exists in a world where people like Louise Rosenblatt, Stanley Fish, Jane Tompkins, Anthony Petrosky, Lucy Calkins, Donald Graves, and many others recognize not only the possibility but the likelihood of variant readings of any text. Yet I, like many of my colleagues and our teachers before us, had traditionally operated on the one-interpretation/one-right-answer model, much as Verna did. It never occurred to most of us that students might be right and we wrong, or, more confusingly, that we might all be right.

I'll exemplify with an incident that occurred in one of my courses this spring. My students had read a short story for homework—"God Sees the Truth but Waits," by Tolstoy. In this story, Aksionov, a young traveling merchant, is falsely accused of the murder of another merchant with whom he shared an inn room. The police find the murder weapon in Aksionov's suitcase and claim to see guilt in his face and manner. Though Aksionov denies having committed the crime, he cannot account for the presence of the knife nor can he account for the murder of the other man. Aksionov is tried, convicted, and sentenced to life imprisonment. Spending the next twenty-six years in Siberia, Aksionov earns the nickname, "the Saint," for his meekness, his piety, and his belief that "only God can know the truth; it is to Him alone we must appeal, and from Him alone expect mercy" (p. 311).

One day, however, a new group of convicts arrives, among them the man who framed Aksionov. This man, Semyonich, begins digging a tunnel to effect his escape. Through a number of oblique references and bragging remarks, Aksionov realizes who this man is and what he is trying to do, and he realizes he can finally avenge what Semyonich did to him so many years before. When asked by the warden what he knows about the newly discovered tunnel, however, Aksionov declares that " 'it is not God's will' " that he tell. Semyonich is overwhelmed by this act of compassion. He begs Aksionov for forgiveness, but Aksionov says only, " 'God will forgive you. . . . Maybe I am a hundred times worse than you,' " making "his heart [grow] light, and the longing for home [leave] him." Though Semyonich proceeds to confess his original culpability to the warden, by the time Aksionov's release is ordered, he is dead.

For someone who knows Tolstoy's work and knows about his religious conversion, this story is easily seen as an outgrowth of his belief that "the evils of life came through ambition, property, and selfishness," and that Christ's teachings can be "reduced to [a] few plain principles [notably] never to resist evil by violence" (Campbell and Stearn 1958, 812). Essentially, in other words, the story is a parable intended to teach a lesson similar to those of the prodigal son, the good samaritan, and other New Testament narratives.

The day this story was due, I spent the first half of our class period eliciting everything my students already knew about parables and then connecting the story to that knowledge. The connections were clear; the point became obvious. But one very brave boy raised his hand to tell me that my interpretation was not even close to what he thought the story was about.

"What did you think it was about?" I asked Doug, impressed by his willingness to risk censure.

"Last night when I read this I thought it was about justice and injustice," he replied, "about how unfair the justice system can be and how a man can be better than the system."

Obviously, Doug had not gotten the word on Tolstoy before he read, and according to the canon, he had misinterpreted the story, missed the true meaning. But had he really? Wasn't Aksionov a man who proved the human spirit could survive oppression, that a man didn't have to follow his least humane instincts instead of his more humane ones? Didn't he experience the impersonality and arbitrariness of institutional justice yet survive with his sense of personal decency in tact? If Tolstoy had known about the Rosenbergs, McCarthy, and Gary Dotson and Kathleen Webb, might not his meaning have been similar to Doug's? And even if it weren't, didn't Doug's meaning make sense anyway?

Not only was I impressed by Doug's chutzpa, but by his thinking, and I told him so. In fact, I spent the rest of that period talking with my students about the various places meaning comes from, why there is more than one way to read any text, and how I wanted them to trust their own interpretations and not be afraid to share and defend them, as Doug had. When the bell rang to end that class, "high-fives," pats on the back, and comments like "Good job!" and "Way to go!" followed Doug into the hall.

My first-period class was never the same again. Not that from that day on everyone shared ideas and had original insights into everything we read, but from then on more people did participate, and the awareness level of the class—their willingness to risk and to initiate, to analyze individually and to synthesize in their groups—increased significantly. And my awareness level increased too, as students began initiating discussions about how accustomed they were to giving teachers only the answers they seemed to want and how they had learned to "psych teachers out." Now, they told me, they wanted to understand how the same text could legitimately have different meanings for different people and, if that were true, how teachers could legitimately insist one meaning was more right than any other. I admit that reader-response theory is not in my curriculum, but I responded by telling them about interpretive communities and other theoretical constructs, attempting to explain the paradox they perceived. I suspect that because those "advanced" ideas articulated what the students had started to intuit themselves and because the ideas were presented in an atmosphere that respected their native intelligence while accepting their topical ignorance, those teenagers understood and appreciated the discussions that ensued.

Yet while I do respect my students as thinking people, like Rosenblatt and other reader-response theorists, I believe some interpretations of literature are too farfetched or too idiosyncratic to be acceptable in an academic English class to anyone but the interpreter, and Doug's could have been one of those. If it had been, and I had been Verna, I would have ignored his response and turned to another student. Or if I were still operating on my old initiation-response-evaluation pattern, I would have done the same thing, but before turning to the next student, I would have offered a "No," a "Not quite," or some other evaluative comment intended to mark Doug's error and perhaps minimize his embarrassment. Now, however, I would do neither of these; instead, I would look for the sense in Doug's reply and its connection to the material at hand.

Perhaps I first clearly recognized the possibility and need to do this when I saw Verna ignore seven-year-old Glen's personal reaction to the textbook picture of farmers picking apples (see chapter 4). When Glen objected to apple picking as a legitimate illustration of farm work, he was reading the text in his mind, not the textbook at hand. From his perspective as a dairy farmer's son, apple picking had nothing to do with farming. When Verna ignored his response completely, I saw her miss an opportunity to both validate Glen's thinking process and expand his awareness of the world. At that moment she reminded me of both the teacher in *The Geranium on the Windowsill Just Died But Teacher You Went Right On*, which made me smile, and of myself in the classroom, which did not.

Another example of a student using previously acquired knowledge to make sense of a text comes from a Shakespeare lesson I taught one spring. Though high school literature and second-grade health may seem to have nothing in common curricularly, the thinking skills they require and the schooling they result in can be markedly the same.

Interpreting the line "My way of life/Is fall'n into the sear, the yellow leafe" (*Macbeth*, act 5, scene iii), a student told me Macbeth was "burned out," emotionally dead. Since the controlling metaphor of the speech in which that line appears is that of the autumn of man's life, the fact that Macbeth may be burned out seems somewhat tangential (though certainly possible at that point in the play) and was not the point I had in mind at the time. But I was struck by the student's chosen metaphor and wondered why she chose it since nothing in the text suggested being burned or used up. With further questioning, I learned that the student had focused on *sear*, associated it with fire, and ended up with the currently colloquial "burned out" as a description of Macbeth's state. While I pointed out the limited application of her metaphor for the speech, noting the other references to old age and the classic Shakespearean life-as-a-year-of-seasons idea, I also credited the thinking that produced her interpretation, her awareness of text and context, and pointed out the power and variety of such metaphorical conceptions. For some people, what I did when I corrected the interpretation was "teaching"; for me, that was only part of the lesson I wanted that student to learn.

(I hope readers will keep in mind that my current teaching assignment involves eleventh and twelfth graders whose preparation for college English falls to me. Were I in the intermediate high school or the middle school again, I would be less likely to dominate my classes even to the limited extent that I do. In those earlier secondary grades particularly, I would not feel the obligation to insure that all my students read the same books, or, more significantly, that they all read the "right" books, and would use a readers' workshop approach similar to the one described by Atwell and similar to the writers' workshops I now conduct. At this point in my experience, however—and I can only speak for now, knowing how experience modifies experience—I still feel constrained not only by my school's curriculum, which lists the texts available for each course, but also by the fact that my college-bound students almost certainly will encounter people like E.D. Hirsch who will expect them to be culturally literate according to traditional definitions. I cannot send my students unprepared to those professors any more than I can send them believing the one-right-answer/one-right-interpretation myth of reading. Much of what I do at this point, therefore, represents the compromise I've struck between my current reality and the reality of academia as I know it.)

Nothing I have suggested here is new or original with me. It is simply my amalgamation and application of Goodman's miscue-analysis approach to misread words in oral reading and Shaughnessy's error-analysis approach to assessing written mistakes, combined with the psychological and learning theories of Vygotsky, Harste et al., and others who contend that what adults may perceive as errors are actually children's approximations of truth. Students do not make random errors, these theorists claim; rather, they err by misapplying or misunderstanding rules, or they make sensible guesses that just happen to be wrong. When teachers respond to such errors by ignoring, discounting, or—worse yet—ridiculing them, they discredit the constructive processes and intentions those answers represent. (This may help explain why students take seemingly objective, unimpassioned criticism to heart: their answers may appear to be just answers to a teacher, but to the students themselves those answers are more deeply rooted personal manifestations.) I have discovered that by not being Verna or my traditional self but attending to student errors instead, I learn a great deal about student models of how the world works, and I can then help them learn to value and modify those models instead of learning to distrust their understanding and themselves.

I admit this approach creates several lesson-management problems. It becomes impossible to predict where class discussion may lead; an apparently simple, obvious question may prompt unanticipated complex responses and subsequent discussion. It may mean all the material allotted to one day's lesson may carry over to a second day (or a third). And, perhaps most disconcertingly, it may lead into unknown, uncharted waters, raising ideas and issues teachers may be unprepared to discuss. All of these things have happened to me since my return from Meadow Brook. My plan book is a perpetual mess; I no longer know at the outset how many days or weeks a unit will take; I frequently have to reschedule reading assignments; and I usually fail to cover all the material my curriculum allots to a particular course. But I've grown accustomed to the lesson-plan disorder; I've developed strategies for moving things around; and I always include a new objective in my list of objectives for each unit—"to increase students' awareness of their reading, writing, and thinking processes and to develop those processes"—that anticipates and justifies inclusion of the unexpected. (Interestingly, I've yet to have an administrator or supervisor observe my class and object to the lack of predetermined structure in my lessons though they've observed some classes only vaguely prefigured in my plans.) When I think back to my more traditional teaching days, I recall many instances in which I also failed to "cover" everything in a particular lesson or unit despite my single-minded devotion to lesson plans and courses of study, so I was probably no more efficient then, and almost certainly less effective.

As to finding myself in uncharted waters, I admit that caused some anxiety at first. Students asked questions I could not answer, raised issues about which I was far from informed let alone expert, and at times I did want to run and hide behind my lesson plan, textbook, and college education. What I slowly discovered, however, was that admitting I did not know an answer made me both a better teacher and a more relaxed human being. Not only did it demonstrate the shared fallibility and humanity of all the people in the classroom community, but it was a great relief for me not to have to worry about knowing everything and always being right as I once did. Even when I could not answer a student's question or intelligently discuss a relevant issue, I found I could talk about how to get the needed information and what to consider in evaluating the issue, modeling research and thinking skills my students, accustomed to being told everything, sorely needed.

Like any discussion of public schooling, all of this leads to the question of testing, of how to assess what students have learned or not learned in the classroom. Traditionally, testing in public schools is little different from testing at Meadow Brook. Students sit in their isolated seats—sometimes moving further apart or building textbook walls to inhibit cheating—and attempt to give back to teachers what teachers and textbooks gave them. Supposedly, this measures how much a student has learned, but from their own experiences on both sides of the desk, most teachers know this actually measures how much a student has memorized the night before. Yet teachers continue to construct so-called objective tests, full of multiple choice, true/false, fill-in-the-blank, and matching-type questions, further decontextualizing and fragmenting whatever subject they are attempting to teach.

As an English teacher whose curriculum emphasizes writing, I had used such objective questions only on quizzes intended to check literal reading progress. On tests I required essay answers instead, and I believed that meant I was requiring higher-order thinking from my students as a result. After seeing Meadow Brook, however, and recognizing the socialization lessons lurking behind straight recall questions, I realized my essay tests were only superficially different from Verna's short-answer variety; an essay test question with one acceptable, expected answer or a formulaic five-paragraph essay amounted to no more than a large blank for my students to fill in. They needed to do no serious analytical thinking, no original synthesizing of ideas; they needed only to use more words to relate recalled information, more words to construct thesis statements and topic sentences, to fill introductions, bodies, and conclusions. As Verna had trained her students to say what she wanted to hear in as few words as possible, I was training mine to do the same in as many words as possible. Her students would make good Amishmen; mine would make good bureaucrats.

But how should I test? Again, I was faced with making pedagogy coherent with goals. My testing like my teaching had to work against the traditional one-right-answer mind-set; it had to assume other than a teacher-dominant, student-subordinate posture; it had to disallow passive, conforming, unthinking student behavior, yet it also had to insure that students knew the facts and ideas involved in the topics studied.

My tests also had to work against the traditional panic associated with testing. Too often, students worry so much about knowing facts that they have neither the time nor the psychic energy left to think about those facts. I wanted them to think about what facts imply and how they relate to each other; to find categories and patterns, causes and effects; and to compare and contrast over time and over genre. To do those things, however, students would have to feel secure about their basic knowledge and control of the text, and I would have to help them achieve this security.

I found three testing procedures that helped solve this panic-producing problem—quizzing, open-book testing, and take-home testing. Occasionally, I gave quizzes with straight-forward questions asking for correctly spelled names of authors and characters, matters of setting and plot, related history and culture, and literary terms and concepts. Students knew exactly how to study for these, felt secure in taking them, and retained supposedly learned information long enough to use it later in the unit or semester and then to really assimilate it.

More often, however, I gave open-book quizzes and tests. If I wanted students to paraphrase poetry or find and explicate metaphors, to analyze two characters' relationship or trace one character's development, or if I wanted them to trace the development of a theme or line of imagery, I allowed them to use their texts for reference. At first they were thrilled, thinking open-book tests meant they didn't have to know anything, but they discovered that one class period left no time for reading what they had not read before; they had to know the material to use the time and the text efficiently. What they did not have to know, however, was how to spell minor characters' names or other facts easily located and used, and that changed the focus of their studying considerably. In addition, paying attention to information they had not considered until during the test became a learning experience; students often knew more when they finished a test than they did when they began.

More than open-book tests, I came to value take-home exams, not the kind completed at home but the kind prepared for at home and written from outlines or notes in class. Such exams eliminate all the excuses students commonly invoke to explain poor essay test performance: no time constraints limit thinking or planning, no "forgetting" specific facts occurs, and little classroom environmental pressure or discomfort exists. Students have all the time and resources they need to fully explore a question, develop a response, find supporting textual evidence, and organize their answers. All they need to worry about is knowing their material well enough to write the finished essay in one class period. Not only does this produce better written, better supported essays for me to read, but it allows me to construct more interesting, more thought-provoking, and—according to my students—more difficult tests. I can ask them to consider a range of material; I can send them back to previous units to compare pieces of literature, trace the development of form, or do any number of things that require more thought and closer text examination than a single class period permits. Perhaps more importantly, however, I can ask them to decide what they think instead of simply to recall information.

Below is an example of a take-home test given at the conclusion of a recent unit on *Macbeth*. The students who took the test were two sections of college-prep juniors and seniors.

Directions:
—This is a closed-book test.
—You will have one class period in which to write your answer. That means you must come to class prepared with some kind of notes or outline. You may not write a full draft of your answer in advance, however.
—Neither of these questions can be answered adequately without specific evidence from the text supporting all generalizations you make.
—Choose only one question to answer.

1. Macbeth is a tragic hero. Beowulf is an epic hero. In a well-developed, well-organized essay, compare and contrast these two different kinds of literary heroes as exemplified by these two characters, and suggest reasons you think early British culture produced one while later British culture produced the other.

2. Both *Macbeth*, the five-act play, and "Beowulf," the epic poem, clearly reflect the values, beliefs, and practices of the societies that produced them. In a well-developed, well-organized essay, explain how each literary piece reflects its society, and highlight the ways in which British culture changed and/or remained the same between the two historical periods.

Though my example comes from a high school English course, open-book and take-home testing can be used at almost all levels and across the curriculum, in any grade or subject where the object is to teach students to use information—to analyze, synthesize, and apply it—instead of just to memorize and recall it.

Testing is not the only possible method of evaluation, however, if the focus is on what students can do with what they learn rather than simply on what they know about it. I have had students write parodies or serious pieces modeled on the literature they have read, and I have had them write short stories and poems to be used as texts by the class. Though these are time-consuming projects to which I devote several class periods and several nights' (or weeks') assignments, they are lessons as much as they are tests. To write such pieces, students must see their reading differently; they must get inside it and determine how it works, so they learn at least as much about literature this way as they do by reading it. And I get to read thirty different original pieces instead of thirty similar boring essays. (Of course, I also have to grade thirty long projects instead of thirty shorter tests, but these are so much more interesting the time passes more quickly and more profitably for me, too.)

Grading these tests and projects differs from grading a more "objective" test, but that makes the process no more subjective, for the criteria remain equally impersonal. On the test, do the students make valid points? Do they explain them clearly and support them sufficiently? On a modeled project, do they know the model well and use it effectively, that is, are their versions similar enough to be successfully compared in terms of structure, topic, purpose, and/or attitude? What matters is not whether I like what they do or agree with it, or whether they choose the "right" point or "right" project idea; what matters is how well they do what they do and whether their work can stand on its own.

"Does spelling count on these?" my students ask at the beginning of each term, and I tell them it does, as do grammar and mechanics. But they do not count until the last minute, until the take-home test goes down in final form or the project enters its last draft, leaving plenty of time to consult dictionaries, texts, grammar books, each other, or me for help. I give every paper two grades—one for content and one for mechanics—and I combine them in a 2:1 ratio to arrive at the recorded grade. I wish I didn't have to grade at all. I wish I lived in a world where learning wasn't reduced to a number or a letter, but I don't. My colleagues, my administrators, my students, their parents, and most colleges all vest great power in grades. I simply try to give students the chance to earn grades that represent more than their ability to memorize and repeat whatever they have been told.

So ethnography changed my Monday mornings in all these overt ways. It affected my classroom management and organization, my lesson plans and activities, and my assignments and tests. But perhaps the most important change ethnography wrought is less clear and less obvious, though it is fundamentally responsible for all the other adjustments I have made and continue to make. At bottom, ethnography changed my perception of myself and my students and why we share a classroom 180 days a year. By changing my perceptions from negative, adversarial, and constraining to positive, collaborative, and liberating, it changed my attitude toward Monday morning from panic-stricken to enthusiastic. And that has made all the difference.

I realize now that the Sunday evening panic attacks I once suffered reflected a view of the education process I no longer hold. When I struggled to come up with clever, attention-getting, period-filling activities, I did so because I saw my students as passive, disinterested, potentially disruptive people who had to be tricked or bullied into paying attention and constantly entertained and monitored to remain so. I had to keep them busy, quiet, and learning, and if I accomplished the first two feats, I assumed the third would follow. According to this model, I was the center of the classroom world, and I was responsible for everything that happened there. I had to be actively engaged, creative, and in control for learning to happen; my students had to be none of these things. Now I am only amazed that despite all this personal involvement I learned nothing until I got away to Meadow Brook, but such is the mind-boggling power of magical thinking.

According to my new model of the teaching-learning process, I am still active, but my students are no longer passive. They now actively engage with ideas, with each other, and with me. They ask questions and seek answers as I do; they, too, make plans and carry them out; they discover things to say and ways to say them, orally and in writing. And through their active engagement, these students become interested in what goes on. The classroom world becomes as much theirs as mine, and they neither have the time nor feel the need to be disruptive, for it is not my lessons but theirs they would disrupt.

To go with this new view of my students and our relationship, ethnography led me to a new view of lesson planning as more than devising a continuous series of activities. While I once thought only about what I would do—my pedagogy—thinking about Verna's teaching led me to think about my own. Before, I had no consciously guiding theory of how people learn, only a subconsciously acquired model from the blank slate/empty vessel school of thought (the same one Verna attended): I had to fill those empty minds—by writing on them or pouring in information—as teachers always had. Now, instead of seeing my plans only in terms of methodology, I judge them according to theories of learning coherent with my new perspective. Polanyi's "tacit knowledge," Vygotsky's "zone of proximal development," Harste et al.'s model of the language learning process all tell me that I need not trick my students into learning. I need not go into class armed with clever plans and reams of dittoed exercises. What I need in that classroom are knowledge of my subject matter and knowledge of how people learn. The rest seems to follow of its own accord.

I now come to class prepared to help my students in their encounters with ideas, not to keep them so busy they have no time to think. I recently heard Donald Graves emphasize the importance of being "present-tense oriented," of engaging with ideas and people in the present moment without seeing each moment as valuable only in terms of future plans. In Graves's terms, I have made each Monday morning one of the series of ongoing moments that is my classroom life. Instead of being a cause of panic and anxiety, a discrete piece I must fit into some larger puzzle,

Monday morning becomes a moment to anticipate, a time to interact with, not operate on my students. I know this may sound corny, but I've honestly rediscovered what it was that made me choose teaching in the first place: the fun and excitement of being with spontaneous, impressionable kids instead of rigid, jaded adults. So I have stopped trying to turn the former into the latter.

Though I still write lesson plans on Sunday night for Monday and every other school morning, they no longer cause panic because while I write them alone, I know I will have help carrying them out. And I no longer need to figure out in advance how I will fill each minute—what I will say and what I will do—because I now plan to listen as much as I plan to talk, to respond as much as I initiate, to support as much as I challenge, and to learn as much as I teach. I plan, in other words, to stay out of my students' way as much as possible. Teaching is the focus of the Old Order; learning is the focus of the new.

ELEVEN

The Old Order as Model and Object Lesson

In the previous chapter I discussed how my experiences as a participant observer in Meadow Brook School affected my subsequent experiences as a teacher in a mainstream classroom. In this chapter I want to consider what my experiences with the Amish imply not only for my classroom but for other mainstream classrooms, schools, and districts as well. Just as Verna served as both role model and object lesson for me, the Fishers, their school community, Meadow Brook, and the Old Order system offer suggestions and warnings for their mainstream counterparts too.

First of all, the Amish experience highlights the need for all those concerned about public education to recognize that every school operates in a cultural context that both creates and maintains it, both shapes and limits the changes possible within it. While the Amish context may be particularly evident, no school—parochial, independent, or public—exists in a vacuum. All schools have histories and administrative agencies as the Amish schools do; every school has a school community as Meadow Brook does. Seeing schools as monolithic, autonomous entities, untouched by and inaccessible to the people they serve, is not only myopic but leads to the sort of tunnel vision evident in such reports as "A Nation At Risk," which sees the schools as responsible for both causing and stemming the "rising tide of mediocrity" about to flood our nation. Were the educators who wrote this report (and those who applauded it) to step back and look again, they might see that schools are socially controlled, not socially controlling, and that the power they attribute to the schools is actually vested in the society that creates, maintains, demands, and tolerates those institutions.

Of course, it is more difficult to see the cultural contingency of mainstream schools than of Meadow Brook perhaps because those looking at public education are usually part of rather than apart from its context, and because public schools have a long history, a large varied constituency, and a complex institutional structure, making them appear distant, impersonal, and unapproachable. Looming over students, parents, and educational researchers for more than a century, public schools seem, like the monolith in *2001*, to have sprung from nowhere and to have self-perpetuating lives of their own, unfathomable by any except those inside. In fact, however, the schools did not spring full-blown from some unknown source, nor are they like the planets in a deistic universe, set in perpetual motion by a creator who then walked away. Instead the schools are created, re-created, and embellished every day by a society that wants them to be exactly as they are, a society with tremendous investment in maintaining the status quo.

Probably the most counterproductive dimension of this usual static perspective is the us-them mentality it inevitably seems to create. In most public school districts, there are insiders and outsiders, professionals and laypeople, those who know and those who don't, those who care and those who couldn't care less. But which group is which? Are the insiders the people in the schools or those in the children's lives? Are "those who know" the people who have been trained to know or those who know from experience? Are those who care the people available daily from 8:00 A.M. to 3:00 P.M. or those not always around but on call twenty-four hours a day? The answers to these questions too often depend on whether the respondent is an administrator, a teacher, or a parent; an Anglo, an Afro-American, or a Hispanic; a white-collar, a blue-collar, or an unemployed worker.

This perceived adversarial relationship, based as it is on the superficial institutionalized features of public schools, not only prevents people from seeing the truly contingent nature of public school systems but takes considerable defensive posturing to maintain. Yet the Old Order experience suggests what might happen were the energy invested in defending against "them" redirected through a new definition of who "we" are. What might happen if public school parents, teachers, and principals got to know each other as adults do at Meadow Brook? What might happen if parents, teachers, and administrators listened to and talked with each other instead of debating with or talking at each other? What might happen if students saw teachers outside the classroom, in the community, or even in each other's homes? What might happen if students saw parents and teachers together, physically and philosophically?

I'm not suggesting that what might happen is the perfection of public education in our time, but given the Old Order model, I would suggest that seeing schools as outgrowths of homes and communities and acting accordingly could benefit mainstream schools in at least four ways. First, this organic view could help eliminate the adversarial relationships that too often exist, allowing everyone to reinvest their energy in more positive, constructive ways. Second, a more cooperative view could enable each group to better understand the others, giving schools a more realistic perception of where their students really come from and where they might be headed, and giving homes and communities reason to be more supportive of their schools. Third, a more coherent view could allow both sides to revise their notions of how homes can support schools and how schools can reciprocate. Homes need not be school centered and schools need not be "relevant" if each is supporting the other through a sense of shared purpose. And finally, aligning schools with homes and communities could provide a more coherent framework for students, minimizing the crossed and mixed messages they now get from parents, teachers, and employers.

The Old Order model also suggests that the appearance of literacy may belie the reality and warns that we should look beneath the surface of apparent reading and writing behavior before we apply labels. Seeing the Amish read James Michener novels and local newspapers, and seeing them conduct literate business makes them seem to read and write just like everybody else. Yet how they understand and apply what they read and how they select and evaluate what they write can be neither superficially observed nor objectively tested. Not until I spent time with the Fishers and at Meadow Brook, not until I attended to people and purposes could I actually discern what constitutes reading and writing in the community and discover what "literacy" really means there.

And the same holds true in mainstream contexts. A student able to read a text orally, able to follow objective test directions, or able to structure a five-paragraph essay may be unable to comprehend what he reads, unable to understand the items he matches on a test, or unable to analyze or explain the line of reasoning he seems to follow in his essay. Conversely, the student who reads every issue of *Automotive News*, who composes original playground rhymes or raps, or who writes elaborate notes to friends and extensively decorates notebooks and lockers may have all the skills and understanding necessary to do school-selected literacy tasks but may simply choose not to do them.

Too often we allow ourselves to be fooled by appearances, to be lulled into thinking that students apparently able to read and write are also able to understand, or that students failing to do the tasks we set for them are actually unable to do so. So concerned about appearances, so adamant about the fact that neatness and spelling count, we often fail to look beneath the neat surfaces of oral reading or mechanically controlled writing to discover what the readers or writers actually think they are doing or to look beyond nontraditional forms to see what they actually represent or entail. The hue and cry heard recently from employers, college professors, and secondary teachers suggests that what passes for literacy at various educational levels may not be literacy at all, and the findings of researchers like Labov, Gilmore, and Fiering suggest that literacy may exist where we are least likely to look for or expect it.

What I saw in Meadow Brook suggests at least one way to begin redefining and rediscovering literacy, a way that would seem more appropriate to mainstream than Old Order classrooms but that the Meadow Brook community recognizes as positive more often than many mainstream communities do. By sanctioning, encouraging, and even "teaching" student-selected reading and student-preferred writing, Verna successfully precluded school problems with "unofficial literacy" (Fiering 1982). By allowing classroom reading and writing to serve personal as well as societal purposes, she increased her students' willingness to cooperate while increasing their ability to read and write as well. This is not to say Verna never taught from basal readers or never required compositions; obviously that wasn't the case. She simply allowed her students to read what they wanted to read every day when they had time; she read to them from books they chose; and she structured some of her writing lessons around models they recognized as appropriate and personally useful. In addition, Verna allowed students to assert themselves in what may seem to be minor ways through their literacy, by embellishing their signatures and their compositions, by having their work displayed in ways that made every student feel like a successful part of the group. Meadow Brook students didn't need to find ways to affirm themselves, to leave their mark on their school either figuratively or literally, for their school insured that each one could.

Certainly allowing students to express themselves through their literacy will not stop the graffiti or other unsanctioned forms of literacy public schools encounter (at least not as long as the society outside school makes it equally difficult for young people to express themselves acceptably there, too), but it may begin to make school a less alien environment and one in which students feel they have a vested interest. Redefining literacy so students can own the definition too may mean not only that we need not ignore what students like or consider important, but that there may be redeeming social and educational value in what seems exclusively student oriented. Encouraging students to read Stephen King novels, Harlequin romances, or *Sports Illustrated*; allowing time in classes for such reading without turning it into a chore by requiring worksheets, book reports, or essays about what they have read; and listening to what they have to say about what they read without minimizing the validity of their responses might help demonstrate that schools value reading, not just schoolwork, while promoting fluency, comprehension, and familiarity with printed text. Similarly, encouraging students to write notes and letters to each other, to tell stories, to write and perform raps, or to do any kind of self-selected writing they choose acknowledges the personal and social value of composing while promoting written and oral fluency that can't help but transfer to more traditional academic writing and speaking.

And student audiences need not be limited to their individual classrooms. As Verna demonstrated, there are older and younger students to communicate with, and there are adults too. The more varied and sophisticated the students' purposes and audiences, the more varied and sophisticated the understandings and skills they will develop. A desirable side effect of all this is that students writing to people they care about and writing because they care will want to be accurate mechanically, for how they are perceived by those others really matters to them.

What is most important, however, is that these kinds of activities be instituted without being institutionalized, that the focus remain on communication, self-discovery, and self-expression, without shifting to recall, usage, grammar, or punctuation. Students should be encouraged to care about and own their ideas, perceptions, interpretations, and essays without having them automatically corrected or co-opted by their teachers. Then success can be measured in terms of students' understanding and sense of accomplishment, reinforcing not apathy and errors but positive attitudes and achievement.

What does this say to people who teach college-prep courses, to English teachers responsible for perpetuating the five-paragraph essay or social studies teachers tied to research papers and reports? To them it says tell your students that these alien forms can and must become less alien, that these seemingly sterile academic purposes can and must become their own if they want the academic universe to be theirs, too. These teachers can point out also that the content of such papers need not be as unyielding as the forms. College-bound students can express themselves through their thinking and their language, through their perspectives and their styles, so they, too, can own school literacy.

Something else the Amish do bears a lesson for public education: they explicitly recognize and accept interpretive communities other than their own. The Amish make no attempt to deny that other people read, write, and think differently than they do; in fact, their very existence is a conscious response to that reality. They acknowledge that alternative literacies exist to serve other people and facilitate other societies, and they in no way demean or diminish the legitimacy of those literacies for those groups. Instead they offer theirs not as superior but as different. Public schools, on the other hand, too often offer their literacy as the only literacy, or at least as the only one that counts. The choice, they suggest, is to be literate or not, not to choose the literacies personally and socially appropriate. As suggested in chapter 10, it may be incumbent upon public schools to be as honest as the Amish, to accept the legitimacy of other interpretive communities and to acknowledge their existence. Given the optional and homogeneous nature of Old Order schools, they can afford to offer only one variety of literacy to their students. Given the requisite, heterogeneous nature of public schools, they cannot afford to be either so limited or so limiting.

Finally, the ways the Old Orders prepare people to teach in their schools offer several suggestions for mainstream teacher preparation. At first glance, it may appear that Old Order teachers are not prepared to teach but are simply thrust into classrooms instead. In comparison to mainstream teacher preparation this may be true, but consider: Old

Order teachers grow up in Old Order homes and attend Old Order schools; they know the values, expectations, and needs of the community and its members, and they know the school is expected to reinforce those values, meet those expectations, and fulfill those needs. They know how children and adults should treat themselves and each other, how skills and ideas are learned, and how they are applied. They know what kinds of situations children may encounter and what kinds of relationships they may enter. In other words, social foundations of education, child development, educational psychology, and teaching methodology are all courses they have taken implicitly throughout their lives. When they enter their first classrooms, then, Old Order teachers need only make explicit and act on what they already know because the schools in which they teach are the schools for which their lives have prepared them.

In a sense, what mainstream teacher preparation does is help prospective teachers make their knowledge explicit before they enter the classroom instead of waiting until they get there as Old Order teachers do. Studying child development, educational psychology, and classroom pedagogy brings to consciousness, highlights, and articulates what students have already experienced and, to some extent, what they implicitly know. Yet this is insufficient for mainstream teachers because the schools and communities that taught them what they know are not necessarily the schools and communities in which they will teach. In the best circumstances, therefore, teacher education also offers students alternate ways to think about growing up and learning, ways to understand the experiences of children whose learning styles and life-styles differ from their own.

Unfortunately, however, not all teacher preparation programs offer these kinds of circumstances. Too many of them present child development and psychology as though they were things to be imposed on or expected of children rather than as necessarily incomplete, decontextualized, simplified descriptions of what children naturally do. Too many of them introduce hierarchical frameworks and implied or even stated value judgments with which teachers can evaluate and label their students, producing teachers who have been taught that growing up is not the complex process they experienced personally but a strictly linear one accompanied by learning in a series of discrete steps and stages. Unlike their Old Order counterparts, these mainstream teachers have a much more extensive vocabulary for discussing development and learning, but their sense of what development and learning entail may no longer have human, experiential dimensions. So while Old Order teachers know no scientific terms for the wonder and complexity they experience in their classrooms, mainstream teachers have a language that reduces the wonder and complexity to sets of scientific terms.

This became particularly apparent to me at the in-service meeting I attended with Verna where problems of introducing preschoolers to school and dealing with adolescent attitudes and rebellion were discussed by professionals in what could be considered layman's terms. The teachers at that meeting recognized the universal dimensions of these problems, for many of them had encountered similar students and similar situations, but not once did they mention self-actualization, separation anxiety, or anything even vaguely reminiscent of developmental psychology. Instead, they approached each problem in its interpersonal context, not going into individual or generic psyches but assessing the social implications and social solutions for each problem instead. It is not that Old Order teachers are unable, constitutionally or intellectually, to analyze child behavior or development; it is that they see growing and learning as social processes and children as social beings, so their analysis necessarily considers behavior and learning in their social contexts. It is not that they know less than mainstream teachers, but rather that they know differently.

Verna, however, forgot that she knew differently, and because of that she provides an interesting object lesson concerning teacher preparation. As noted earlier, when Verna decided to become a teacher, she attended a New Order Mennonite high school for several years, hoping that would better prepare her for the classroom. When she came to Meadow Brook, Verna's Old Order ideas and perspective had been extended and modified by exposure to the values, expectations, and needs of a different, more academically oriented society. So while she still knew what the Old Orders demanded and expected, she was unaware of the impact her high school experience had had on her thinking. When Meadow Brook parents objected to the stringency of her academic demands and her somewhat impersonal, decontextualized relationships with and understanding of their children, Verna had difficulty understanding their objections.

She had made no major changes in Meadow Brook's preexisting curriculum nor had she modified its social organization and social expectations. All she had done was make what seemed to her to be minor but desirable changes in what and how she taught as compared to her predecessors and colleagues. What she added was minimal: original student stories in the school newspaper, formal essays in the composition lessons, a "dress up" lesson on Clara Barton. Though parents objected to the former, the latter went unnoted if not unnoticed. So the central issue was not what Verna did. Rather the conflict developed over how she did it—not her formal pedagogy, but her slightly superior attitude, her more formal demeanor, and her more formal expectations. In other words, Verna's high school education had not taught her to think differently in substantive ways but had suggested, perhaps subliminally, that school is more of a separate, elevated institution than the Old Orders want it to be. She had tried to elevate Meadow Brook—to make it a more important and more powerful presence in her students' and community's lives—but her students and community objected. Unfortunately, however, Verna did not understand their objections. She thought they wanted Meadow Brook to be better, so she worked harder at being a better teacher, never realizing that her definition of better was not the same as theirs. Gradually, frustrated by her inability to please the school community despite her concerted efforts, Verna began adopting an adversarial attitude that the community eventually shared.

Verna's problem, in other words, was not that she did not know enough, but that she knew too much. Having learned more than necessary, she could recognize less of what was necessary. Had she been consciously aware of both the overt and subtle differences between New and Old Order situations, she might have been able to put her additional knowledge in context instead of letting it intrude where it was not only irrelevant but counterproductive. And that, it seems to me, may be a major problem for mainstream teachers, too. Armed with the impersonal, decontextualized concepts of psychology; the unanalyzed, interchangeable possibilities of methodology; and the values, expectations, and needs of academe, they enter schools and school communities where such knowledge may be not only irrelevant but counterproductive. Having learned more than necessary, they are unable to recognize what is truly necessary, and they, like Verna, may lack the awareness and ability to put their education in context, particularly if that means putting aside much of what they were taught or putting it in the background to be drawn on only as called for by particular situations.

Instead of producing graduates who believe they know how to teach school, teacher preparation programs may be well advised to tell their students what they cannot learn in college, to let them know what they cannot know before they begin to teach. In other words, perhaps teacher education should prepare teachers to approach individual students, classrooms, schools, and districts on their own terms rather than as generic manifestations of "student," "school," or "district." Perhaps, as Old Order teachers are, they should be taught to see children in their contexts—as social beings and social products—rather than seeing them as embodiments of skills, abilities, and developmental processes. And perhaps prospective teachers should be allowed to realize that different communities, institutions, and individuals have different values, expectations, and needs that no single curricular philosophy or methodology can serve and no single expert can predict or modify.

In other words, perhaps the social foundations of education may be presented as more than the social history or the sociology of education. Social history is too easily reduced to Jean-Jacques Rousseau, Benjamin Franklin, John Dewey, and the development of the public school system in America; sociology too easily reduces to the generalized ecology of "children" and "adolescents" interacting with "parents" and "teachers" in elementary or secondary "school cultures," without ever wondering which students, which adults, or which schools in which communities such glosses represent. As the Fishers, Verna, and Meadow Brook suggest, the social foundations of education are within communities, not necessarily across them, and involve particular belief systems and life-styles, not the homogenized versions offered by many textbooks, lecturers, and curricular syllabi.

I am suggesting that the social foundations of education may be presented from a series of diverse perspectives—from that of Labov's New York street corners to Heath's Piedmont Carolinas, from Ogbu's perception of social gate-keeping to Rodriguez's view of bilingual education. Of course, no course, whether occupying one semester or two, could possibly present all the kinds of social foundations underlying American public (and private) schools, but that is precisely my point: prospective teachers should know what they cannot possibly learn in advance and should have a sense of the variety and possibilities that await them, a sense traditional teacher preparation courses rarely offer.

In addition to these suggestions for teacher preparation, the Amish experience suggests reconsidering teacher in-service education, as well. From my vantage point, it seems that "inservicing" teachers often involves top-down decisions to bring in outside "experts" who can address a district's faculty on a topic the administration thinks they do, might, or should care about. Like their students, teachers are rendered passive; they have little input in the planning of their own education and even less involvement in its process. Yet consider the Old Orders: there, teachers decide what teachers want or need to learn more about, and there, teachers not only plan but usually carry out their own programs. There, teachers and administrators respect the accumulated wisdom of their own ranks. They realize that more experienced teachers can speak to the needs of others because they know and share those needs, and those speakers know what to suggest not because they have done or read the research, but because they have been in the schools. This gives them not only respect but credibility, something outside experts may be hard put to establish.

Of course, there are some issues of serious teacher concern no staff member may be able to address. In mainstream schools, identifying and dealing with students who use drugs, students who come from abusive homes, or students who are potentially suicidal are teacher skills best taught by someone specially trained in those areas. And the Old Orders recognize this fact. As noted earlier, when those teachers wanted to know more about identifying and dealing with learning-disabled students, they brought in an outsider who offered knowledge no insider could supply.

Perhaps surprisingly, given their attitude toward superfluous education, Old Order teacher in-service programs come not once or twice a year but every six weeks. These teachers and administrators seem to perceive some value in continuing education when it addresses immediate teacher needs and interests, when teachers are actively involved in the solution of their own problems, and when the very acts of planning and coming together give them a sense of professionalism and a network of support. For those of us who feel isolated in our classrooms, caught up in bureaucratic and hierarchical systems, these alone would be reasons enough to modify current in-service practice.

Of all the implications the Amish experience has for mainstream education, the most important one—the one that may facilitate all the others—may also be the most difficult for the larger society to accomplish. What enables the Amish to create and maintain a coherent, cooperative approach to education, what enables them to meet students' needs, desires, and interests while simultaneously meeting those of the school and the community, and what enables them to effectively prepare and support their teachers is a clear, explicit understanding of what they want and need from their schools. The Amish know what they want their schools to do and how they want those goals accomplished, so they create and maintain schools capable of achieving those ends. They experience no significant conflict between parents and school people, students and school people, or among school people themselves because the goals of the home and the children are the goals of the teachers and administrators, and the objectives of the classroom teacher and curriculum are coherent with those of the encompassing educational philosophy as well.

While the larger American society served by public schools is notably pluralistic, has no singular identity or sense of itself, and may neither be able to nor desire to achieve one, some shared sense of goals, some agreement on intentions, some consistent attitudes seem necessary to replace the mixed and crossed messages currently abundant. Such coherence need not be national or even regional; it may only be necessary—or possible—locally, within a district or within a school community. The most outstanding American schools—the schools with the most satisfied constituencies—seem to be the private ones established to serve particular religious or secular philosophies and the public ones in which parents, children, teachers, and administrators, no matter how heterogenous a group they may be, decide cooperatively to determine what they expect to accomplish and what they expect from each other, how they define literacy, and how they define education.

Unfortunately, too many educators look at these successful schools the way the blind men saw the elephant. Some see their facilities and hardware and say, "If we had more classrooms, a better gym, and more computers, our problems would be solved"; some see supplies, textbooks, and software and say, "If we had a new reading series, more consumables, and more library materials, our problems would be solved"; others see curricula or pedagogy and say, "If we had more elective courses or if our teachers asked better questions, our problems would be solved"; still others see administrative organization and policy and say, "If we had an assistant principal whose only job was tracking down truants or if we had a more clearly articulated disciplinary code and demerit system, our problems would be solved"; and still others see PTA's and involved parents and say, "If we had more caring, more involved parents, our problems would be solved."

But like the blind men describing the elephant, each of these visionaries sees only one part of one example. Not only will simply improving the physical plant or revising the curriculum fail to magically solve a school's problems; transplanting all the facilities and methods of a successful school to a less successful one will fail to solve them, too. The reasons new facilities, hardware, curricula, textbooks, methods, or programs work in a particular school or district is not because they have special efficacy in and of themselves but because they serve the purposes, meet the needs, and mesh with the attitudes of the people in that situation. Shiny new books will not automatically improve the education of students who see no reason to read them; banks of computers will not magically educate children who see the machines as extensions of an alien culture to which they may never have access; and new models for clinical supervision or lesson construction will not necessarily improve the performance of teachers who feel alienated from or threatened by their supervisors or students. Schools need a coherent sense of purpose and a purposeful sense of coherence before any reading series, computer program, lesson plan or individual staff member can work most effectively.

Consider the Meadow Brook example. Meadow Brook's second-hand library more than sufficed not because books did not matter but because thrift is valued while appearance does not count; Meadow Brook's students cooperated with and learned from a teacher who conducted impersonal "classes" but whom they called by her first name because they perceived no contradiction between the formal and informal dimensions of their relationship; and Meadow Brook's teacher and parents ultimately became dissatisfied with each other and their relationship failed because her values, needs, and expectations did not coincide in significant ways with theirs. Both these successes and these failures were possible because of the agreed-upon premises on which Meadow Brook was established and according to which it functions.

To develop a truly unifying, guiding philosophy and to articulate goals, intentions, and attitudes, a school or district must attend to the schools, the homes, and the communities it serves and should call on the people in those schools, homes, and communities to participate. Educational researchers are not needed to discover what a school community knows or needs or, worse yet, to tell them what they should have. While such experts can suggest what to look at or how to begin, their findings cannot substitute for the realities of a particular situation. In fact, the people who live with the questions are the ones best suited to search for the answers. The too prevalent belief of our highly specialized society that only experts or professionals know how to get things done is an unfortunate misleading notion. Not only do outsiders need to become insiders before they can discern the reality of a school or a district, but insiders are often nascent experts waiting for an opportunity to use their expertise. People with eighth-grade educations created and maintain Meadow Brook school and the Old Order system because they need and want to. Witness the Amish.

TWELVE

Getting Here from There: A Look Back at the Ethnographic Process

To those who have read the eleven preceding chapters, the data and findings of this study may well appear self-evident. It may seem that all I had to do was spend enough time with the Fishers and in their communities to learn—inevitably and unavoidably—what I finally learned. In fact, that may seem to be the nature of any ethnographic study when encountered in its final published form. Yet that is not the reality of ethnography as I experienced it, so I want, in this last chapter, to share some personal truths about this kind of research with those who read it and those who plan to try it themselves. I agree emphatically with Calkins when she says "the research process is in need of demythologizing," in need of "honest accounts . . . with the texture and complexity and tentativeness of reality" (1985, 126), and it is such an account I hope to offer here.

I first realized that the presentation of any ethnographic study as a fait accompli may be misleading when I was asked to talk about "doing ethnography" to a seminar of soon-to-be ethnographers at the University of Pennsylvania. While trying to determine the best way to tell them about my work in terms of the process that produced it, I considered handing out copies of my findings and telling them how I found each one. That seemed an easy-to-follow, logical method of presentation which would highlight the important dimensions of what I had done. As I started to plan further, however, I knew something was wrong; the approach was clear and logical but somehow it seemed too clear and too logical—too neat, too pat, and too simple to convey any but a misleading sense of how ethnography happens. I would be a study come to life for that group but not a study lived, and if nothing else, I wanted to give them a sense of living through research, or at least what I as one ethnographer survived. Handing them my findings from the outset would suggest they were always just that evident to me. But I did not have my findings from the beginning of my research experience; in fact, I didn't "find" them until very near the end. Those findings were not apparent when I went into the field, nor did they pop full-grown from the data as I collected it. They remained hidden, implicit, until I was on my third draft.

And that is the problem with reading completed ethnographies, like this one, before going into the field; they make ethnography look relatively simple. While they look like they took a long time to produce, and while few people would claim lengthy writing is easy, these finished products are so well organized, so to-the-point, that their conclusions seem too easily reached, almost self-evident and unavoidable. A reader looks at the data presented and says, "Of course, those are the categories; of course, those are the themes and relationships," or at least that is what I said when first I read them. My early reading made me think the trick to ethnography was finding the right culture, the right situation to study. Once I did that, I thought, everything would become apparent if only I looked hard enough; then I would just have to write up what I saw.

I'm not saying I should not have read ethnographies before doing my own. Reading ethnographies helps contextualize intended studies and intended ethnographers; it showed me what is possible, where I might begin, and where I might fit into the field as it already existed. What I should have done in addition to reading those studies, however, was realize that by the time an ethnography appears in final form, the ethnographer has her findings, and the writing process has reverted from being inductive to being deductive. Everything for that last draft is reevaluated, reorganized, and rewritten in light of the finally discerned and finely phrased findings. Final writing, in other words, starts with closure and works backwards, but doing ethnography does not. As noted in chapter 1, ethnography is inductive, open-ended, and interactive/adaptive. So while a straight line from data to conclusions may be desirable and possible in a final report, it misrepresents the research process that produced it. As Donald Murray (1980) has said about trying to deduce the writing process from a written product, such attempts are like trying to discern the pig in the sausage. Both impossible tasks.

So I did not give that seminar group my findings and work backwards because while that would have told them a lot about Amish literacy, it would have told them nothing about how I learned what I did about Amish literacy. And my learning process did not move in a neat straight line or even in a neat "ethnographic spiral" (Spradley 1980). Ethnography, for me, turned out to be more inductive, open-ended, and interactive/adaptive than I ever imagined or wanted it to be, making this the first point I want to emphasize about ethnographic research: doing ethnography is not at all like reading ethnographies.

Just as the ethnographic process is not nearly as neat or self-evident as the product, this ethnographer was not nearly as certain about what she was doing in the field as she may appear to have been in the final report. My second point, therefore, is that even though I thought I knew what I was doing during my research experience, often I actually did not. For much of my time among the Amish, I felt like a child lost in an amusement park or a teenager lost in Bloomingdale's; I was so excited that I didn't know I was lost. I was in a wonderful place surrounded by all sorts of fascinating things, and I thought I knew where I was and what I was doing there. I was in the world of the Amish, and I was there to collect the data that would someday become the doctoral dissertation I had proposed, a dissertation called "Three Children at Home and at School: A Literacy Study Among the Amish."

Not until I tried to put together all the pieces I had collected—pieces that made so much sense as I collected them—did I discover I wasn't where I thought I was and, worse yet, I couldn't get where I wanted to be from there. I couldn't write "Three Children at Home and at School" for two reasons: First, I couldn't maintain my focus on the three school-age Fisher children. No matter how hard I tried to concentrate my vision, they kept slipping in and out. I was faced with a figure-ground situation in which the children were not only not the figure; they were but a portion of the ground. The second reason I couldn't write "Three Children at Home and at School" was that home and school turned out to be only two parts of a six-part puzzle, only two of the six categories I ultimately "discovered." In other words, I suddenly became aware that over time my focus had changed, or, more accurately, my focus had been changed—shaped by what I had seen.

So when I report that the name of the dissertation I finally did write is "Reading, Writing, and Meaning: A Literacy Study among the Amish," the name change should not be considered merely cosmetic, for it represents the more profound change in understanding I experienced. Throughout my research the only thing that remained constant was my interest in and focus on reading and writing. I was so certain of this, in fact, that not until somewhere in my second draft did I realize I had been looking at meaning too. Just as the people and settings had shifted, what they revealed had shifted too.

I write about these changes now as though they were relatively simple matters, discrete clicks of consciousness raised, prompting simple readjustments in thinking. They weren't. The move from the proposed study to the actual one was so slow, so subtle, I didn't realize it was happening. And when it did begin to dawn on me, through a vague felt sense that something was amiss, I fought the coming realization with a vengeance. I *knew* what I was writing, and by God and by Geertz, I was going to write it. I was going to *make* the pieces fit. I had to! But try as I might, I couldn't. Because they just didn't.

And that is one particularly frustrating but potentially exhilarating aspect of most naturalistic research. Though it may make the researcher feel or appear to be out of control and unscientific, without the impressive, quasi-omniscient vision seemingly possible with more deductive methods, inductive research in naturally existing settings with naturally functioning subjects is as unpredictable, capricious, complex, and exciting as the real life it studies.

Recognition of this truth makes it both possible and important for me to acknowledge that not only did I not always know what I was doing while I was doing it, but I didn't always know why I was doing what I was doing while I was doing it, even though I usually thought I did. As noted before, I was doing a literacy study, and that was the one unchanging thing about my research throughout. While I was collecting data for my literacy study, however, I was having experiences that required analysis of a seemingly unrelated kind. As explained in chapter 1, a good ethnography answers two primary questions: "What is going on here?" and "What the devil [do] they think they're up to?" I knew from the courses I had taken, the reading I had done, and the conversations I had had with faculty ethnographers, that one of my ethnographic tasks would be to discover what an individual had to know to be a good successful Amishperson, to lead a good Amish life and get along successfully in Amish society. I had to discover what was going on, to ferret out the rules operating beneath the surface of Amish daily living whether or not they had any apparent connection to literacy because they would contextualize anything else I found. Or so I had been told.

So I started to look for the unseen and listen for the unspoken, and I was fascinated. Working in the realm of communicative competence, of speech events, of language and social context, I felt like a real ethnographer. I had files labeled "data analysis" and "notes to myself," and they were quickly filling with thoughts about sex roles, Amish/English relationships, adult/child differences, technology, and ethnic boundaries. My advisor and I were having wonderful discussions, and he seemed really pleased. My research was rolling.

But, once again, something bothered me. Increasingly, I had the feeling there was something wrong with what I was doing. I was rolling, but it seemed to be in the wrong direction down the wrong hill. Although my work correlated well with major ethnographic theorists and practitioners—with Hymes, Heath, Shultz, Florio, Erickson, Mehan, Michaels, and even the other Fishman—it did not seem to correlate very well with me, first because by background and interest I was neither anthropologist nor linguist, and second because I thought I was interested in reading and writing, not speech and social relationships.

So one day I marched into my advisor's office and demanded that he stop making me look at all the speech and culture stuff and let me start concentrating on my topic. After all, I told him, I wasn't doing a comprehensive ethnography but a topic-oriented one. He was relatively patient; he both insisted and reassured me that I had to look at all this "stuff," but it was okay if I wanted to refine my focus at some point. I was relieved, even joyous. I still didn't believe context so seemingly far afield could ever possibly be relevant, but that didn't matter because I finally had permission, I thought, to get down to work.

As readers familiar with foreshadowing have surely guessed, what I thought was irrelevant turned out not to be, but the ways it actually helped may be less predictable. Some of the social and language data were directly relevant and helped me understand and explain what I saw, particularly in Meadow Brook School. Some of it, however, became relevant not through any direct application but by enabling me to participate more appropriately and interact more effectively, and while that may never have gotten into my dissertation as such, it made me a better participant observer and thereby affected the quality of my work. And finally, some of that stuff became relevant by helping me decide what else was not relevant. What I mean, for example, is that I looked at, read about, and thought about speech pragmatics and discourse analysis enough to know that I didn't want to consider them in my study. If I hadn't had that context in my head, I might have tried to include some discussion of, for instance, the use of the Pennsylvania Dutch language, which would not only have expanded my focus untenably but would have taken me into a field in which I had no long-term interest.

Yet neither these changes in focus nor these forays into potentially extraneous areas were the biggest problem or challenge I encountered. The biggest problem for me came not in doing the research but in writing about it, in organizing and analyzing the data I collected. When I had more data than I could possibly use—after six months in the school and a formal year in the larger field—I decided I had better start writing. Of course, I had been writing all along—writing out field notes and making lengthy notes to myself—but I had not actually started drafting the data chapter of the dissertation, and I really didn't know how or where to begin. So I went back to a description of the Fisher farm I had written for an earlier paper, hoping that revising that piece would give me a running start, and it did. Describing the house led to describing the evidence of literacy in the house, which led to describing the literacy activities I had seen going on in the house. From there it was easy to move from what I had seen the family do in the house to what I had seen them do outside the house, from there to what I had seen other Amish people do, and from there to the newspaper Amish people write. The text grew, in other words, almost organically, certainly without any artificially imposed constraints. When it had stopped growing, I sent four hundred pages to my advisor at Penn, and I followed those pages to Philadelphia for a conference soon after.

I could turn what happened in that conference into a long, suspenseful narrative—of the thick description variety—but I won't. Suffice it to say that my advisor looked down at my four hundred pages stacked on his desk, looked up at me, and said, "Well, Andy, I think you're ready to start writing."

I thought he was kidding. He had to be. So I said something like, "Very funny. Start writing. I think I have *started* writing."

My advisor then very gently explained that what I had written represented the full-blown version of my field notes, and while they were interesting to read and not badly written, they didn't say anything. What point was I trying to make? he asked me. What was I trying to say about Amish literacy? He acknowledged that I had said some things about its function and use, about its meaning to participants, but what was my point?

Any student writer can imagine how I felt, and any teacher can imagine how my advisor felt. While we were both sitting there, feeling, another professor, also on my committee, came in unexpectedly, and my advisor briefly described our problem to her. The second professor responded with the suggestion that ultimately saved my sanity and my study: "Outline what you've written," she said. "That way you'll discover what it is you have to say, and then you can revise to say it."

Though I thanked her for the idea at the time, I didn't begin to appreciate it until later, and I can only fully appreciate it now, in retrospect. Which is why I recount this story. The point is that while I knew I couldn't predict what I had to say before I did my research, what I discovered did not jump out at me and scream, "Here I am!" as I must admit I expected it to. I had to write it down, at length, then read what I'd written, before I actually realized what I had to say about what I knew. I don't know if Shirley Heath had this kind of experience on her first ethnographic foray; I don't know if her Roadville and Trackton data yielded immediately evident findings. But I do know my data did not. As good as my situation was, and as interesting as it was, I have never had to think as hard or as complexly as I did then. It may be cognitive insufficiency on my part, but I don't think so. I think, rather, that original ethnographic thinking is a lot harder than it looks, and it can't be done with mirrors. I'm not relating this to frighten potential ethnographers or to send them running to more traditional varieties of educational research—for that's the last thing I think anyone should do. I relate this here because it so terrified and disconcerted me when it happened. The studies I had read made it look so easy, and as a result I have never felt as intellectually or academically incompetent and alone as I did then. And I suspect I'm not the only person who has ever felt that way in the course of an ethnographic project, nor the only one who ever will.

So I took my advisor's questions—What points did I want to make? What did I want to say about Amish literacy?—and tried to answer them using my other professor's method, guided by levels of description frequently used in ethnographic research (form and feature; function and use; meaning to participants; and interpretation of that meaning). I was off and writing. Again. But this time I stopped when I realized something was wrong. I wasn't going the organic route twice; I would exercise more control this time. I paid attention to the problem I was having and realized I could write about only some parts of my data according to the new system; other parts refused to be included. It didn't take me long to realize I needed new categories; I needed some sort of overall organization that would encompass all my data and allow me to trace themes, point out similarities, and contrast differences.

As the original working title reveals, I started with home and school as my major divisions but they turned out to be insufficient. I added "church," but that was not enough. I needed other places that would incorporate other data. So I tried adding "Lancaster," but that was neither sufficient nor parallel. After I gave up struggling with places, I tried people—relatives, friends, Amish, Mennonite—but those categories failed; so I tried activities—farming, quilting, cooking, traveling—but those failed, too. Neither places nor people nor activities were the answer. I needed categories that would encompass all those things without depending on any one of them. What I came up with, somehow (and I emphasize the unpredictable almost Joycean epiphany quality of the discovery), was the notion of community as a group of people who relate to each other for particular reasons on a regular basis—regardless of or because of the fact that they're Amish, English or Mennonite; regardless of or because of the fact that they're relatives, friends, neighbors, or strangers; and regardless of or because of the fact that they live nearby or far from each other.

Finally, I ended up using the family as one category, as the focal one to which all others relate. (Notice I chose *family*, not *home*, as the operative word although home had been the tag for my entire data collection period. Ultimately, I had to admit to myself that it just didn't work and I had to discard it.) I retained the school as a place for students and their teacher, but I did not call them the school community because I needed that term for another group whose existence revolves around them. Between the family and the school, I identified the four communities all described earlier.

And while these six categories overlap somewhat, they actually proved to be quite elegant. They embraced all of my data, and, more importantly, they turned out to have tremendous explanatory power. They said a great deal about Amish life and Amish society in a background, contextualizing way. Their separation facilitated my analysis of reading, writing, and meaning, making my otherwise overwhelming data manageable. And in addition, their separation and their overlapping made it possible for me to highlight both the complexity and the coherence I discovered through my analysis.

In fact, it is probably the ways these organizing categories work that make the results of this study seem at all polished or complete. And while I don't know how I would have finally written up my research without them, I would caution any reader against trying to transplant these categories to another setting or to assume that my findings may be found intact anywhere else. What this study can do for its readers is what I finally realized the ethnographies I read could do for me. While reading published ethnographies may lead to a skewed view of the research process, focusing on their content may help contextualize and orient other ethnographers and ethnographies. Knowing particular kinds of communities exist in a particular culture where literacy serves particular functions and is defined and approached in particular ways gives readers and researchers things to consider in looking at other settings and studies. My findings add to but do not supplant what is already known about literacy; they simplify one study while simultaneously contributing to the complexity and richness of the field as created by others.

There are those who would note that had I identified these six domains earlier I would have saved myself considerable time, effort, and anxiety. I should have found them before I started writing, as cookbooks for doing ethnography suggest. And I agree that starting out with those categories would have simplified my life significantly. But I would point out to anyone who offers "everything required to begin research, collect data, analyze what you find, and write up your report" (Spradley 1980, v) that few inductive learning experiences progress in such a smooth linear fashion, and I would refer them to Murray, Perl, and others who discuss writing as a discovery process and not merely a reportorial one. Of course, I envy any ethnographers able to do neat, step-by-step research with never a step mis-taken and any able to write only one rough draft. Perhaps in time and with practice I will be more ethnographically agile, too. I suspect, though, that first-time ethnographers may operate less gracefully than practiced ones and that ethnography may be, in any case, not a line dance but a ballet.

Regardless of the complexity of its choreography and performance, however, ethnography works, and that is the final point I want to make. Though it took what seemed an interminable period, my data did yield its own categories and my faith in the process was rewarded. But faith is not enough. Ethnography is work. It is more than the collection of data or even the description and explanation of data. It is making the implicit explicit, articulating the ineffable. It means seeing the invisible and then making it visible to others. In a sense this final chapter is an ethnography of my ethnographic experience, and I expect readers to do with it what I would expect anyone to do with any ethnography: consider it one more county heard from, compare and contrast it to others reporting, and apply it as applicable to their individual situations.

NOTES

CHAPTER TWO: THE FAMILY AT HOME

1. For a detailed discussion of the *Ausbund*, see William I. Schreiber, "The hymns of the Amish *Ausbund* in philological and literary perspective," *The Mennonite Quarterly Review*, 1962, XXXVI, 36–60.

2. *The Amish Directory of the Lancaster County Family, extending to Chester, York, Lebanon, Dauphin, Montour, Lycoming, Clinton, Centre, Franklin, Cumberland, Adams Counties of Pennsylvania and St. Mary's County, Maryland* alphabetically lists all Amish individuals living in those areas by nuclear family groups. Pequea Publishers, in Gordonville, Pennsylvania, issues the directory every five years. In addition to the individual listings, the book contains maps of the eighty-seven church districts, which show both where families live and where schools are located. The family locations are coded M or D if a male in the family is a minister or a deacon. The 1980 edition has 304 pages.

CHAPTER THREE: THE FAMILY AND THEIR COMMUNITIES

1. Between the time of my original study and the time this book went to press, a box appeared in the lower right corner of the front page of one issue of *"Die Botschaft."*

A MESSAGE FROM YOUR BOTSCHAFT COMMITTEE

It seems there has again been some confusion as far as what is proper and acceptable for inclusion in Die Botschaft. With this in mind, we are again printing the Guidelines and ask everyone to please abide by these provisions.

Guidelines
1. Scribes are entitled to free envelopes and subscription for the asking. Please do this at the beginning of the year.
2. For prompt delivery service, have at least six (6) subscribers to one postal address.
3. For extra slow delivery, contact your local post office. If you are convinced that it is not the local post office, contact [name], Circulation Dept. of Die Botschaft.
4. Unaffiliated or improper poems, love or murder stories should not be printed in Die Botschaft.
5. Unreasonably long letters or news not important to the majority of readers should be avoided as we wish to keep the cost of Die Botschaft down.
6. Letters with religious discussions, criticism or unsigned letters should not be printed in Die Botschaft.
7. Questionable advertisements in Die Botschaft should have the approval of the Botschaft Committee.
8. No money showers should be printed in Die Botschaft.

We thank all of you for your co-operation with Die Botschaft Committee.

Your Botschaft Committee

A modified version of these guidelines, without the explanatory preface and with two additional items—one prohibiting photographs of people in advertisements, the other insisting "Old Order Amish and Mennonite writers only"—has appeared occasionally since the first version was printed, but it has been relegated to the second page. I have noticed no significant differences in the length or content of the paper since these guidelines began appearing.

2. When the Amish schools were looking for ways to compromise with Pennsylvania's compulsory attendance law, they developed what they called their vocational program, which was cited and endorsed by the Supreme Court in *The Wisconsin v. Yoder* decision. Amish students completing eighth grade but not old enough to leave school under the law must attend only three hours each week to study English, math, health, and social studies. The rest of what would be their school time is spent learning agricultural and homemaking skills at home and keeping a diary of these activities. The schoolteacher theoretically visits each three-hour pupil's home periodically to insure the value and completion of these ongoing projects.

CHAPTER FOUR: THE FAMILY AND THE SCHOOL

1. Prior to 1930, all Old Order children attended public schools. Then, slowly, Amish parents began questioning the appropriateness of public education to their children's lives. Public schools had been acceptable when they retained a human scale, when each child was responsible to the group, when teachers used "old-fashioned" methods, when the curriculum and pedagogy had religious components, and

when the schools were more part of than apart from daily life, but things began to change. Intellectual achievement and technological knowledge became more important than leading a good life and acquiring wisdom; competing for individual worldly success became more important than cooperatively working for community welfare; and public schools became counterproductive and potentially destructive to the Old Order way of life. So in the 1930s, a few Amish families established their own schools. Few more followed suit until the 1950s and 1960s when public school districts began consolidating, leaving many Amish with what they saw as no choice but to withdraw their children from the new, large, modern institutions. This led to legal pressure from and legal battles with school districts, finally ending in the Supreme Court where, in 1971, *The Wisconsin v. Yoder* case recognized for all times the adequacy and necessity of separate Old Order schools for the maintenance and preservation of Old Order society. Now virtually all Old Order children attend Old Order schools.

Chapter Five: The Teachers' Community

1. An advertisement appearing almost monthly in *Blackboard Bulletin* offers the only other community-produced teacher training resource I discovered. Pathway Publishers, the Amish company that produces the reading series used at Meadow Brook, offers three texts for teachers (available for two dollars a piece or all three for five dollars): *School Bells Ringing*, "a teacher's manual which shares some lessons that have been learned during the parochial school movement"; *Teacher Talk*, "containing 35 choice articles" from the *Bulletin*; and *Tips for Teachers*, "containing many tips on games, bulletin boards, primary grades, compositions, discipline, and free points," compiled by Pathway from actual teacher contributions.

REFERENCES

Akinnaso, F. N. 1981. The consequences of literacy in pragmatic and theoretical perspectives. *Anthropology and Education Quarterly* 12: 163–200.

Anderson, Alonzo B., and Teale, William H. 1981. Literacy as cultural practice. Paper presented at Simposia Internacional: Nuevas Perspectivas en los Procesos de Lectura y Escritura, Mexico City.

Atwell, Nancie. 1987. *In the middle*. Upper Montclair, NJ: Boynton/Cook Publishers.

Baker, Carol. 1982. Locating the process of socialization for literacy. Paper presented at Forum for Ethnography in Education, University of Pennsylvania.

Barth, Fredrik. 1969. *Ethnic groups and boundaries*. Boston: Little, Brown and Co.

Basso, Keith, and Selby, Henry. 1976. "Introduction." In *Meaning in anthropology*, eds. Keith Basso and Henry Selby. Albuquerque: University of New Mexico Press.

Bissex, Glenda L. 1980. *GNYS AT WRK: A child learns to write and read*. Cambridge: Harvard University Press.

Brannon, Lil, and Knoblauch, C.H. 1982. On students' rights to their own texts: A model of teacher response. *College Composition and Communication* 33: 157–66.

———. 1984. *Rhetorical traditions and the teaching of writing*. Upper Montclair, NJ: Boynton/Cook Publishers.

Bruffee, Kenneth A. 1984. Collaborative learning and the "Conversation of mankind." *College English* 46: 635–52.

Buck, Roy C. 1978 Boundary maintenance revisited: Tourist experience in an Old Order Amish community. *Rural Sociology* 43: 221–234.

Calkins, Lucy McCormick. 1983. *Lessons from a child*. Portsmouth, NH: Heinemann Educational Books.

———. 1985. Forming research communities among naturalistic researchers. In *Perspectives on research and scholarship in composition*, eds. Ben W. McClelland and Timothy R. Donovan. New York: Modern Language Association of America.

———. 1986. *The art of teaching writing*. Portsmouth, NH: Heinemann Educational Books.

Campbell, O.J., and Stearn, E.C., eds. 1958. *Adventures in world literature*. New York: Harcourt, Brace, & World.

Cazden, Courtney. 1980. Peekaboo as an instructional model: Discourse development at home and at school. In *Papers and Reports of Child Language Development*, 17, 1–29.

———. 1982. Four comments. In *Children in and out of school*, eds. Perry Gilmore and Allan A. Glatthorn. Washington, DC: Center for Applied Linguistics.

Cazden, Courtney, and John, Vera. 1971. Learning in American Indian children. In *Anthropological perspectives on education*, eds. Murray Wax, Stanley Diamond, and Fred Gearing. New York: Basic Books.

Chomsky, Carol. 1971. Write first, read later. *Childhood Education* 47: 296–99.

Coffman, S. F., ed. 1952. *Confession of Faith*. Scottdale, PA: Mennonite Publishing House.

Cole, Michael. 1981. The zone of proximal development: Where culture and cognition create each other. Unpublished manuscript.

Cook-Gumperz, Jenny, and Gumperz, John. 1981. From oral to written culture: The transition to literacy. In *Variation in writing: Functional and linguistic-cultural differences*, ed. Marcia Farr Whiteman. Hillsdale, NJ: Lawrence Erlbaum Associates.

Cooper, Marilyn. 1982. Context as vehicle: Implications in writing. In *What writers know: The language, process, and structure of written discourse*, ed. Martin Nystrand. New York: Academic Press.

Coser, Lewis. 1956. *The functions of social conflict*. New York: Macmillan Co.

Cronk, Sandra. 1981. GELASSENHEIT: The rites of the redemptive process in Old Order Amish and Old Order Mennonite communities. *The Mennonite Quarterly Review* 55: 5–44.

Davidson, Marshall, ed. 1973. *The writers' America*. New York: American Heritage Publishing Co.

DeFord, Diane. 1980. Young children and their writing. *Theory Into Practice* 19: 157–62.

Emig, Janet. 1981. Non-magical thinking: Presenting writing developmentally in schools. In *Writing: Process, development, and communication*, eds. Carl H. Frederiksen and Joseph F. Dominic. Hillsdale, NJ: Lawrence Erlbaum Associates.

Ericksen, Eugene P.; Ericksen, Julia A.; and Hostetler, John A. 1980. The cultivation of the social as a moral directive: Population growth, family ties, and the maintenance of the community among the Old Order Amish. *Rural Sociology* 45: 49–68.

Erickson, Frederick. 1977. Some approaches to inquiry in school-community ethnography. *Anthropology and Education* 8: 58–60.

Erickson, F., and Shultz, J. 1982. *The counselor as gatekeeper*. New York: Academic Press.

Esh, Levi. 1977. The Amish parochial school movement. *The Mennonite Quarterly Review* 51: 69–75.

Ferreiro, Emilia. 1982. On the underlying logic of literacy development. Paper prepared for University of Victoria Symposium on Children's Response to a Literate Environment: Literacy Before Schooling, Victoria, B.C., Canada.

Fiering, Sue. 1982. Unofficial writing. Ph.D. diss., University of Pennyslvania.

Fish, Stanley. 1980a. Interpreting the *Variorum*. In *Reader response criticism: From formalism to post-structuralism*, ed. Jane P. Tompkins. Baltimore: Johns Hopkins University Press.

———. 1980b. Literature in the reader: Affective stylistics. In *Reader response criticism: From formalism to post-structuralism*, ed. Jane P. Tompkins. Baltimore: Johns Hopkins University Press.

Fishman, J. A. 1982. The sociology of language. In *Language and social context*, ed. Pier Paolo Giglioli. Harmondsworth, England: Penguin Books.

Flower, Linda. 1979. Writer-based prose: A cognitive basis for problems in writing. *College English* 41: 19–37.

Friere, Paulo. 1983. The importance of the act of reading. *Journal of Education* (Winter): 5–11.

Geertz, Clifford. 1973. *The interpretation of cultures*. New York: Basic Books.

———. 1976. "From the native's point of view": On the nature of anthropological understanding. In *Meaning in anthropology*, eds. Keith Basso and Henry Selby. Albuquerque: University of New Mexico Press.

Gibson, Walker. 1980. Authors, speakers, readers, and mock readers. In *Reader response criticism: From formalism to post-structuralism*, ed. Jane P. Tompkins. Baltimore: Johns Hopkins University Press.

Gilmore, Perry. 1978. Ethnography and education: A description of trends and issues with special emphasis on the ethnography of communication. Paper submitted to the National Institute of Education as part of a Final Report from The Basic Skills Component, Research for Better Schools, Inc., Philadelphia.

———. 1982. Literacy and attitude. Unpublished manuscript.

Gilmore, Perry, and Glatthorn, Allan A., eds. 1982. *Children in and out of school*. Washington, DC: Center for Applied Linguistics.

Gilmore, Perry, and Smith, David A. 1982. A retrospective discussion of the state of the art in ethnography in education. In *Children in and out of school*, eds. Perry Gilmore and Allan A. Glatthorn. Washington, DC: Center for Applied Linguistics.

Goodlad, John A. 1984. *A place called school: Prospects for the future*. New York: McGraw-Hill.

Goodman, K.S. 1969. Analysis of oral reading miscues: Applied psycholinguistics. *Reading Research Quarterly* 5: 9–30.

Grice, H. P. 1975. Logic and conversation. In *Syntax and semantics*, Vol. 3, eds. Peter Cole and Jerry Morgan. New York: Academic Press.

Gundlach, Robert. 1982. Children as writers: The beginning of learning to write. In *What writers know: The language, process, and structure of written discourse*, ed. Martin Nystrand. New York: Academic Press.

Harste, Jerome C.; Burke, Carolyn; and Woodward, Virginia. 1981. *Children, their language and world: Initial encounters with print*. Bloomington, IN: Indiana University.

Harste, Jerome C.; Woodward, Virginia; and Burke, Carolyn. 1984. *Language stories and literacy lessons*. Portsmouth, NH: Heinemann Educational Books.

Heath, Shirley Brice. 1978a. *Outline guide for the ethnographic study of literacy and oral language from schools to community*. Philadelphia: University of Pennsylvania.

———. 1978b. *Teacher talk: Language in the classroom*. Arlington, VA: Center for Applied Linguistics.

———. 1980. What no bedtime story means: How children learn to use language to read. Paper prepared for Terman Conference, Stanford University (November).

———. 1981. Toward an ethnohistory of writing in American education. In *Variation in writing: Functional and linguistic-cultural differences*, ed. Marcia Farr Whiteman. Hillsdale, NJ: Lawrence Erlbaum Associates.

———. 1982. Ethnography in education: Defining the essentials. In *Children in and out of school*, eds. Perry Gilmore and Allan A. Glatthorn. Washington, DC: Center for Applied Linguistics.

———. 1983. *Ways with words: Language, life, and work in communities and classrooms*. Cambridge: Cambridge University Press.

Holiday, Albert. 1972. The Amish and compulsory education. *The Education Digest* 37: 21–23.

Horton, Rod W., and Edwards, Herbert W. 1952. *Backgrounds of American literary thought*. New York: Appleton-Century-Crofts.

Hostetler, John. 1974. Education in communitarian societies—the Old Order Amish and the Hutterite Brethren. In *Education and cultural process: Toward an anthropology of education*, ed. George Spindler. New York: Holt, Rinehart and Winston.

———. 1977. Old Order Amish survival. *The Mennonite Quarterly Review* 51: 352–61.

———. 1980. *Amish society*. Baltimore: Johns Hopkins University Press.

Hostetler, John A., and Huntington, Gertrude Enders. 1971. *Children in Amish society*. New York: Holt, Rinehart and Winston.

Hymes, Dell. 1967. Models of the interaction of language and social setting. *Journal of Social Issues* 23: 8–27.

———. 1972. Toward ethnographies of communication: The analysis of communicative events. In *Language and social context*, ed. Pier Paolo Giglioli. Harmondsworth, England: Penguin Books.

———. 1982. What is ethnography? In *Children in and out of school*, eds. Perry Gilmore and Allan A. Glatthorn. Washington, DC: Center for Applied Linguistics.

Jackson, George P. 1945a. The American Amish sing medieval folk tunes today. *Southern Folklore Quarterly* 10: 151–57.

———. 1945b. The strange music of the Old Order Amish. *The Musical Quarterly* 31: 275–88.

Labov, William. 1972. The logic of nonstandard English. In *Language and social context*, ed. Pier Paolo Giglioli. Harmondsworth, England: Penguin Books.

———. 1982. Competing value systems in the inner-city schools. In *Children in and out of school*, eds. Perry Gilmore and Allan A. Glatthorn. Washington, DC: Center for Applied Linguistics.

Loomis, Charles. 1975. *Social systems: Essays on their persistence and change*. Cambridge: Schenkman Publishing Company.

Loomis, Charles, and Beegle, S. Allan. 1975. *A strategy for rural change*. Cambridge: Schenkman Publishing Company.

Magoon, A. John. 1977. Constructivist approaches in educational research. *Review of Educational Research* 47: 651–93.

McDermott, Ray. 1977a. Social relations as contexts for learning in school. *Harvard Education Review* 47: 198–212.

———. 1977b. The ethnography of speaking and reading. In *Linguistic theory: What can it say about reading?* ed. R. Shuy. Newark, DE: International Reading Association.

McDermott, Ray; Gospodinoff, Kenneth; and Aron, Jeffrey. 1978. Criteria for an ethnographically adequate description of concerted activities and their contexts. *Semiotica* 24: 245–75.

Mehan, Hugh. 1979. *Learning lessons: Social organization in the classroom*. Cambridge: Harvard University Press.

———. 1982. The structure of classroom events and their consequences for student performance. In *Children in and out of school*, eds. Perry Gilmore and Allan A. Glatthorn. Washington, DC: Center for Applied Linguistics.

Michaels, Sara. Forthcoming. Teacher/child collaboration as oral preparation for literacy. In *Acquiring literacy: Ethnographic perspective*, ed. Bambi Schieffelin. Norwood, NJ: Ablex.

Michaels, Sara, and Cook-Gumperz, Jenny. 1979. "A study of sharing time with first grade students: Discourse narratives in the classroom." In *Proceedings of Fifth Annual Meeting of the Berkeley Linguistics Society*.

Mischler, Elliot. 1979. Meaning in context: Is there any other kind? *Harvard Education Review* 49: 1–19.

Moffett, James. 1981. *Coming on center*. Upper Montclair, NJ: Boynton/Cook Publishers.

Murray, Donald M. 1980. Writing as process: How writing finds its own meaning. In *Eight approaches to teaching composition*, eds. Timothy R. Donovan and Ben W. McClelland. Urbana, IL: National Council of Teachers of English.

Ogbu, John. A review of literacy in subordinate cultures: The case of black Americans. Department of Anthropology, University of California, Berkeley.

Old Order Book Society, Old Order Amish School Committee, and Old Order Mennonite School Committee. 1973. *Standards of the Old Order Amish and Old Order Mennonite Parochial and Vocational Schools Of Penna*. Gordonville, PA: Gordonville Print Shop.

Olson, David. 1977. From utterance to text: The bias of language in speech and writing. *Harvard Educational Review* 47: 257–81.

Perl, Sondra. 1980. Understanding composing. *College Composition and Communication* 31: 363–69.

Petrosky, Anthony. 1982. From story to essay: Reading and writing. *College Composition and Communication* 33: 19–36.

Read, Charles. 1981. Writing is not the inverse of reading for young children. In *Writing: Process development and communication*, Vol. 2, eds. Carl H. Fredericksen and Joseph F. Dominic. Hillsdale, NJ: Lawrence Erlbaum Associates.

Resnick, Daniel P., and Resnick, Lauren B. 1977. The nature of literacy: An historical exploration. *Harvard Educational Review* 47: 370–85.

Reutter, E. Edmund, Jr., and Hamilton, Robert R. 1976. *The law of public education*. Mineola, NY: Foundation Press.

Rist, Ray. 1973. *Urban school: A factory for failure*. Cambridge: MIT Press.

Rodriguez, Richard. 1983. *Hunger of memory*. New York: Bantam Books.

Rosenblatt, Louise. 1978. *The reader, the text, the poem*. Carbondale, IL: Southern Illinois University Press.

Sanday, Peggy Reeves. 1982. Anthropologists in schools: School ethnography and ethnology. In *Children in and out of school*, eds. Perry Gilmore and Allan A. Glatthorn. Washington, DC: Center for Applied Linguistics.

Schieffelin, Bambi B., and Cochran-Smith, Marilyn. 1984. Learning to read culturally: Literacy before schooling. In *Awakening to literacy*, eds. H. Goelman, A. Oberg, and F. Smith. Portsmouth, NH: Heinemann Educational Books.

Schreiber, William. 1962. The hymns of the Amish *Ausbund* in philological and literary perspective. *The Mennonite Quarterly Review* 36: 36–60.

Scollon, Ron, and Scollon, Suzanne. 1981. *Narrative, literacy, and face in interethnic communication*. Norwood, NJ: Ablex Publishing Corporation.

Scribner, Sylvia, and Cole, Michael. 1981. Unpackaging literacy. In *Variation in writing: Functional and linguistic-cultural differences*, ed. Marcia Farr Whiteman. Hillsdale, NJ: Lawrence Erlbaum Associates.

Seiverling, Richard, ed. 1976. *Educational quality assessment: Manual for interpreting secondary school reports*. Harrisburg, PA: Pennsylvania Department of Education.

Shaughnessy, Mina P. 1977. *Errors and expectations: A guide for teachers of basic writing*. New York: Oxford University Press.

Shultz, Jeffrey. 1983. Paper presented at the Ethnography in Education Research Forum, April, at the University of Pennsylvania, Philadelphia, Pennsylvania.

Shultz, Jeffrey; Florio, Susan; and Erickson, Frederick. 1982. Where's the floor? Aspects of the cultural organization of social relationships in communication at home and at school. In *Children in and out of school*, eds. Perry Gilmore and Allan A. Glatthorn. Washington, DC: Center for Applied Linguistics.

Sindell, Peter. 1969. Anthropological approaches to the study of education. *Review of Educational Research* 39: 593–605.

Smith, David M. 1982. Reading and writing in the real world. University of Pennsylvania.

———. 1983. The anthropology of literacy acquisition. In *The acquisition of literacy: Ethnographic perspectives*, eds. Perry Gilmore and Bambi Schieffelin. Norwood, NJ: Ablex Publishing Corporation.

Spiller, Robert E., ed. 1963. *Literary history of the United States*. New York: Macmillan Co.

Spindler, George. 1974. Why have minority groups in North America been disadvantaged by their schools? In *Education and cultural process: Toward an anthropology of education*, ed. George Spindler. New York: Holt, Rinehart, and Winston.

Spradley, James P. 1980. *Participant observation*. New York: Holt, Rinehart, and Winston.

Spradley, James, and McCurdy, David. 1972. *The cultural experience: Ethnography in complex society*. Chicago: Science Research Associates.

Stubbs, Michael. 1982. Written language and society: Some particular cases and general observations. In *What writers know: The language, process, and structure of written discourse*, ed. Martin Nystrand. New York: Academic Press.

Szwed, John F. 1981. The ethnography of literacy. In *Variation in writing: Functional and linguistic-cultural differences*, ed. Marcia Farr Whiteman. Hillsdale, NJ: Lawrence Erlbaum Associates.

Taylor, Denny. 1983. *Family literacy*. Portsmouth, NH: Heinemann Educational Books.

Thomas, Robert, and Warhaftig, Albert. 1971. Indians, hillbillies, and the "education problem." In *Anthropological perspectives on education*, eds. Murray Wax, Stanley Diamond, and Fred Gearing. New York: Basic Books.

Tierney, Robert, and LaZansky, Jill. 1980. *The rights and responsibilities of readers and writers: A contractual agreement* (Reading Education Report No. 15). Urbana-Champaign, IL: University of Illinois Center for the Study of Reading.

Tolstoy, Leo. 1970. God sees the truth but waits. In *A pocket book of short stories*, ed. M. Edward Speare. New York: Washington Square Press.

Tompkins, Jane P. 1980. The reader in history: The changing shape of literary response. In *Reader-response criticism: From formalism to post-structuralism*, ed. Jane P. Tompkins. Baltimore: Johns Hopkins University Press.

Van Braght, Thieleman J., ed. 1975. *Martyrs Mirror*. Scottdale, PA: Herald Press.

Vygotsky, L. S. 1962. *Thought and language*. Cambridge: MIT Press.

———. 1978. *Mind in society: The development of higher psychological processes*. Cambridge: Harvard University Press.

Wagner, Daniel A. 1983. Rediscovering "rote": Some cognitive and pedagogical preliminaries. In *Human assessment and cultural factors*, eds. S. Irvine and J. W. Berry. New York: Plenum.

Wax, Murray, and Wax, Rosalie. 1971. Great tradition, little tradition, and formal education. In *Anthropological perspectives on education*, eds. Murray Wax, Stanley Diamond, and Fred Gearing. New York: Basic Books.

Wilson, Stephen. 1977. The use of ethnographic techniques in educational research. *Review of Educational Research*, 47: 245–65.

Wittmer, Joe. 1970. An educational controversy: The Old Order Amish schools. *Phi Delta Kappan* 52: 142–45.

———. 1972. The Amish and the Supreme Court. *Phi Delta Kappan* 54: 50–52.

Wolcott, Harry. 1967. Anthropology and education. *Review of Educational Research* 37: 82–95.

———. 1971. Handle with care: Necessary precautions in the anthropology of schools. In *Anthropological perspectives on education*, eds. Murray Wax, Stanley Diamond, and Fred Gearing. New York: Basic Books.

Zinsser, Caroline. Forthcoming. For the Bible tells me so: Teaching children in a fundamentalist church. In *Acquiring literacy: Ethnographic perspectives*, ed. Bambi Schieffelin. Norwood, NJ: Ablex Publishing Corporation.